FRENCH MUSEUM ARCHITECTURE

ICI CONSULTANTS **Planning Editor**
Alison CULLIFORD **English Translator**

Editorial Consulting
ICI CONSULTANTS

Direction
Chia-Ling CHIEN

Communication / Documentation
Nicolas BRIZAULT

English Translation
Alison CULLIFORD

Art Direction
Karine de La MAISON
Wijane NOREE

FRENCH MUSEUM ARCHITECTURE

ICI CONSULTANTS **Planning Editor**
Alison CULLIFORD **English Translator**

DESIGN MEDIA PUBLISHING LIMITED

INNOVATIONS IN HISTORIC SPACES

DIALOGUES BETWEEN OLD AND NEW

BRAND NEW EXPRESSIONS

Würth Museum: Architect Jacques & Clément Vergély / Sculptor Bernard Venet / photgrapher Erick Saillet

FUTURE PROJECTS

INNOVATIONS
IN HISTORIC SPACES

CHAMPOLLION MUSEUM – SCRIPTS OF THE WORLD

Architect: Moatti-Rivière
Location: Figeac
Completion Date: 2007
Photographer: Luc Boegly (pp.8-9), Matthieu Deville (pp.10-13)

The Champollion Museum is housed in four Medieval buildings in the protected sector of Figeac's town centre, one being the birthplace of Champollion, the decipherer of Egyptian hieroglyphics. On its main façade, the arcades partly date back to the 12th century while the upper floors are 18th-century. Covering 1,400m², the museum is composed of a main space displaying the permanent collections, with a temporary exhibition room and an educational workshop situated in independent buildings nearby.

In Moatti et Rivière's renovation, the buildings have been totally restructured to free the museography of all constraints and to open up large visual perspectives. The beams of the new concrete floors are hung from the old façade using metallic struts. These also compose the structure of the loggias and the sun terraces, whose

1

metallic trellis floors allow one to walk in the space between the two façades.

The existing outer façade has been renovated and ensures the urban continuity with the houses of the town. The second façade, set back around 1m, is made up of 48 glass panels averaging 3.5m by 1.2m. A 0.5-micron copper leaf cut into 14cm x 14cm panels was laid by hand on a polymer film. Each letter was hand-

cut out of the copper. The layered glass contains the copper polymer film between two sheets of PVB. The layers of glass and the different films are combined using a chemical process. This glass was then assembled with a sheet of 8mm safety glass to form a traditional double glazing. The Champollion Museum's aim was to bring the work of artisans together with an industrial process, and the façade conveys the imagination and beauty of the letters to give the project its identity.

The permanent exhibition takes one through seven distinct rooms over four levels. Each room has a thematic unity conveyed by a single colour – black, red orange, blue, ivory – that links the floor, the ceiling and the painted signage on the glass cabinets and the information panels. It allows one to focus on the artefacts in a setting of peaceful unity.

1. Scripts of the Mediterranean room
2. Exterior façade
3. The "soleilo", a typical feature of the region's architecture
4. Master plan
5. The façade of a thousand letters, a play of shadows and light
6. Ground floor plan
7. Typical floor plan

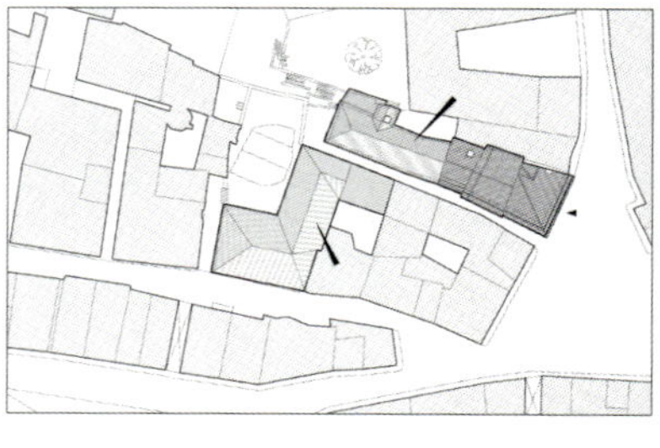

4

5

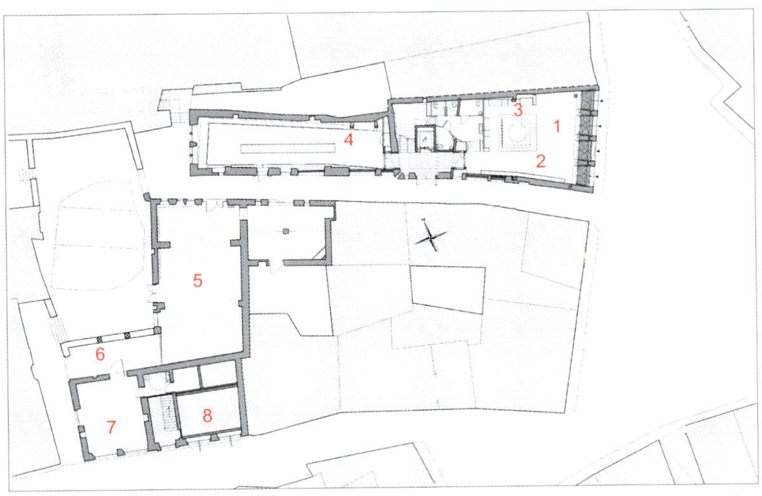

6

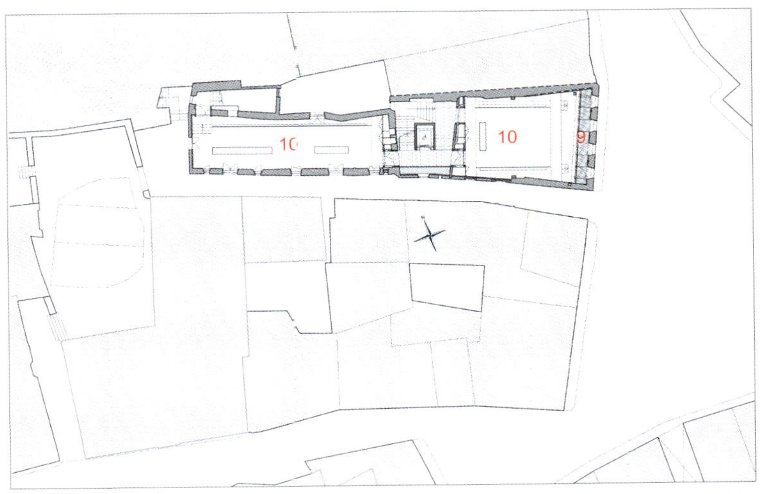

7

1. Waiting/meeting area
2. Reception
3. Ticket desk
4. Champollion room – permanent exhibition
5. Scripts room – temporary exhibitions
6. Gallery
7. Educational workshop
8. Béteille Café
9. Loggia
10. Permanent exhibition room

8

9

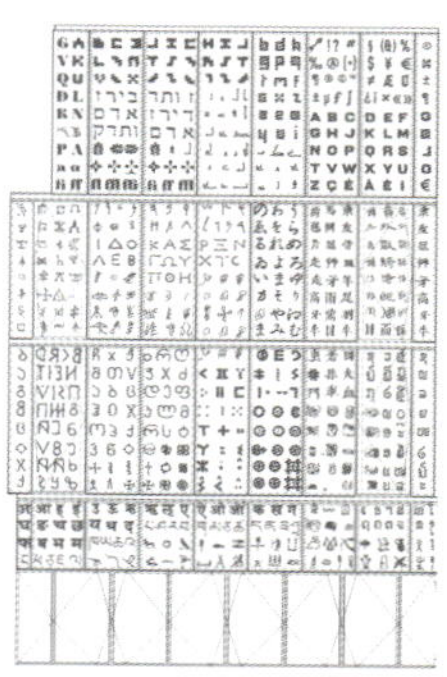

10

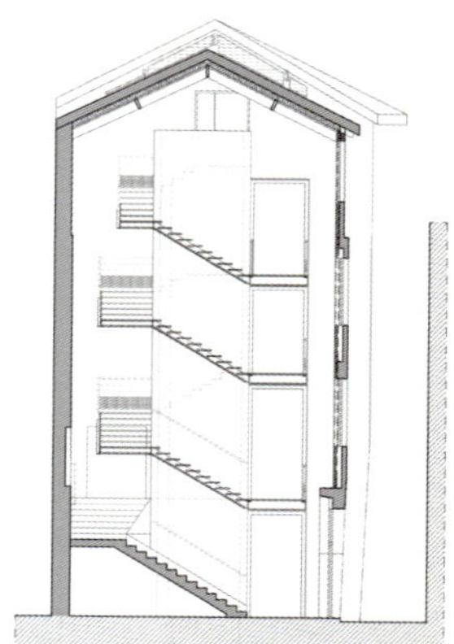

11

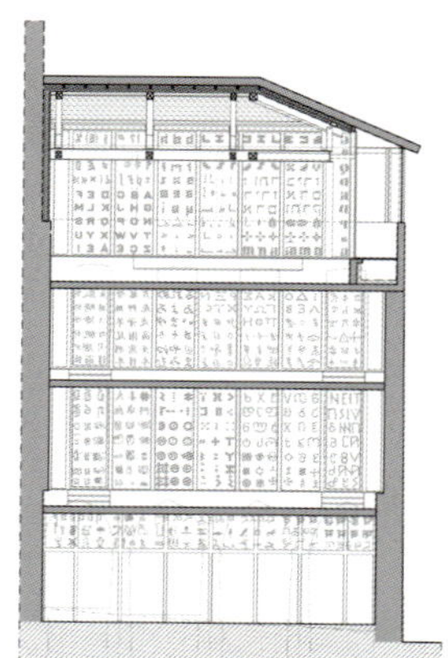

12

8. Scripts of the Mediterranean room
9&13. The palimpsest of the two façades
10. Façade of a thousand letters
11-12. Cross sections

COMIC BOOK MUSEUM

Architect: Bodin & Associés
Location: Angoulême
Completion Date: 2009
Photographer: Enrico Bartolucci (except n°2), Magelis (n°2)

The Comic Book Museum in Angoulême opened its doors in June 2009, in a series of old wine warehouses beside the Charente. Entirely renovated and enlarged with a new space of 5,000m^2, it hosts the prestigious permanent collection for which Angoulême is known around the world. One of the major languages of popular art, in the most profound sense of the term, needed to be exhibited, and this called for a museum of contemporary art, no less.

A vast space, clearly lit but respectful of the works, welcomes the visitor at street level to wander among the collections. Its curved route follows the history of the comic book and its major exponents. Through these sinuous presentation areas, the comic book takes on life, presence and sense. Exhibition cabinets at a height that is accessible for all visitors show books, plates and documents marking the great moments and major trends through which this art made its mark on contemporary culture.

Installing itself in the new spaces, the Comic Book Museum has reorganised the whole

1

of its permanent collections over a space of around 1,300m^2. With a sober and elegant design that shows the original works to their best effect, the new itinerary is organised in four sections: the first part is devoted to the history of the comic book in the French-speaking world, America and Japan; next "the workshop" is devoted to the different techniques and stages in the creation of a comic strip; "the salon" presents the aesthetic of the comic book; and finally "the gallery" presents thematic exhibitions linked to current events.

2

3

1. Masters of Drawing area – reading point
2. Façade of the museum housed in the 19th-century wine warehouses
3. Perspective view of entrance hall
4. Longitudinal section
5. Entrance hall – staircase leading to the museum

4

administration
administration
administración
auditorium
auditorium
auditorium

5

6

7

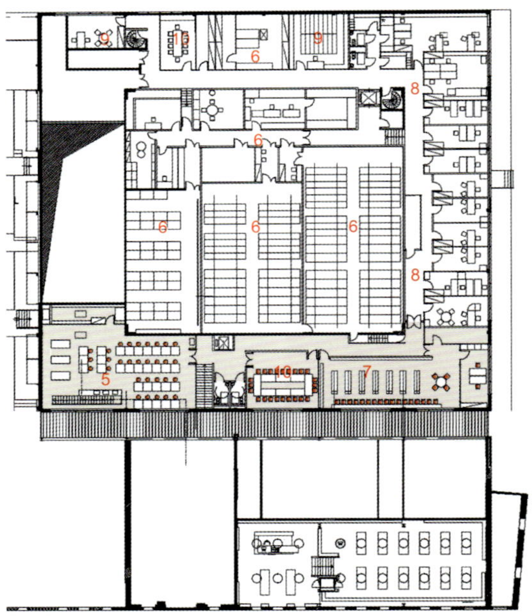

8

6. Perspective view of bookshop
7. Ground floor plan
8. 1st floor plan
9. Bookshop

1. Entrance hall
2. Bookshop
3. Permanent exhibition space
4. Temporary exhibition space
5. Mediation service for the public
6. Heritage centre
7. Centre for documentary research
8. Offices
9. Surveillance, technical, upkeep and maintenance
10. Common areas

9

10

11

12

10. Reading point
11. Comic Books and Society area – daily life reading point
12-13. Comic Book News area – manga reading point

13

14

15

14. History area: plastic art – multimedia point and display case
15. History area: display case of "toys"
16-18. Museum reserves

16

17

18

FABRE MUSEUM

Architect: Brochet Lajus Pueyo
Location: Montpellier
Completion Date: 2007
Photographer: Hervé Abbadie

The renovation of the Fabre Museum aimed to interpret an ambitious project in spatial terms while respecting the "spirit of the place". Comprised of an urban block that brings together three large buildings from different eras, which exhibit different architectural techniques, the project aims to link them together while revealing the uniqueness and the quality of each of its parts.

This main objective was tackled through simple principles. Each of the museum's parts preserves its integrity, is shown in its best light and becomes the basis for a museographical and architectural path through the museum. Each path is clearly identifiable from the entrance hall, imposing a unity of time and unity of place. The courtyards stand out as the strong points of the approach: the "Soulages courtyard", open to the city, together with the interior courtyards of Bourdon, Cabanel, Bazille and Vien, form the high points and the breathing spaces of the composition. The placing of the welcome

1

hall was crucial, given the number of different floors that it serves. This project establishes it naturally under the Bazille courtyard, the compositional centre of the Jesuit college, on the same level as the Soulages courtyard. It forms the fulcrum of the museum, from which an understanding of the different paths through the museum and of its general organisation extends. The success of the project also comes from the orchestration of the different sequences, which is why great attention was paid to the treatment of the transition

2

3

spaces and breathing spaces that are the courtyards.

The "light wing", a real glass showcase, enclosed by the Bourdon courtyard, houses the works the artist Pierre Soulages recently donated to the museum.

The north façade of the Soulages wing is composed of scales of textured glass, lined on the interior by panels of transparent glass. With this "tracing paper" effect the architects have made a contemporary statement in this composite historic building in the heart of the city.

1. The restored grand gallery
2. The Soulages wing (on the right) faces a historic building
3. The Soulages wing – a double glass wall flooded with light serves as a façade to the extension
4. Stone façade facing the street
5. Longitudinal section of the hall and the temporary exhibitions beneath the old courtyards
6. Interior courtyard of the library

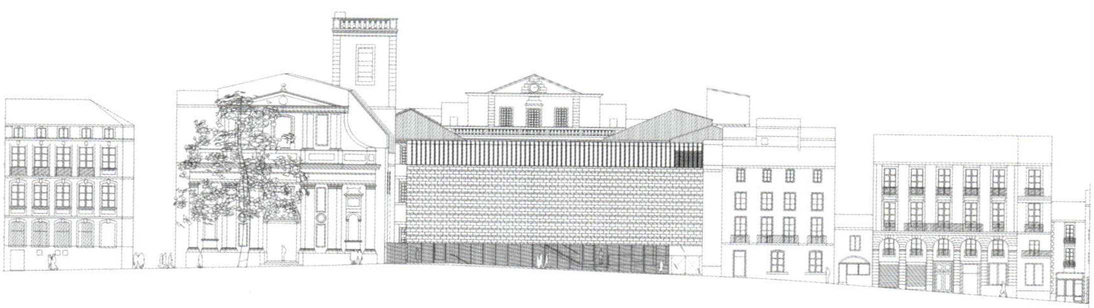

4

5

7. The entrance hall opens onto a room worked in colour by Daniel Buren
8. The entrance hall in concrete poured in situ slides under a courtyard of the old museum
9. 2nd floor plan
10. 1st floor plan
11. Ground floor plan

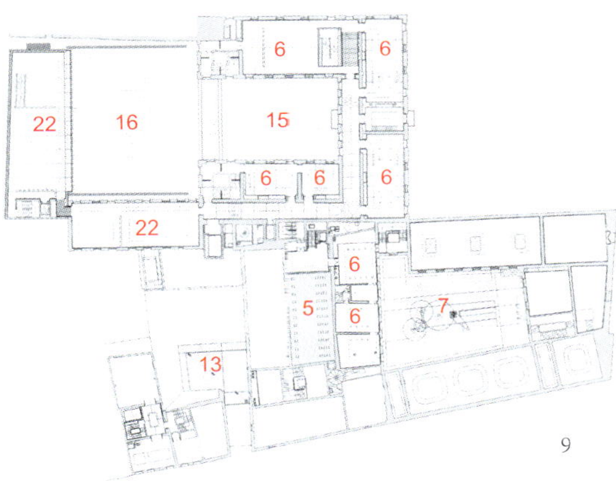

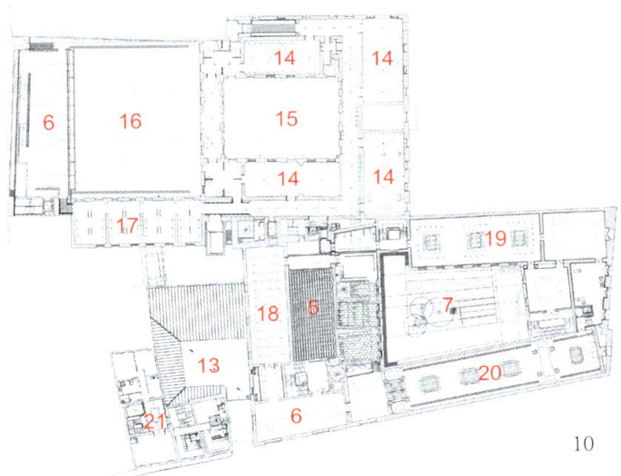

1. Soulages courtyard (Entrance courtyard)
2. Library
3. Bookshop
4. Entrance hall
5. Sculpture courtyard
6. Exhibition room
7. Vien courtyard
8. Auditorium
9. Restaurant
10. Educational workshops
11. Temporary exhibitions
12. Workshops
13. Cabanel courtyard
14. Permanent collections
15. Bazille courtyard
16. Bourdon courtyard
17. Contemporary gallery
18. Griffins gallery
19. Houdon gallery (old library)
20. Columns gallery
21. Administration & workshop
22. Soulages collection

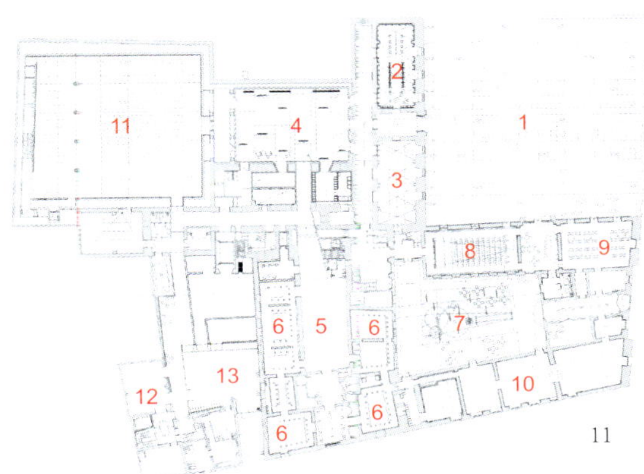

12

13

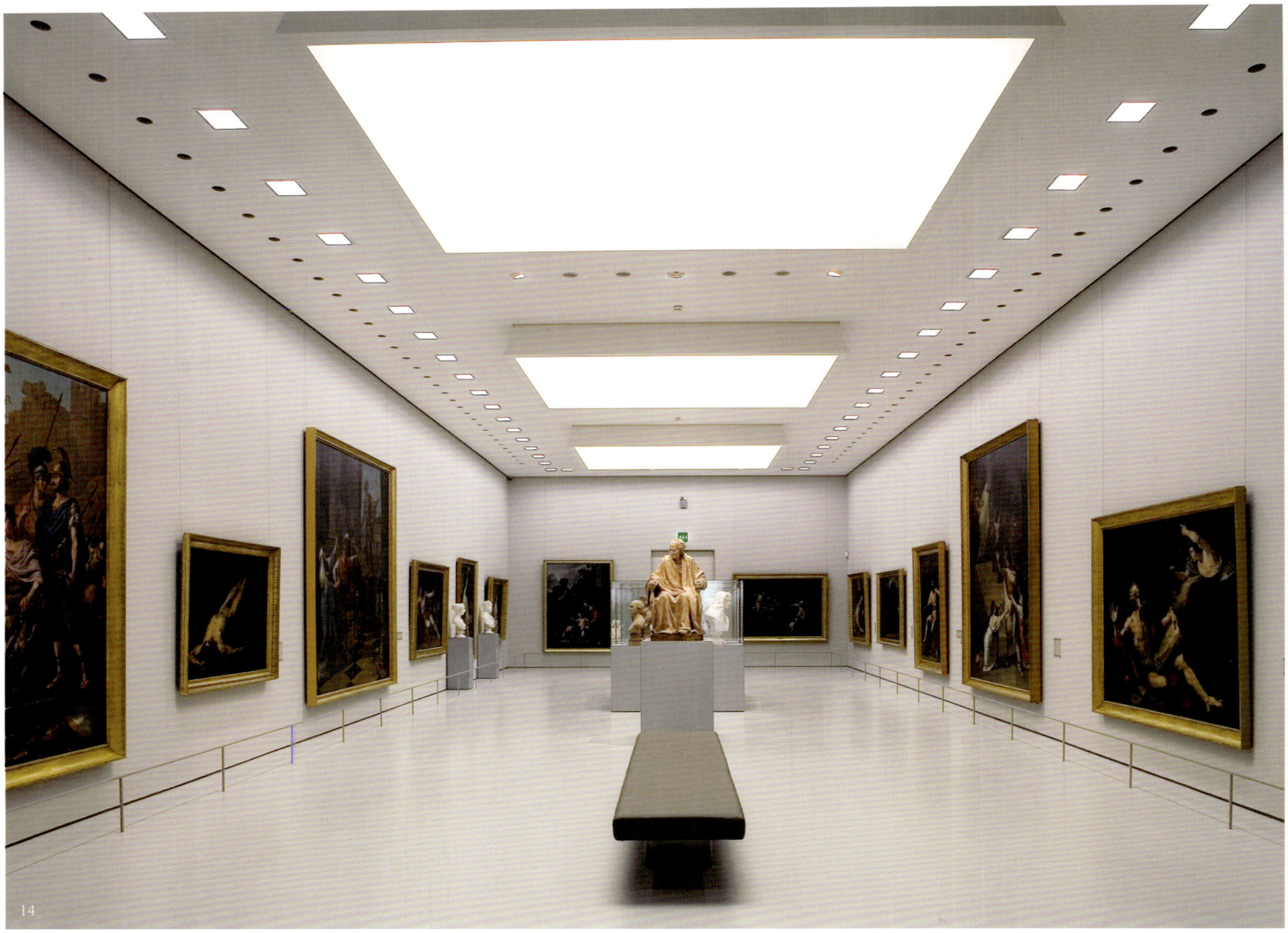

14

12. The restored Griffins room
13. The Griffins gallery and its restored interior decoration
14. The restored old library
15. Transverse section of the reclaimed and covered courtyards
16. Vaulted galleries of the old convent
17. The restored beams of the galleries
18. Axonometric drawing
19. An old courtyard covered in glass for a sculpture room
20. Simon Hantaï in a concrete alcove
21. The Soulages rooms and natural light distilled by a double skin

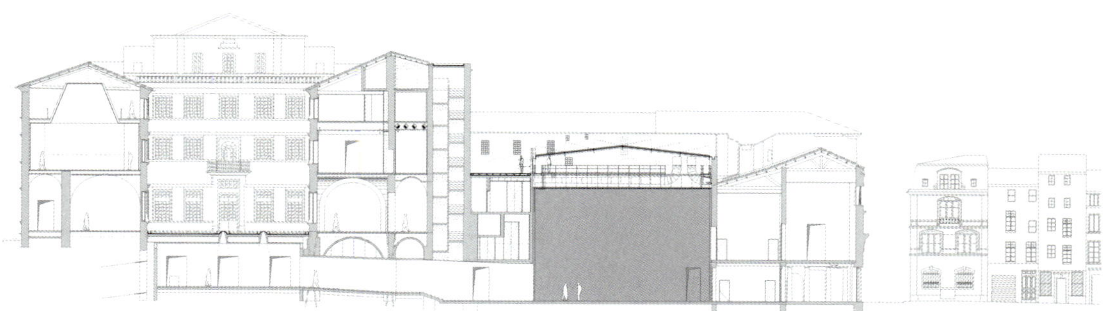

15

16

17

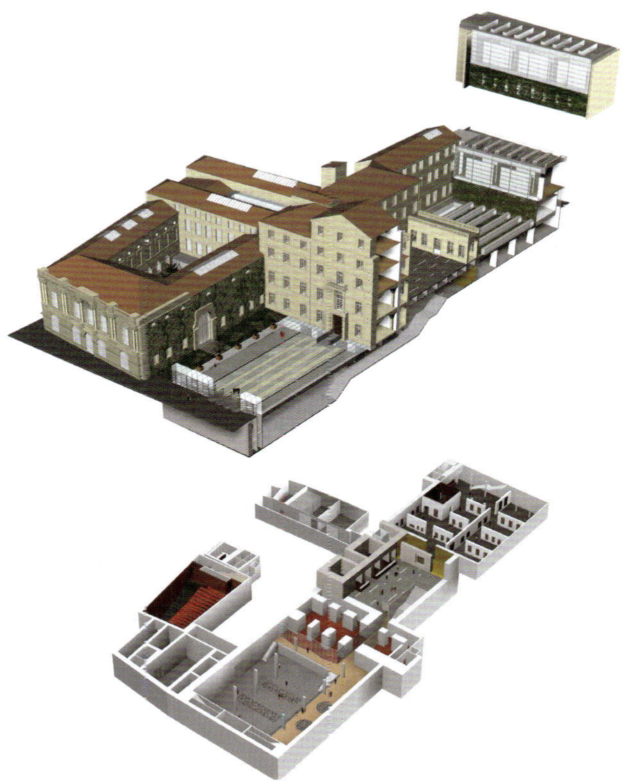

18

19

20

21

1

HISTORIAL CHARLES DE GAULLE

Architect: Moatti-Rivière
Location: Paris
Completion Date: 2008
Photographer: Hervé Abbadie

The Historial Charles de Gaulle is situated in the Army Museum, under the Valeur courtyard of the Hôtel des Invalides in Paris. Here, a double challenge is inherent in inserting modernity into a piece of heritage: historical, in terms of communicating the work of Charles de Gaulle; and architectural, with the creation of a contemporary project at the Invalides. The digital architecture of the 21st century has been inserted into a 17th century stone building. Using architecture to create scenes and atmosphere, conveying knowledge and emotion, the Historial is a kind of "audiovisual architecture", where the light of images reveals the material. Interactivity, multimedia and art installations are used to bring archive images to life, as a present-day witness to historical events.

This place of memory is intended to link past and present. Of all the educational tools available to us – books, CD-roms, internet – only museums allow people to immerse themselves physically in the subject. Visitors will compose their own path

2

of knowledge, whether they are neophytes, curious, passionate about the subject or specialists. Here, space structures time, here an architectural itinerary merges with immersion in the images, monochrome materials merge with multimedia, and historical figures merge with the spectators of history.

The Historial is structured into three sections in successive strata, which complement each other. They represent three ambiances, three experiences for

3

5

the visitor and three types of access to knowledge. First of all an inverted dome, the multi-screen room where the visitor receives information via a documentary film; next the ring of history, an artistic intervention that delivers us the symbolic images of the 20th century; and finally the three heritage doors, through which the visitor passes from emotion to understanding.

6

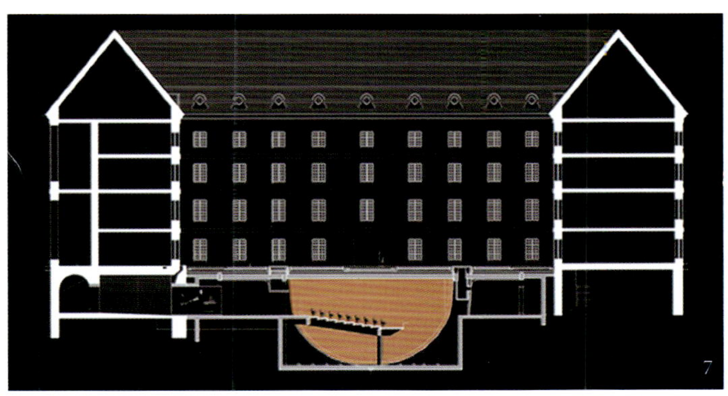

7

1. The entrance and the corridor leading to the alcoves
2. The ring of history, a junction between the multi-screen room and the alcoves
3. A curved glass screen, crossed by the image. both halts it and remains transparent
4. The multi-screen room
5. General axonometric drawing
6-7. Longitudinal section

RETOUR
A LA NORMALE...
NOUS SOMMES TOUS
DES JUIFS
ET DES ALLEMANDS
MAI 68
LA POLICE
CHEZ VOUS
ÉLECTIONS
INFORMATION
LIBRE
L'INTOX
VIENT
A DOMICILE
8

Radiola
PHILIPS
CRS
SS
INFORMATION
LIBRE
L'INTOX
VIENT
A DOMICILE
MAI 68
9

10

8. In a red space between rooms, the events of May'68
9. The 1960s in France
10. Museographic space dedicated to the Fifth Republic

ORANGERIE MUSEUM

Architect: Brochet Lajus Pueyo
Location: Paris
Completion Date: 2006
Photographer: Hervé Abbadie

Guarding the south-west corner of the Tuileries garden, the Orangerie Museum overlooks the River Seine. It is mirrored by the Jeu de Paume Gallery du in the north-west corner, the two buildings standing either side of the garden's main entrance on Place de la Concorde. The renovation of the Orangerie, completed in 2007, aimed to synthesise the history of the building, which originally housed an orange grove. The architects set out to restore some of its initial character, while respecting the general form of the building and its main lines. The symmetry between the north and south terraces – the Orangerie and the Jeu de Paume Gallery – prevented any addition to the existing building so instead additional gallery space was found by building underground. Wishing to restore some of its original spirit, the architects settled on the idea of an envelope of glass on the south side, towards the Seine, and closed, opaque walls on the north side.

The Orangerie first became a museum after the First World War, when it was

1

specifically designated to house Claude Monet's large-format Waterlily paintings. In the 1960s, the installation of a second floor for the Walter Guillaume collection literally put Monet's Waterlilies in the shade, thus going against the wishes of the artist. The unique character of Monet's work guided the architects towards an exceptional setting, which provides this museum's main attraction for the public. The work is once again exhibited in natural light, as Claude Monet had originally recommended.

2

3

4

1. The north façade with windows onto the garden
2. Skylight along the north façade
3. The administration offices in a concrete block suspended in the existing volume
4. Entrance hall, north façade with windows onto the Tuileries garden
5. South façade, Seine side. The volume initially planned in wood was built in concrete.

The Waterlilies remain in place, and their setting has been restored. The interpretation of the 'oval hall" described by Monet was the keystone to the approach to light in the whole building. The hall forms a light shaft at the heart of the project, linking all the levels of the museum. It contains the teaching elements needed for an understanding of the work exhibited. This staging of the Waterlily paintings, the reinstating of natural light at the heart of the work, gives the Orangerie its place in the "Grand Louvre" project. Forming the foreground of the perspective towards the Louvre from the quays of the Seine, the Orangerie Museum acts as a lighthouse or a beacon.

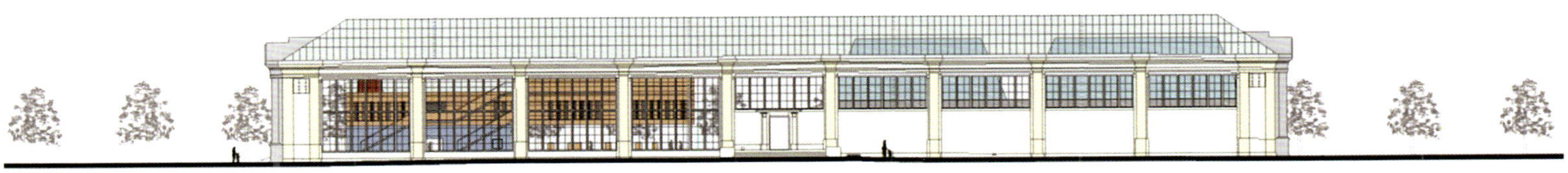

5

Les Nymphéas

6. Approach to the Waterlilies via a wooden bridge
7. The Waterlilies room with its natural light restored
8. Ground floor plan

1. Entrance hall
2. Ticket desk
3. "Drawbridge"
4. Vestibule
5. Waterlilies room
6. Skylight over the permanent exhibition gallery

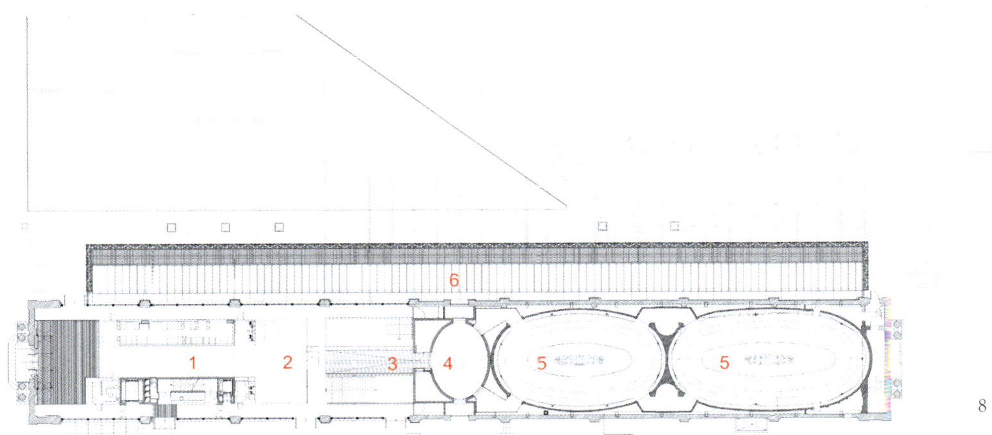

8

9

9. The mezzanine bookshop
10. Basement floor plan
11. Longitudinal section of the entrance hall and the Waterlilies room
12. North gallery created beneath the Tuileries garden
13. The Soutine room beneath the garden

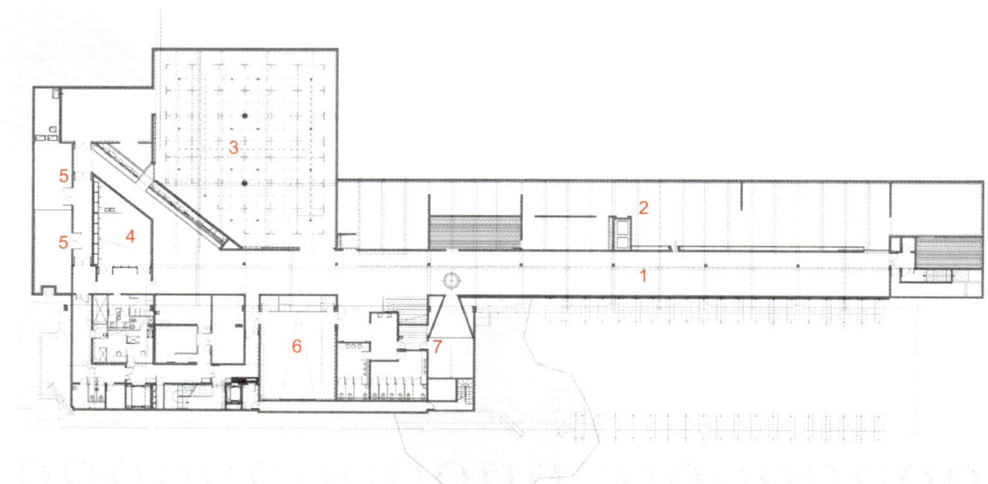

10

1. Permanent exhibition gallery
2. Permanent exhibition rooms
3. Temporary exhibition rooms
4. Educational room
5. Reserves
6. Auditorium
7. Introduction room

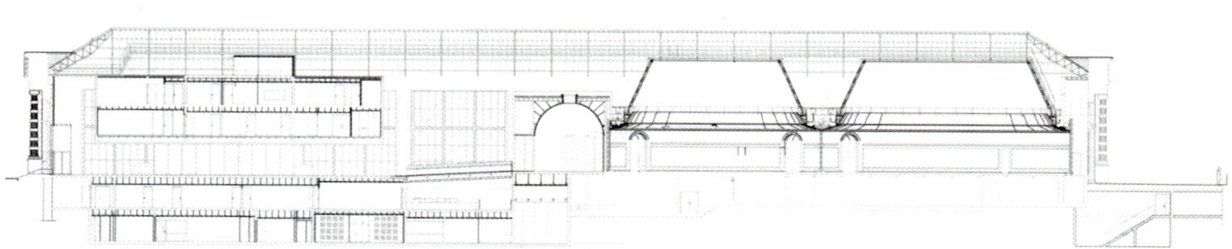

11

12

13

ORSAY MUSEUM

Architect: Jean-Paul Philippon
Location: Paris
Completion Date: 1986
Photographer: Wijane Noree (pp.50-51), Deidi von Schaewen (pp.52-55)

In 1979 the three architects Renaud Bardon, Pierre Colboc and Jean-Paul Philippon won the competition to transform the former Orsay train station into a museum. Their approach, which grew out of their research paper "Metamorphosis of the Architectural Object", presented to the Ministry of Culture in 1977, was based on three principles:

- the city is a work in constant metamorphosis, which has an effect on every building;
- transforming a building to recycle it in urban life is legitimate;
- the dialectic between the pre-existing architecture and contemporary contributions will generate a new architecture.

Since the unloved station had been earmarked for destruction only a short time before, demonstrating that it could be transformed into a museum was decisive in saving it. The project addressed the enormity of the vast hall and brought the immensity of the whole building down to the scale of the artworks exhibited, it

1

remodelled the large space under the glass roof of the old station into a succession of rooms and galleries spread over two floors, along an inclined central avenue from which the visitor could easily move from place to place.

A geometrical transformation has been achieved, based on the station's original architect Victor Laloux's very clear composition. Used along its longitudinal axis, the full scale of the grand nave can be appreciated, with the Bellechasse forecourt

2

and the glass canopy dedicated to welcoming visitors. Overlooking the Seine on its north side and lit by overhead natural light in the old eaves of the station hall, the Impressionists gallery runs between the Amont and Aval pavilions, opposite the Louvre. Natural light infiltrates the building through the station's glass roofs. It is made more atmospheric, finished and assisted by indirect lighting. Vertical planes of ochre Buxy stone reflect the light and add warm tones. They frame Laloux's architecture in surprising ways. Inventing his own itinerary, the visitor simultaneously takes in the old building, the new construction and the artworks exhibited. The station has given the museum its unusual spaces, and the museum has saved the station.

5

1. A Parisian station transformed into a museum – view of the entrance
2. Seine side façade
3-5. The nave with its sculptures. Natural light infiltrates the building through the station's glass roofs
6. Axonometric drawing of the nave
7-8. Statues in the nave, a central avenue from which the visitor could easily move from place to place

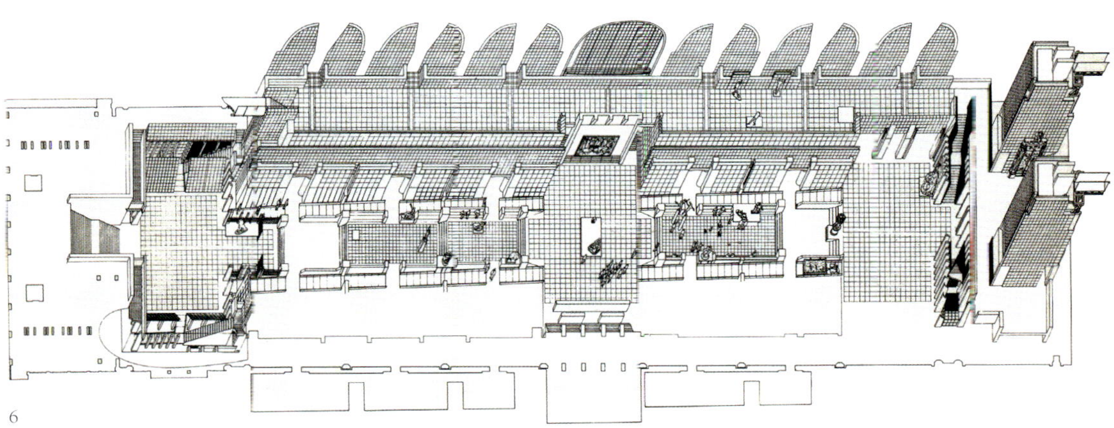

6

8

1

AMONT PAVILION AT THE ORSAY MUSEUM

Architect: Atelier de l'Ile
Location: Paris
Completion Date: 2011
Photographer: Atelier de l'Ile, Hervé Abbadie

In 2011, Atelier de l'Ile redesigned the Amont Pavilion to provide a new setting for decorative arts, the Nabis painters and the large format paintings of Gustave Courbet. Drawn in by the red of the wall at the end of the nave, the visitor enters a pared down environment where everything has been designed to show the artworks to their best advantage.

The Pavilion was open to the rest of the museum and linked to it via passages and a footbridge. A simple and legible circuit for visitors has been created through a new approach to vertical circulation and a circular route on each floor. From the ground floor, the way up to the Impressionists gallery at the foot of the tympanum has been made more legible by grouping the staircase and lift with the escalators at the end of the nave, thus reducing the number of pillars and

2

obstacles in this part of the museum. From the larger surface area of the rooms to the uncluttered and discreet museography, everything works to provide an improved setting for the artworks. The organisation of each floor is now much clearer thanks to a sharp distinction made between the exhibition spaces and the circulation hubs: for the latter, a clear path through the space is strengthened by natural light, while state-of-the-art artificial light is deftly

3

1. Vertical view down the well of the central staircase
2. Sculpture and light
3. Exterior of the pavilion
4. Staircase and footbridge linking to the nave
5. 2nd floor, the red theme and the light wells
6. Axonometric drawing
7. Position of the Amont Pavilion

employed in the exhibition rooms.

The space is brought alive by the use of different scales. The floors dedicated to the different schools of decorative arts have been reworked on the scale of the furniture and objects exhibited. The structure of the rooms and the display supports (plinths, display cases…) are conducive to representing the works "in situ", recreating the intimate atmosphere of a private home. Conversely, to reveal the clock and the exceptional view over the Seine in all their glory, the 5th floor space has been cleared of obstacles. In the same way, Courbet's large format paintings have been given a room that they deserve, with a large circular seat the only furniture. Finally, work on colour has been done, with the red wall serving as a clarion call, a landmark, a means of getting one's bearings, and a backdrop to the vertical circulation, while a dark "taupe" hue has been used for the gallery walls, the better to show the artworks.

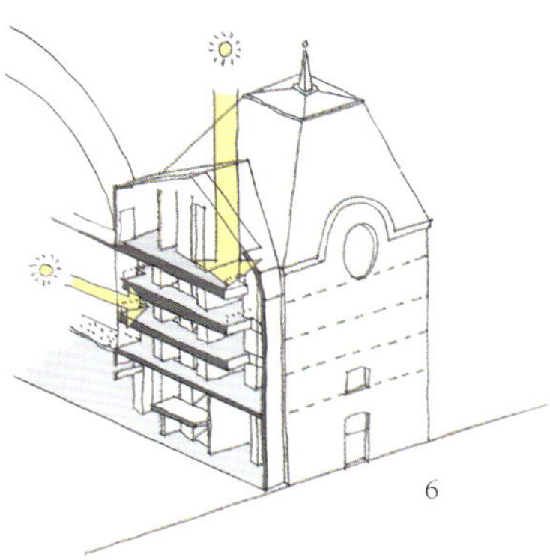

8

8. Natural light and a red wall (red line)
9. New vertical circulations
10. Vertical view of the atrium and red walls (red line) on a grand scale

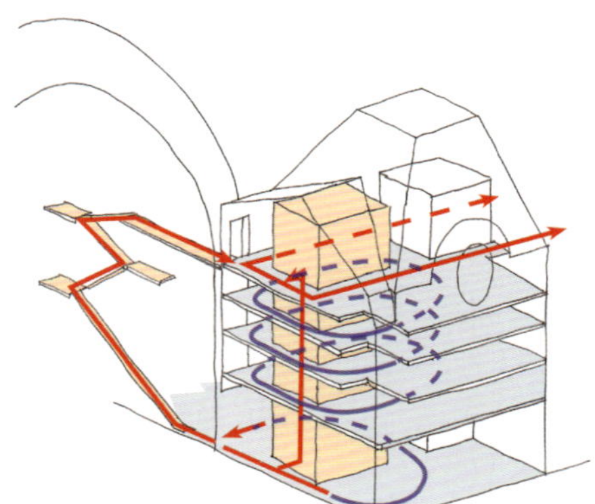
9

10

11

12

13

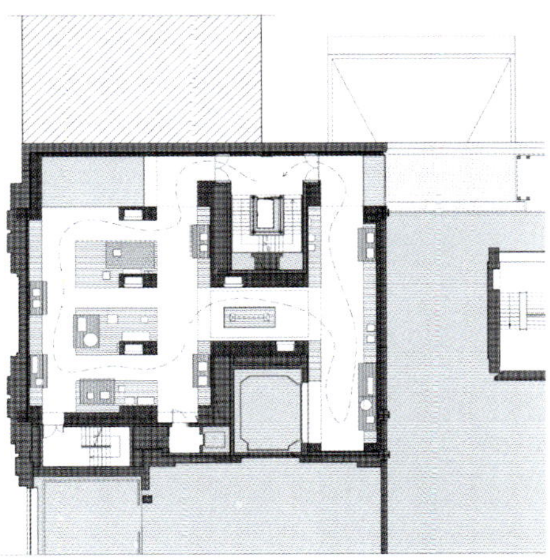

14

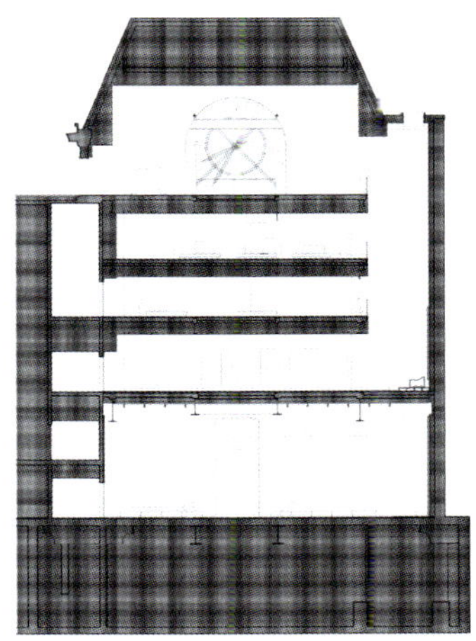

15

11. 2nd floor, the Nabis
12. 4th floor, European furniture
13. 2nd floor, the Nabis, the different arts brought together
14. 3th floor plan, thematic exhibition room
15. Section

16

17

16. 4th floor, display cases and European furniture (Austria)
17. Natural light and artificial lighting, on a domestic scale
18. The central staircase and the lift shaft in metallic mesh
19. 5th floor, the clock, the skylight and the atrium
20. 5th floor, the clock and the view of Paris

18

19

20

INTERNATIONAL PERFUME MUSEUM

Architect: Frédéric Jung
Location: Grasse
Completion Date: 2009
Photographer: Frédéric Jung (pp.66-67, 69, 70, 75), Éric Laignel (pp.68, 71-73, 76-77)

The challenge in designing this museum was to convey the subject of perfume, newly recognised as a form of heritage but nevertheless intangible. This museum does not limit itself to conservation, but sees itself as a tool – an "interpretation centre" housing a collection and offering the means to read it in a contemporary way. The permanent exhibition of the collections is fed by satellites: a lecture room, temporary exhibitions, an osmotheque, an archive, educational workshops for children and adults, etc.

This gave rise to a complex project, spread over multiple buildings, marked by the history of the town and its successive additions. Placed on a hillside, perpendicular to a topographical fault, on the edge of the old city fortifications, the museum had to make good use of this spatial and historical richness. The primary stake in its reorganisation was how to create a relationship across the 3,000m^2 spread over five buildings and seven floors. A major reference point creates a synergy for the many different spaces. It

2

has been created around the uncovered 14th-century city wall, enshrined at the heart of the block by a "fault" that offers a clear view of the exhibition floors and organises the movement through the museum.

Paradoxically, it is a wall around two metres thick that becomes the point of contact, the link for the new organism. This axis of fortification is revived and protected by a glass "nave" running alongside it and supported by it. The nave appears as the

3

4

contemporary face of the museum from Boulevard Fragonard, while not interfering with the lines of the Hôtel Morel-Amic, the master building of the site. The itinerary through the museum is extremely varied. Neither a temple-museum or not forum-museum, it tells a series of "stories" in a living way, in seven very different settings.

5

1. Façade on Jeu de Ballon boulevard
2. South façade
3. The fault
4. Entrance hall
5. Master plan
6. Entrance to the temporary exhibitions

7

7. The terrace
8. Longitudinal section (contemporary displays + rooftop conservatory)
9-10. Rooftop conservatory

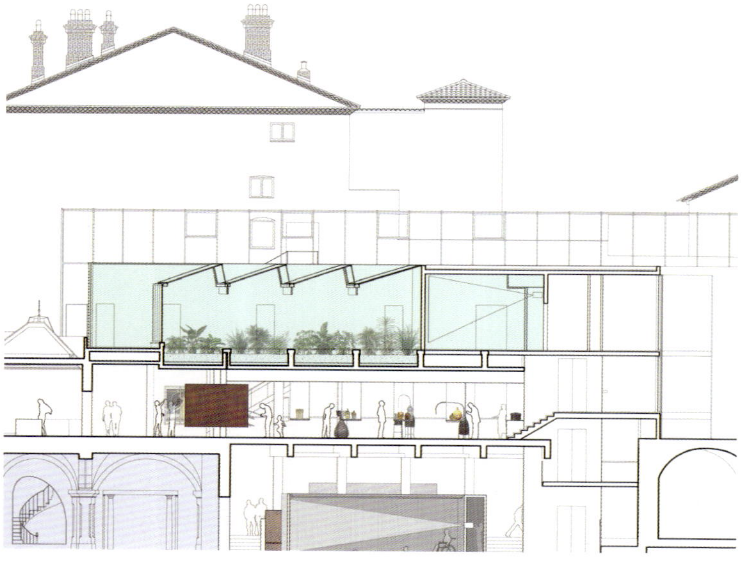

8

11. The fault
12-14. Industrial machinery in the fault

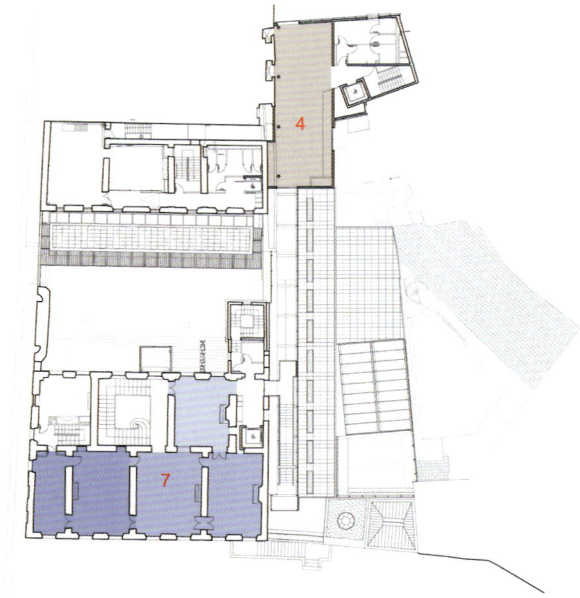

15

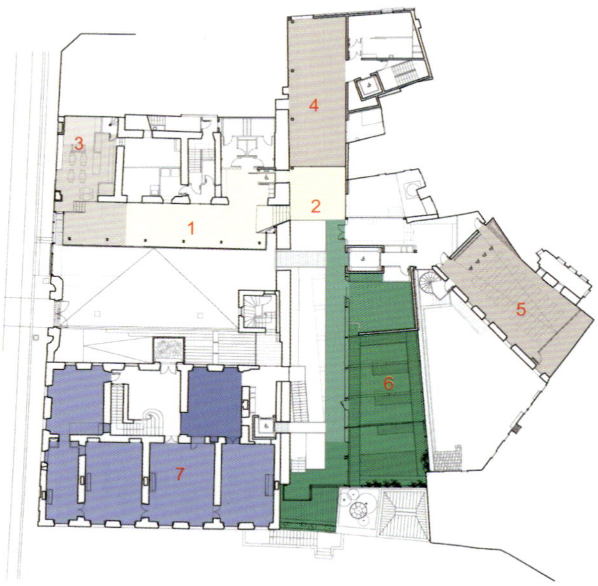

16

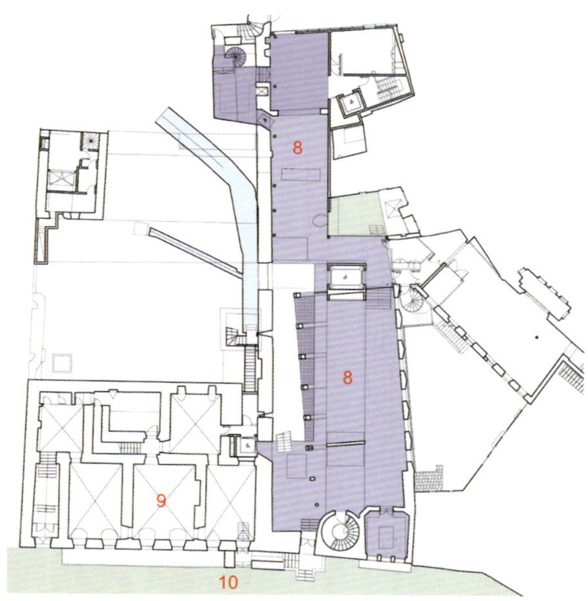

17

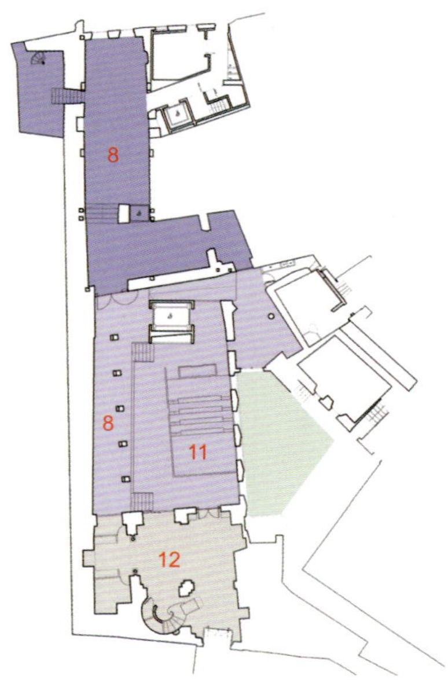

18

15. 1st floor plan
16. Ground floor plan
17. 1st basement floor plan
18. 2nd basement floor plan
19. The fault and the 19th century displays
20. Longitudinal section of the fault (the city wall)
21. Longitudinal section of the fault (contemporary displays)

1. Entrance hall
2. Entrance to the temporary exhibition room
3. Children's area
4. Temporary exhibition room
5. Auditorium
6. Botanical conservatory: aromatic plants
7. Thematic exhibition room: Historic look – from Antiquity to the Revolution
8. Thematic exhibition room: 19tth-20th centuries – manufacturing and distribution
9. Café
10. Gardens of the 18th and 19th centuries
11. Projection room
12. Shop

19

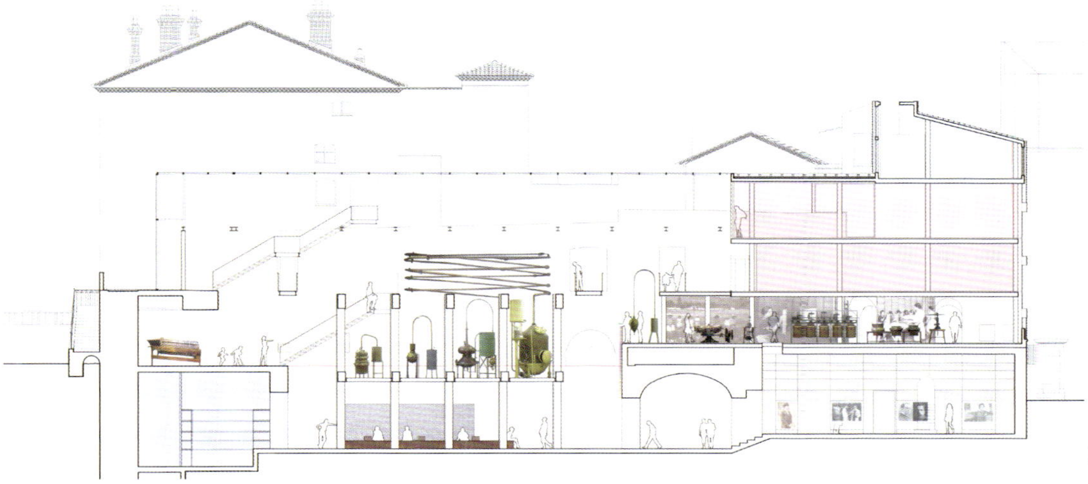

20

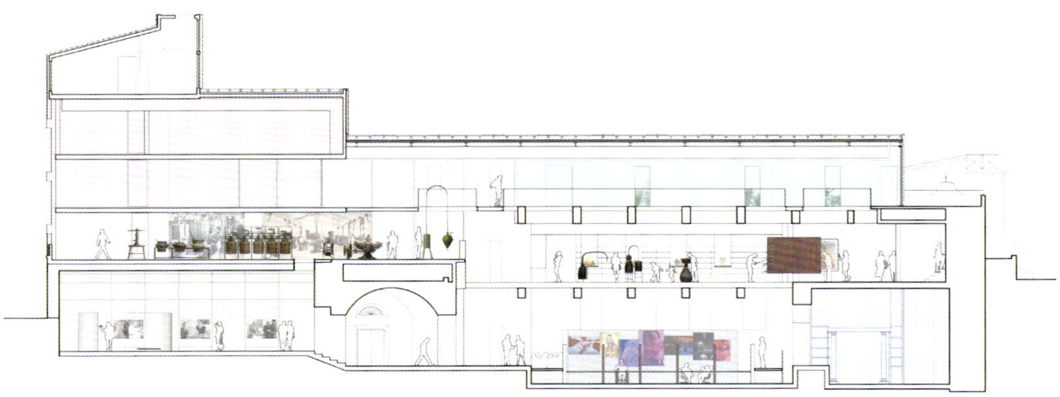

21

22. 19th century displays
23. Early 20th century displays
24. 20th century: a perfume for each year

1984
1983
1982
1981
1980
1979
1978
1977
1975
1974
1973
1972
1971
1970
Chloé
24

TOMI UNGERER MUSEUM

Architect: ECDM – Emmanuel Combarel Dominique Marrec
Location: Strasbourg
Completion Date: 2007
Photographer: Luc Boegly

Situated in the heart the Ville Neuve district, near Place de la République, the Tomi Ungerer Museum and International Centre for Illustration is housed in the Villa Greiner, which was built in 1884 by the architect Samuel Revel. The building's neo-classical style is typical of the late19th-century architecture of this German Imperial neighbourhood and as such had to be respected, whilst adapting it to its new role as a major cultural destination for Strasbourg and its region.

The bourgeois residential building thus changed its status to become a public building, a space to welcome visitors ranging from researchers and academics to the simply curious. The architects endeavoured to take on board the regulatory demands and technical contingencies while giving the building a specific identity, that of a cultural space in an overall architectural context.

It is a contemporary intervention in a 19th-century setting. The integrity of the exterior

1

of the building has been preserved, the only change being to the windows, which, as an interface, had to be updated to respond to the specifications of the museum, and the installation of a curved walkway across the garden.

2

Inside, the proportions of the original rooms have been preserved, but white ceilings, floors and walls give them a "white cube" aesthetic suitable for the display of graphic works. Visitors can easily move between the four floors of the museum via

3

4

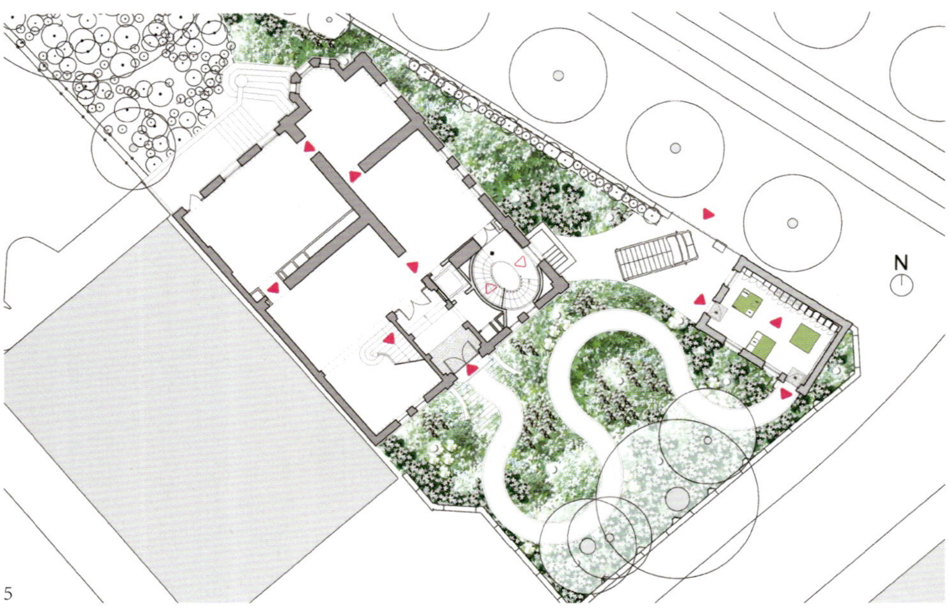

5

a lift or a white spiral staircase forming an internal column to the left of the entrance.

While remaining true to its historical context, the Villa Greiner has acquired a new identity as a cultural centre through weaving its specificity and constraints into the poetry of the whole.

1. Exhibition room, in a “white cube” aesthetic suitable for the display of graphic works
2. Creation of a second interior staircase
3&4. The renovated staircase
5. Plan of the lower ground floor and garden
6. Exhibition room

7

8

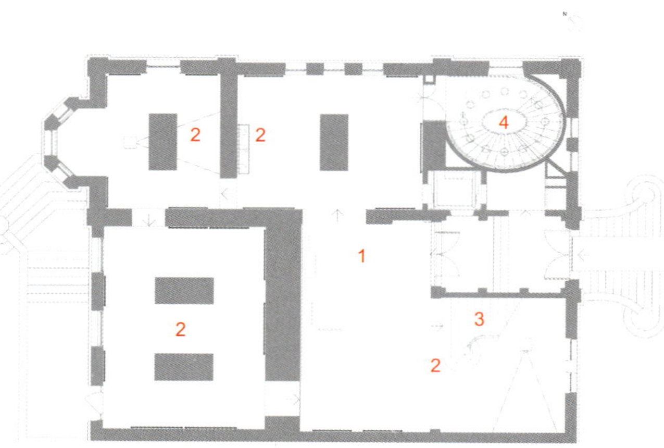

9

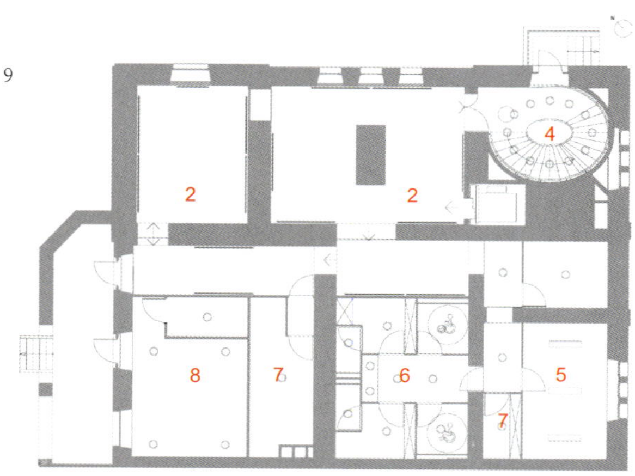

10

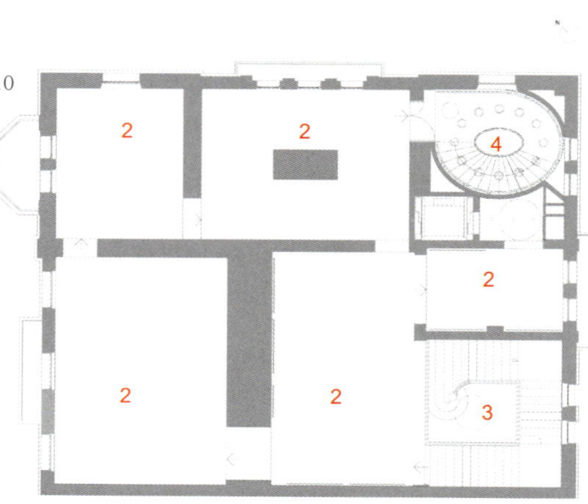

1. Entrance hall
2. Exhibition room
3. Renovated existing staircase
4. New staircase
5. Relaxation room
6. Coat check / WC
7. Maintenance room
8. Technical area

7&11. Exhibition rooms with white ceilings, floors and walls
8. Higher ground floor plan
9. Lower ground floor plan
10. 1st floor Plan
12. Cross section
13. Landing of the new interior staircase

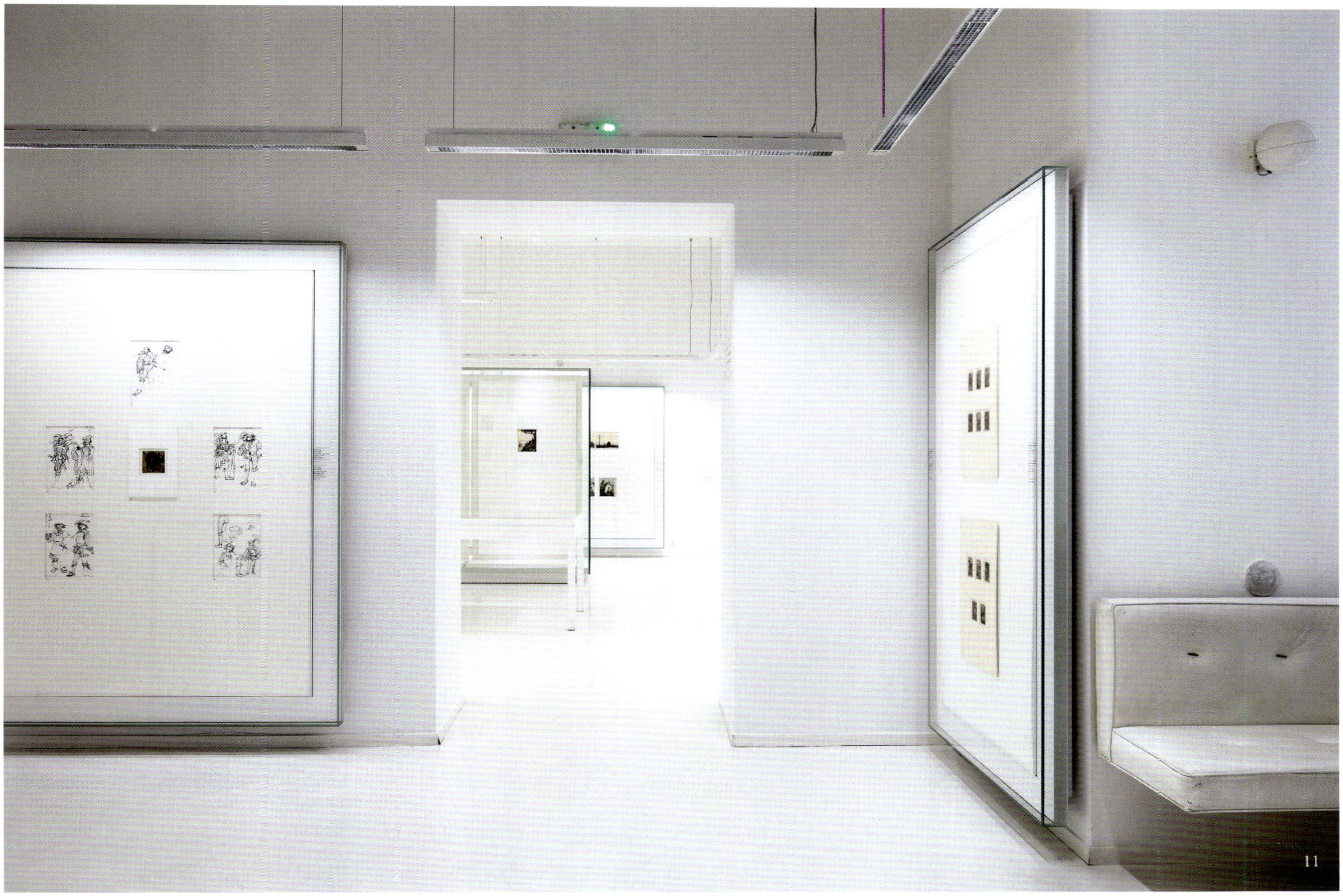
11

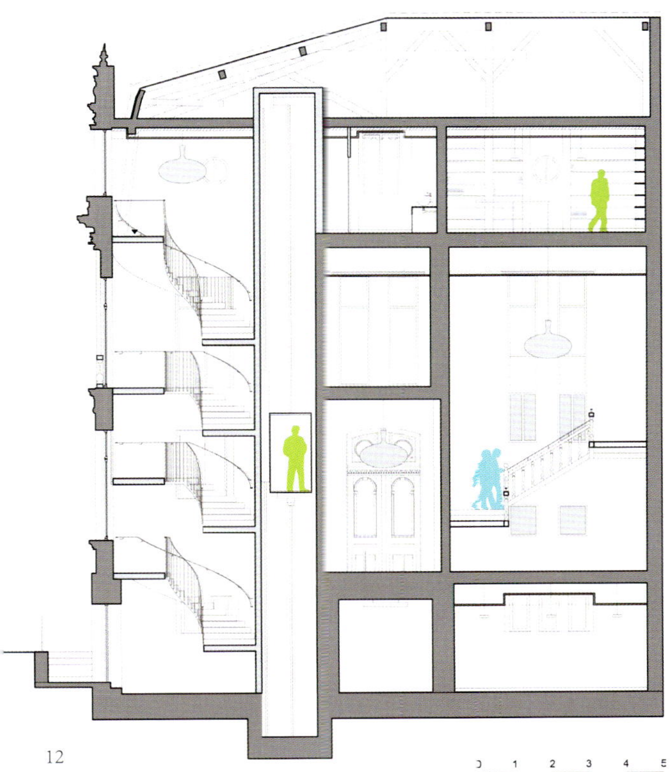
12

13

DIALOGUES
BETWEEN OLD AND NEW

VALENCE MUSEUM OF FINE ART AND ARCHEOLOGY

Architect: Jean-Paul Philippon
Location: Valence
Completion Date: in progress
Visual documents: Michaël Belolo

The museum is housed in the old episcopal palace, facing the cathedral. This site, which has been in constant transformation since the Gallo-Roman period, is like a palimpsest preserving all the imprints of its successive evolutions. Now the 21st century is making its own mark.

The look-out tower over the Rhône is the crowning glory of a "palindrome walk". Situated at the crossroads of two of Valence's historic strata, the project makes the most of the views the building commands across the old city and the 19th-century town.

The focus of the museum is the Hubert Robert collection, where fine art and archeology meet. This painter was a unique figure in the history of art, passionate about ruins and landscapes. By respecting and developing the spirit of the place, the project opens up possibilities for the museum concept to evolve, increasing

1

its appeal for visitors. The impressive collections and the spaces that house them have lent themselves to several different itineraries around the museum: one that is directly chronological, one with a reverse chronology and a third, architectural itinerary. The solidity and complexity of the existing volumes has been preserved, while the new parts adopt the form of successive planes.

2

1. Perspective drawing of the museum in its setting
2. The museum, the cathedral and the loop in the Rhône
3. Perspective drawing of the museum entrance on Ormeaux Square
4. Gallo-Roman archeology room

5

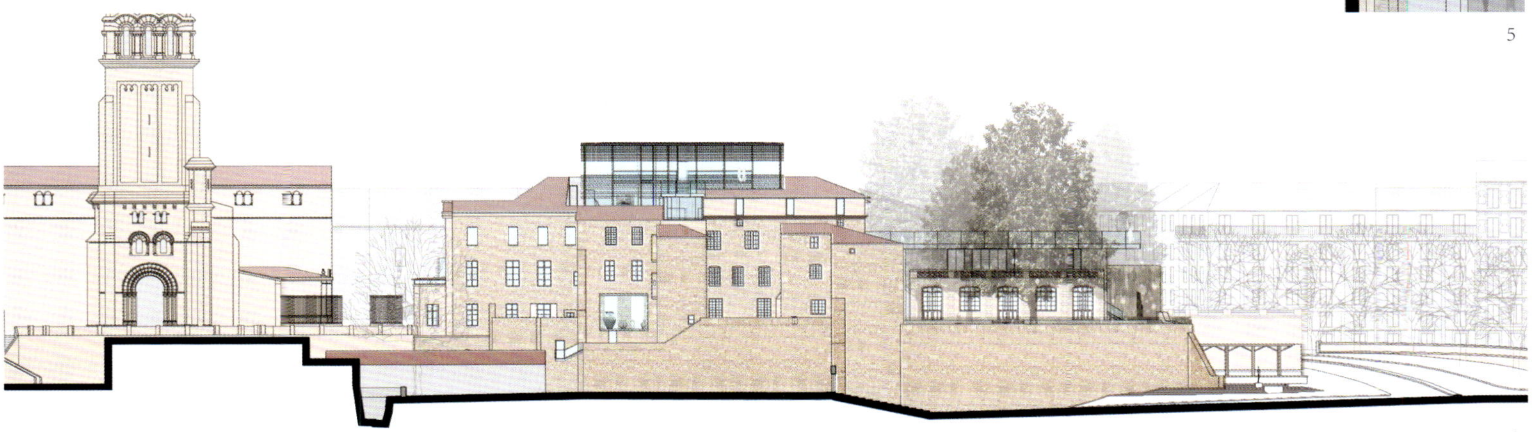

6

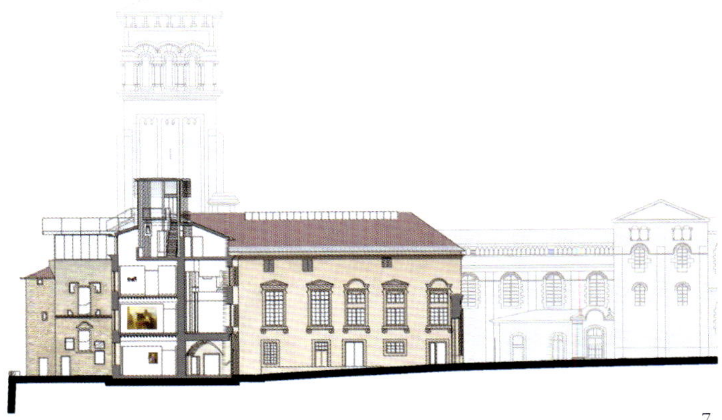

7

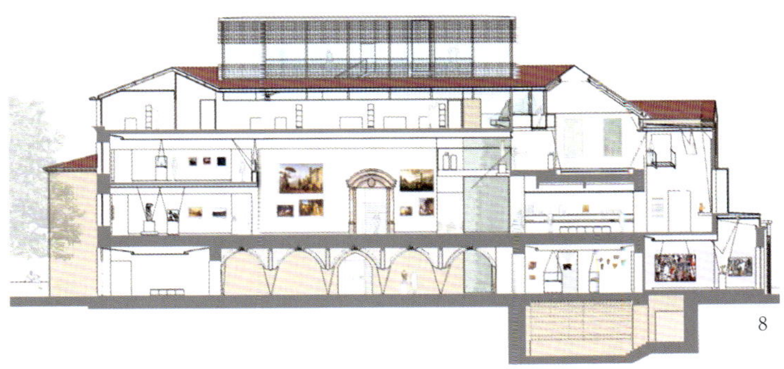

8

5. Façade overlooking the Rhône and look-out tower
6. Museum façade in front of the cathedral
7. Section of the look-out tower and the cour d'honneur
8. Museographical cross section

1

QUIMPER MUSEUM OF FINE ARTS

Architect: Jean-Paul Philippon
Location: Quimper
Completion Date: 1993
Photographer: Jean-Marie Monthiers (except n°3)

The current museum, which houses the important Silguy collection and the Max Jacob fund, is an extension and restructuring of the old museum, a neo-Tuscan building designed in 1864 by Joseph Bigot that faces Quimper cathedral. Creating a dialogue between two forms of architecture from different eras, the building has been totally reinterpreted on the theme of split-personality.

The granite staircase has been displaced from the main axis, as if "carried by a wave", leaving the axis, now extended to rue Verdelet, as an opening onto the reception spaces at the heart of the museum. The Fauvist decor of the old Hôtel de l'Épée by Jacques-Julien Lemordant has been reinstated in a transversal wooden nave, floating between two floors. Jean-Paul Philippon's project was based on the principle of transparency and free movement. Brittany's ethereal and changing light enters the building, playing

on the concrete, granite and beech wood.

A majestic central nave, harmonious in its volumes, gives onto the exhibition rooms and all the reception services. Openings in the concrete and granite provide interior and exterior reference points for the visitor, particularly those that reveal a view of the cathedral.

5

6

1. Painting rooms
2. Lemordant room
3. Entrance façade on Saint Corentin Square
4-5. Façade on Rue Verdelet
6. Entrance gallery
7. Section

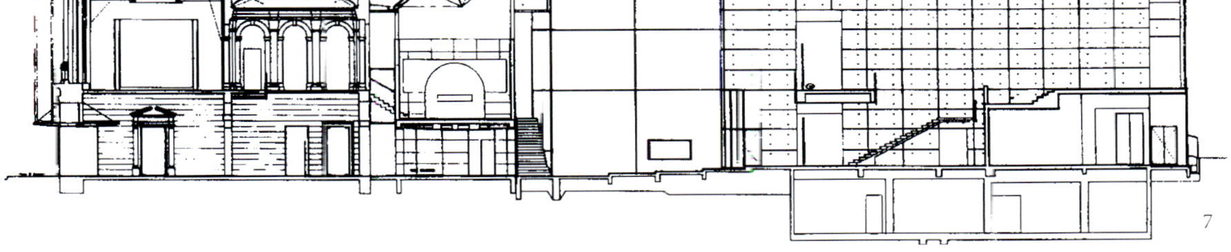

7

8

9

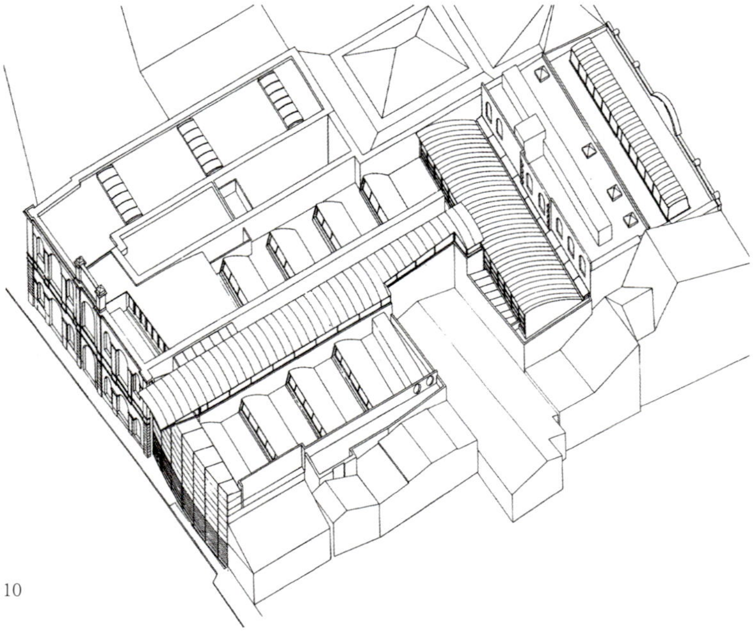

10

8. The nave, lateral view
9. Lemordant room
10. Axonometric drawing
11. Footbridge

11

BONNARD MUSEUM

Architect: Frédéric Ferrero & Sylvie Rossi
Location: Le Cannet
Completion Date: 2011
Photographer: Claire Palué

The Villa Saint-Vianney is a fine example of Belle Époque architecture. It was built in 1908 as a private residence, became a guest house and then a hotel until 1990. After being saved from demolition by the state heritage department, it was bought by the town of Le Cannet in 1998 in order to turn it into a museum.

From the beginning, the focus was on preserving the spirit of the place. The project forms part of a larger development of the old town centre of Le Cannet, and is linked to Bonnard's former home, the Villa Le Bosquet, by a walk in the steps of the painter. The renovation of the Villa Saint-Vianney develops almost 890m^2 of useable space, including 495m^2 in the existing building. An extension has been built on the sloping ground in front of the villa, containing the reception area, shop, educational room and a large terrace. The façade opens onto the Boulevard Sadi Carnot and marks the entrance to the museum.

A glass column containing a staircase and a lift, connecting to the existing building via a footbridge, takes visitors to the exhibition floors while offering a view over the landscape. The internal structure of the Villa Saint-Vianney has been entirely altered. Air conditioned throughout, the museum unfolds over five floors including three floors of exhibitions, a projection room and a terrace overlooking the garden.

3

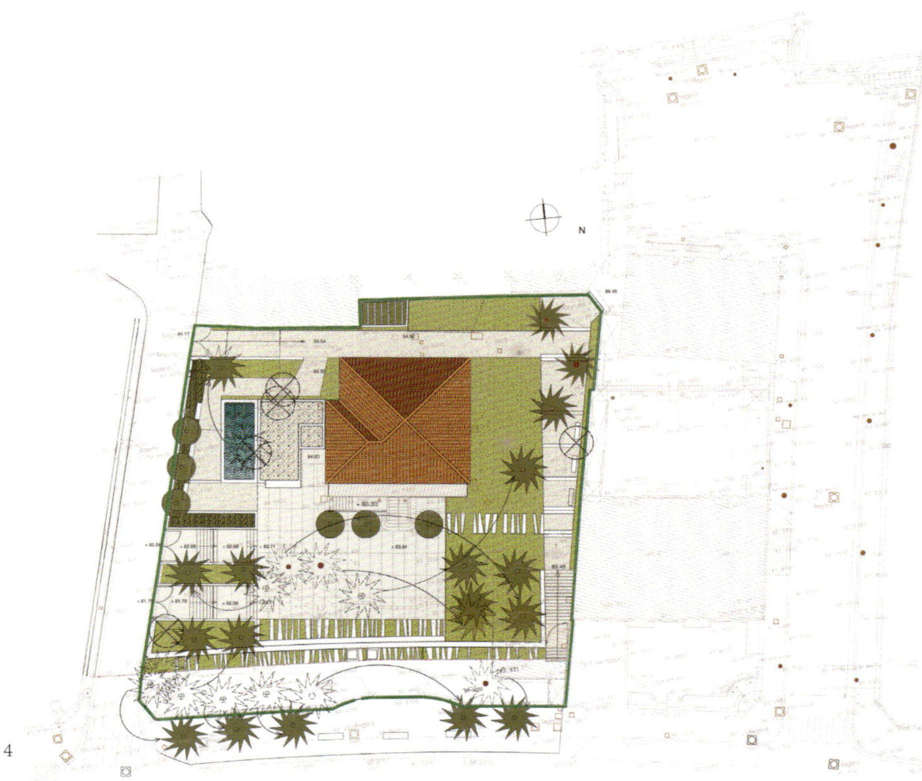

4

5

1. Exhibition room
2. Museum entrance, Boulevard Sadi Carnot
3. View of the museum from Boulevard Sadi Carnot
4. Master plan
5. View from the terrace
6. South façade
7. West façade

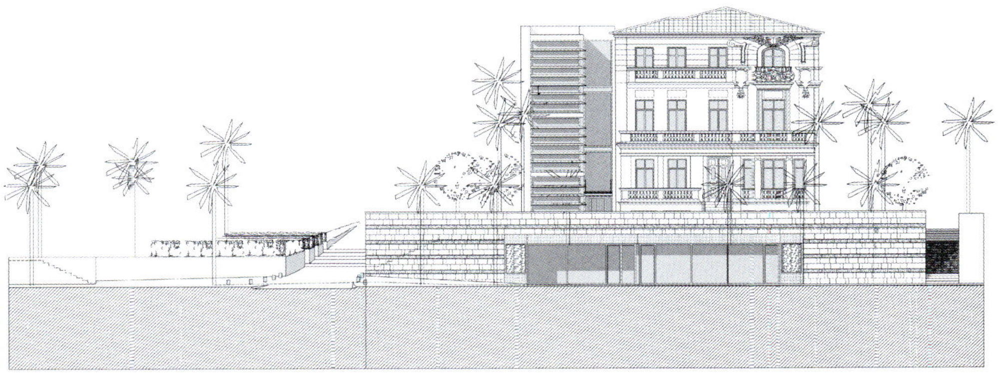

6

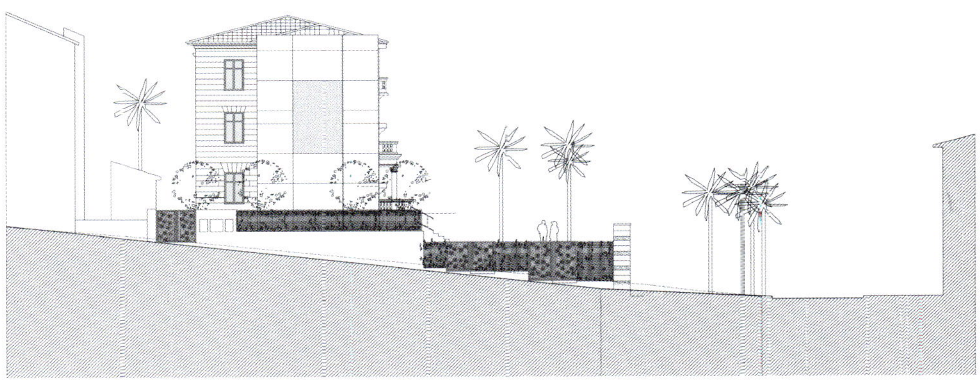

7

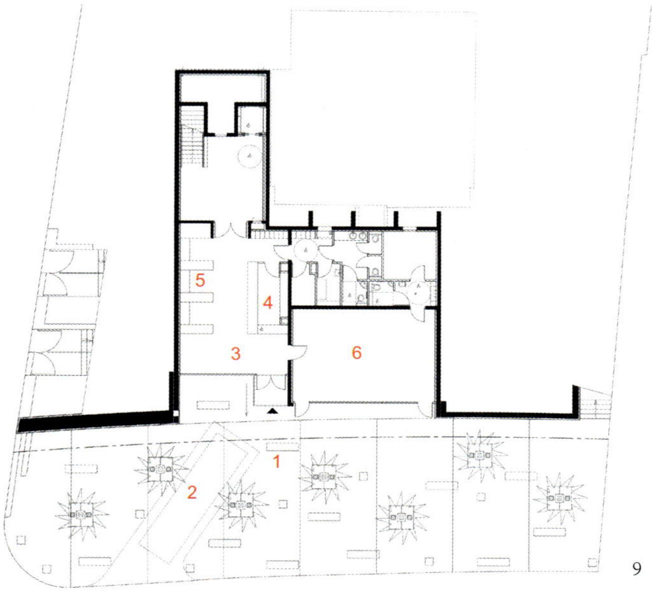

9

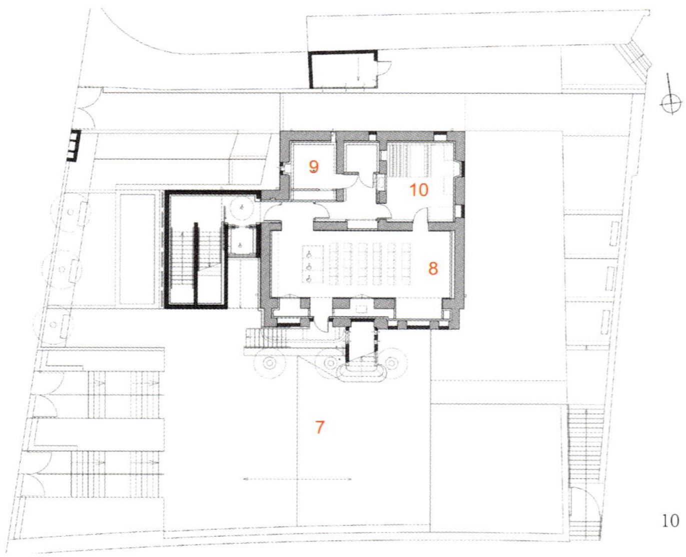

10

8. The museum's garden terrace
9. Ground floor plan
10. 1st floor plan

11. Exhibition room
12. Old staircase of the Hôtel Saint-Vianney
13. 2nd floor plan
14. 3rd floor plan
15. 4th floor plan
16. Roof plan

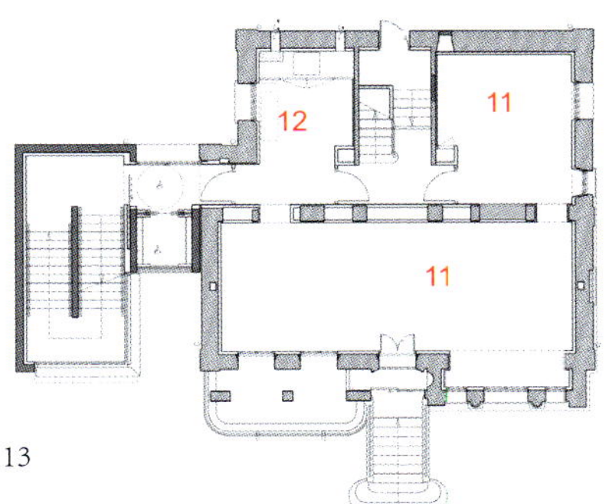

13

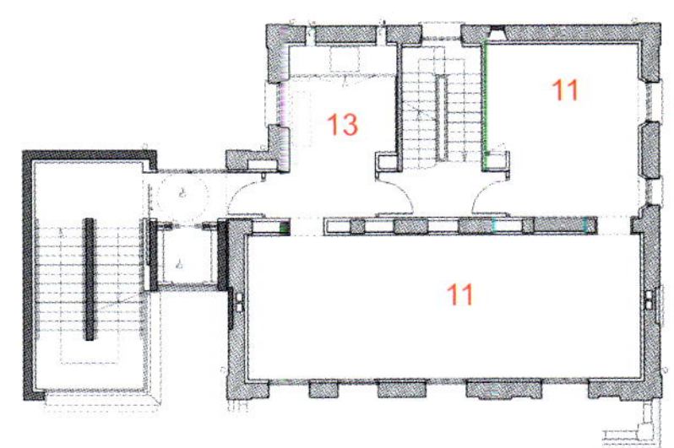

14

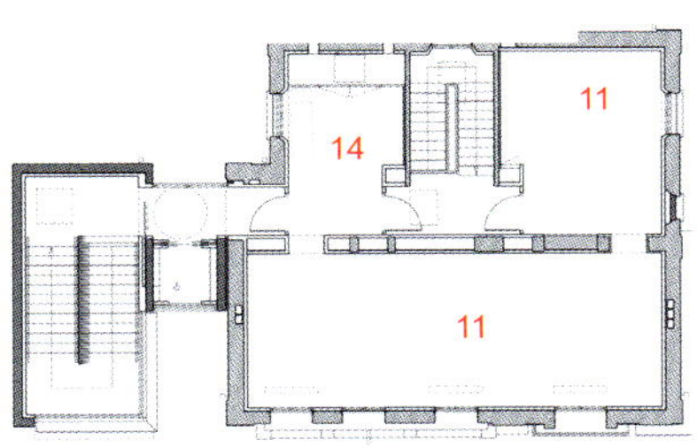

15

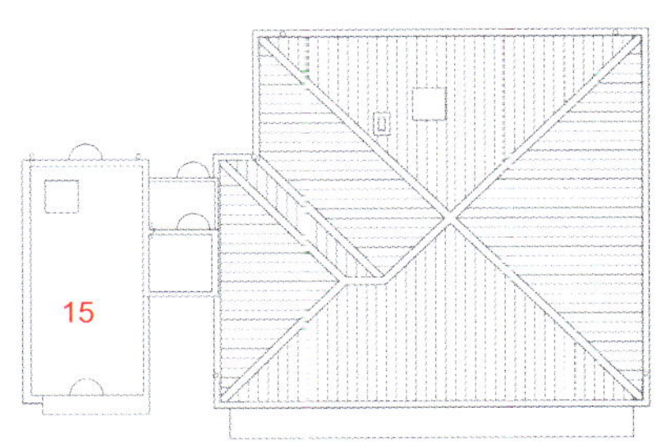

16

1. Forecourt
2. Delivery area
3. Entrance Hall
4. Reception
5. Shop
6. Activities room
7. Garden terrace
8. Projection room
9. Technical area
10. Stock room – reserves
11. Exhibition room
12. Introduction room
13. Biography room
14. Workshop
15. Roof terrace

COURBET MUSEUM

Architect: Ateliers 234
Location: Ornans
Completion Date: 2011
Photographer: Nicolas Waltefaugle

The Courbet Museum has left the limited space of its original location in the Maison Hébert to expand into two adjoining buildings: the Maison Borel and the Hôtel Champereux. These three entities rejoice in a remarkable location right beside the River Loue in Ornans, between the Great Bridge, the fountain and Robert Fernier Square. The building has been opened up to the light, colours and materials of "Courbet country".

The previous façade gave no indication of the museum's presence. Today a large stainless steel box juts out, suspended from the height of the entrance hall, announcing the museum to the city. On the river side, a horizontal sequence also proclaims the building's new dimensions: a thin glass roof built into the tiles highlights the position of the hall, then a glassed-in gallery forms a link between the houses, continues through the Maison Hébert and protrudes from the end wall. This long horizontal sequence on the river symbolises the new ambition of the

1

museum. At nightfall, this line becomes a luminous thread between the houses and the garden reflecting on the water.

One of the basic tenets of the project was to preserve the atmosphere of the Maison Hébert. The parts of the museum that called for large-scale restructuring, such as the welcome area, are kept "at a distance" and connect with the public space. This house, a succession of historic rooms of which some are heritage listed, is plunged into the atmosphere and colours

2

musée COURBET
Bienvenue
Welcome
Willkommen
Bienvenidos
ようこそ

3

4

5

1. The museum's new dimensions; a luminous thread
2. The old courtyard houses the entrance hall. The black box metaphorically reaches out to the town
3. The black box floats above the reception
4. The gallery, a place of immersion into the landscape
5. Footbridge to the black box
6. Situation plan

of Courbet's time. The Maison Hébert leads into the Revolutions rooms, where the scene is first set in space and time: a display case/gallery visible from both sides evokes the revolution of 1848 on one side and on the other, at the end of the visit, the revolution of 1870. Thanks to this transparency the building is readable through its entire depth.

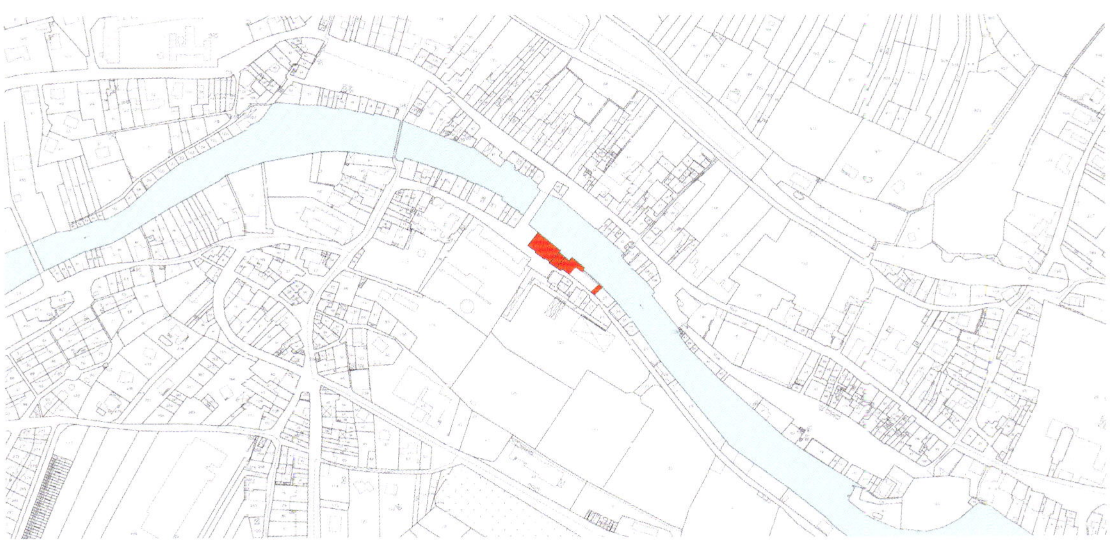

6

7

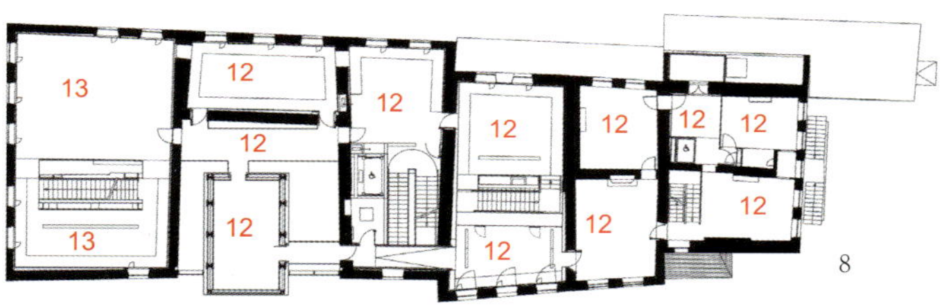

8

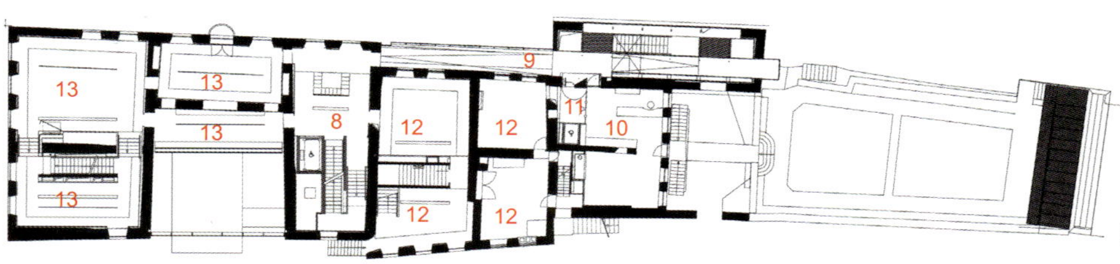

9

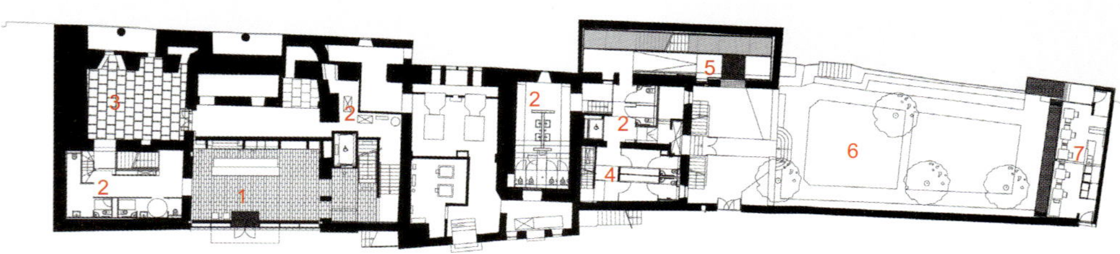

10

1. Entrance hall / reception
2. Rest rooms
3. Vaulted cellars
4. Staff cloakrooms
5. Gallery, exit to the garden
6. Garden
7. Summer cafeteria
8. Coat check
9. Gallery overlooking the Loue
10. Shop
11. Entrance to the permanent exhibition
12. Permanent exhibition
13. Temporary exhibition

7. Revolutions room, a place of rupture
8. 1st floor plan
9. Upper ground floor plan
10. Lower ground floor plan
11. The walls cut at an angle show their historic thickness
12. Display tables protect precious drawings

13

14

15

16

13. The passage from one house to another, in serenity
14. Restrooms in the old vaulted cellars
15. The exit hall, a place of reflection(s)
16. Near the museum exit visitors can look down on the water
17. Cross section
18. Longitudinal section

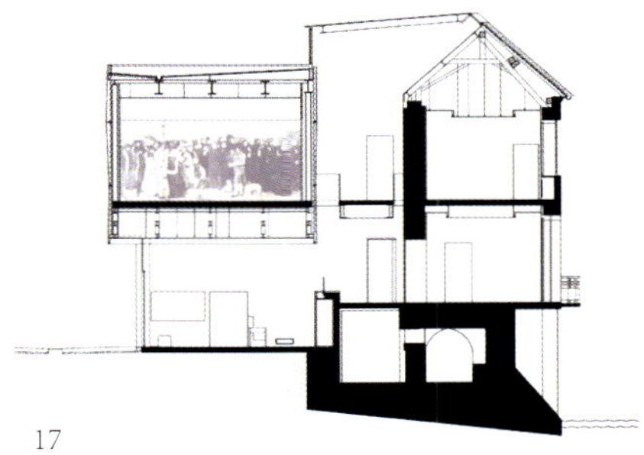

17

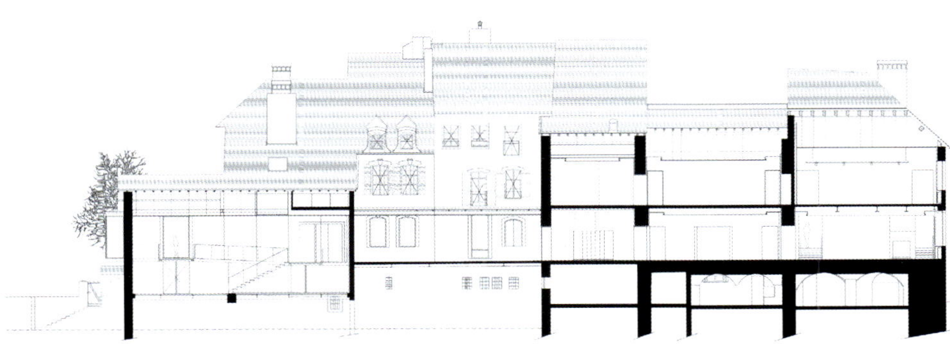

18

LA PISCINE MUSEUM OF ART AND INDUSTRY

Architect: Jean-Paul Philippon
Location: Roubaix
Completion Date: 2001
Photographer: Florian Kleinefenn

The Museum of Art and Industry has given a new dynamism to the town of Roubaix, which was proud of its old Art Deco swimming pool designed by Albert Baert. This building has been redeveloped and extended into a neighbouring disused industrial site, thereby offering the potential for cross-fertilisation with the worlds of industrial creation (fashion shows, textile design), culture (performance arts, music) and education (teaching workshops).

The project has made use of the original materials, bricks and enamelled stoneware tiles of the cabins, found in situ and has reconfigured them. Through a dialogue that respects the existing building, down to the very detail of the its vocabulary, this project has given a central place to creative mutations and scenographies that are the height of creativity. The thin stream of water preserved in the central swimming pool area reflects the works presented on the horizontal pontoons and can also be covered

1

over for an exhibition or a fashion show.

With an auditorium, and logistical spaces that are entered from the street, the vast temporary exhibition space enables extremely varied exhibitions (Picasso, Degas, Signac, Marimekko) that make use of a large-scale hanging system that is both fixed and mobile. It is a new kind of museum that brings together art and economics, memory and modernity.

2

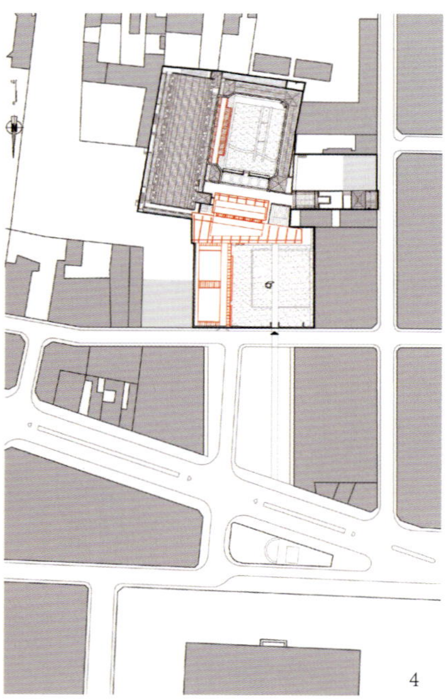
4

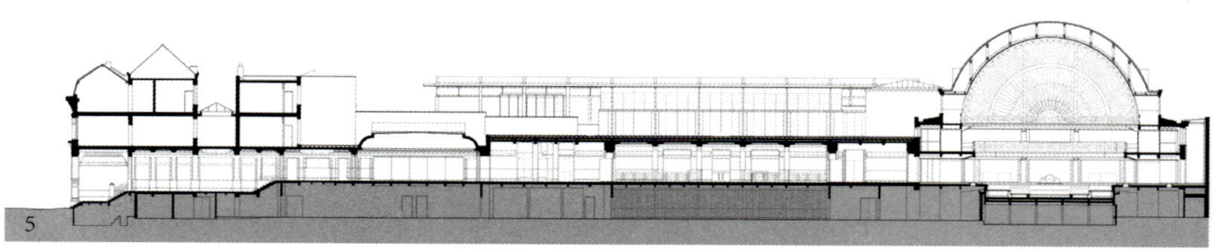
5

1. Exterior view
2. Façade of the museum
3. The entrance through the garden on the old industrial site
4. Master plan
5. General section
6. Entrance hall

6

7

8

7&8. Entrance to the temporary exhibition
9. Section of the entrance hall

9

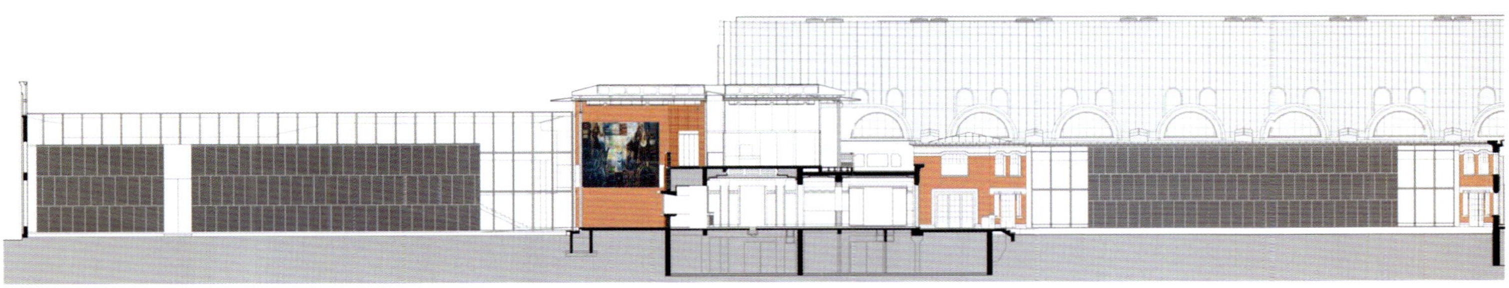

10

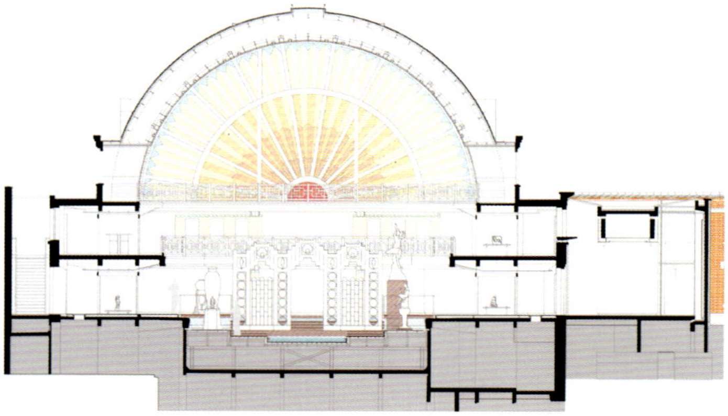

11

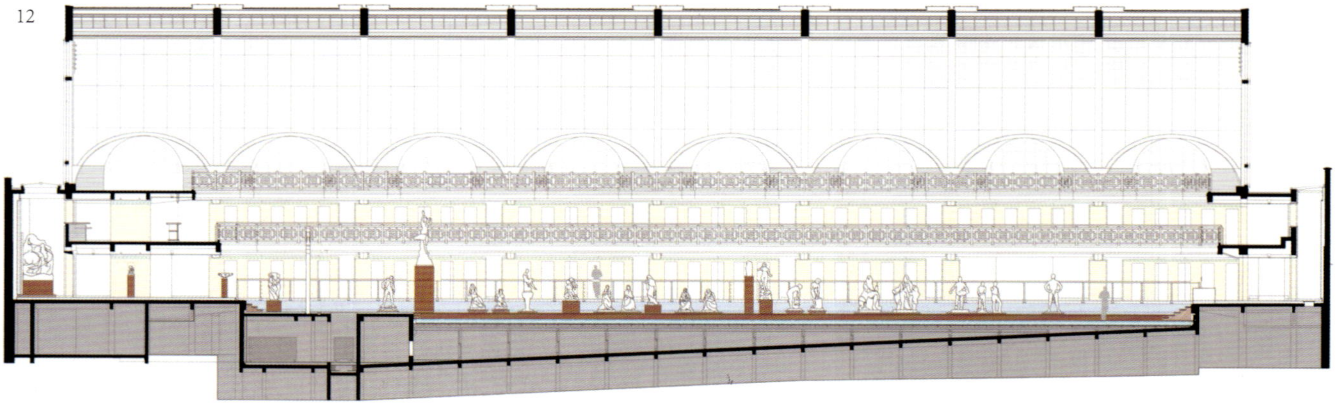

12

10. The swimming pool
11. Cross section of the swimming pool
12. Longitudinal section of the swimming pool
13. The swimming pool, sculpture pontoon and changing rooms

13

14. A Carolyn Carlson performance in the swimming pool
15. Entrance through the compass room and the bust of Albert Baert

15

LA MAISON ROUGE

Architect: Amplitude Architectes, Jean-Yves Clément
Location: Paris
Completion Date: 2004
Photographer: Luc Boegly

Originally, the Maison Rouge (the Red House) was a shop open to the street. The back wall of the shop was demolished, opening up a courtyard, in the centre of which was found a small house encircled by a glass roof and surrounded by warehouses from the beginning of the 19th century, whose riveted metal beams retained a historic value. Behind were two industrial buildings, one from the 1950s-60s and the other in concrete, over three floors. Jean-Yves Clément's idea was to remove the floors of the latter to create a large volume.

The heterogeneity of this site has become one of its strengths. It has been used according to the specificity of each place within. Some spaces are large on the lower part, like the current polygonal room. Further on, the architects find what is known as a "White Cube", and down a few steps you feel as if you are under a tent where the nave of the original industrial structure has been preserved. The idea was that on entering you could

forget that you were in Paris and lose any geographical notion of the city. For Clément it was about offering a place that could evoke certain buildings from other large capitals, which would aid the appreciation of contemporary art.

The false ceilings that in the past unified the spaces and made this into a typically Parisian building have been avoided. For the restaurant, the idea was that it would be discovered, in a democratic way, at the heart of the Maison Rouge. Anyone can

2

1. Gallery, patio and café
2. Skylight
3. Gallery with a view of the patio
4. Upper mezzanine gallery
5. Mezzanine

enter, without a ticket, and have a cup of coffee at the heart of the exhibition. The city and the public space are thus invited in to the private foundation. This kind of neutrality of spaces is what distinguishes the Maison Rouge from other Parisian environments. We are nowhere and we could be anywhere... Here, in this non-referential space and time, contemporary art meets post-industrial architecture.

6

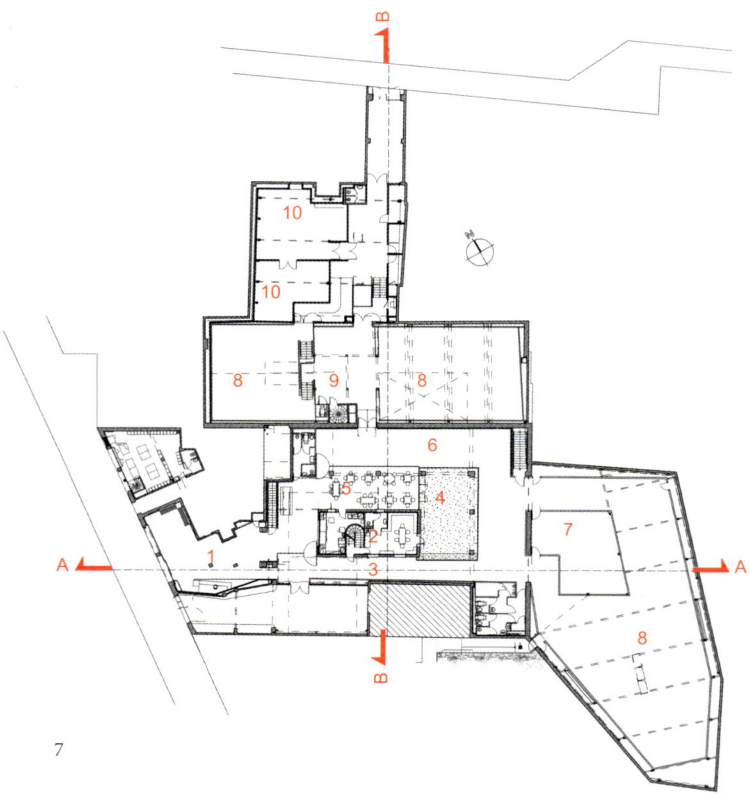

7

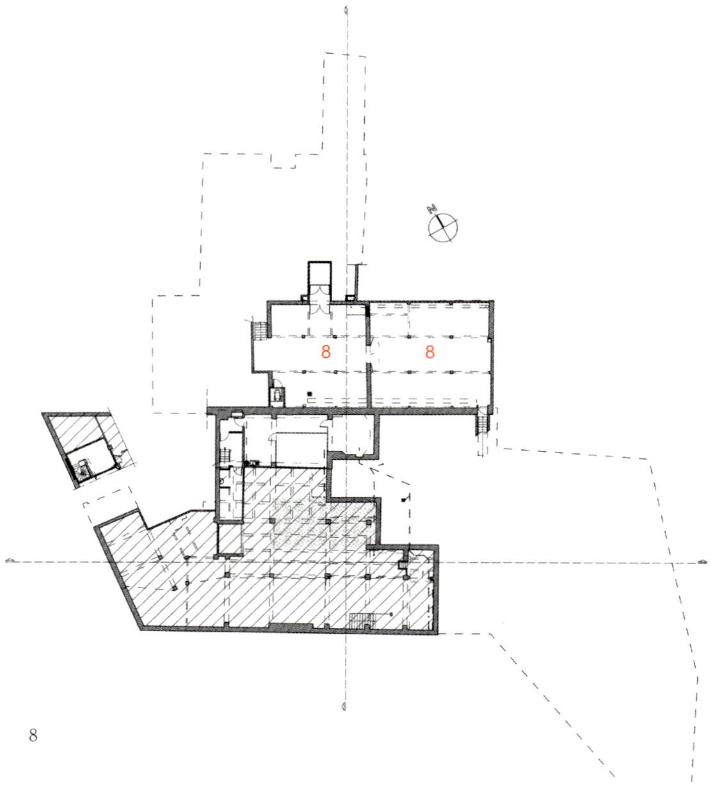

8

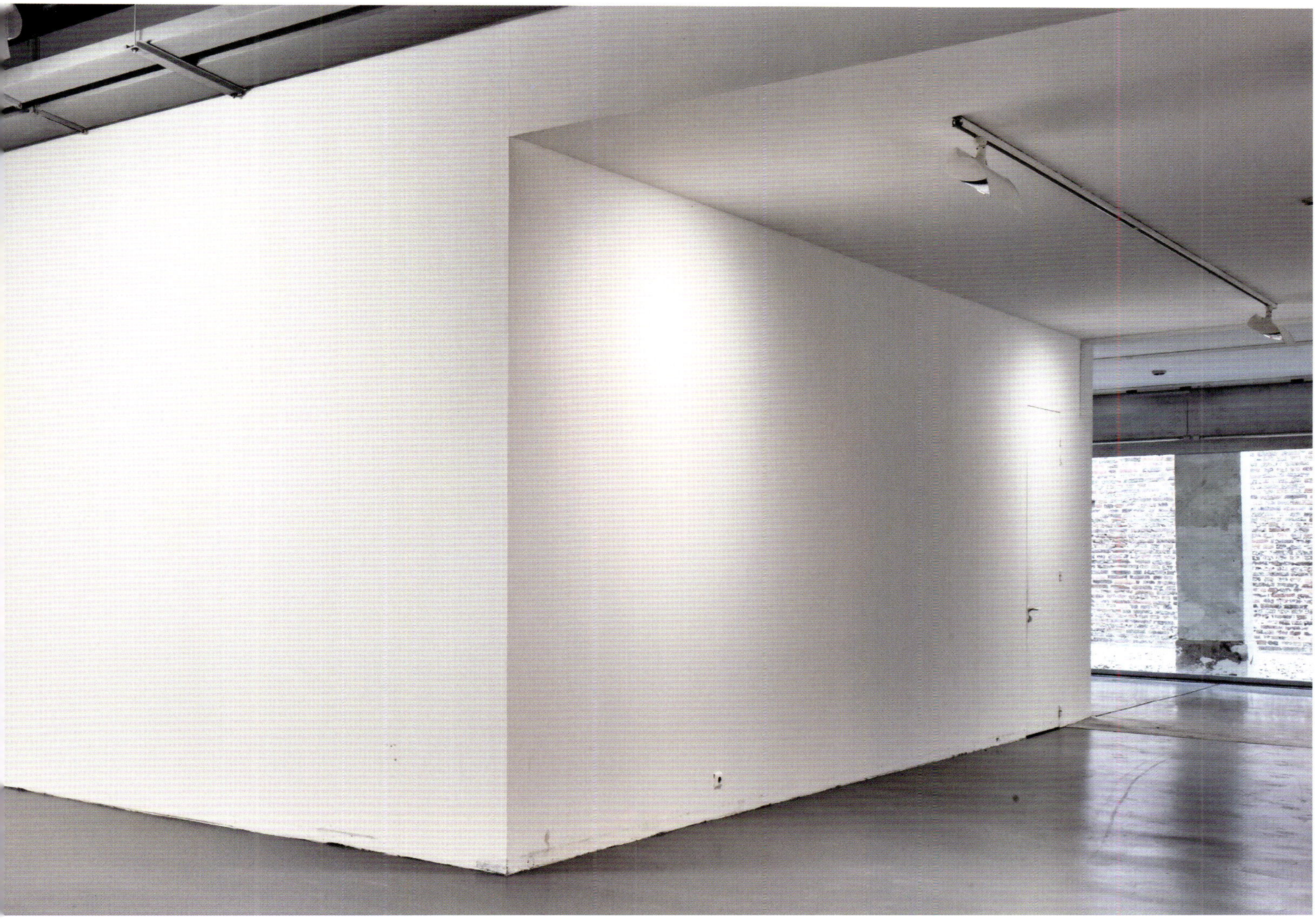

1. Entrance hall
2. Maison Rouge
3. Interior street
4. Patio
5. Terrace café
6. North gallery
7. Multimedia room
8. Exhibition room
9. Balcony
10. Reserves

6. Polygonal room
7. Ground floor plan
8. Basement floor plan
9. Section AA
10. Section BB

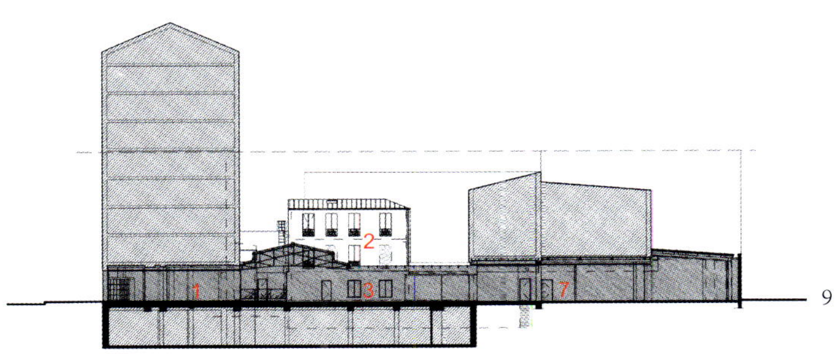

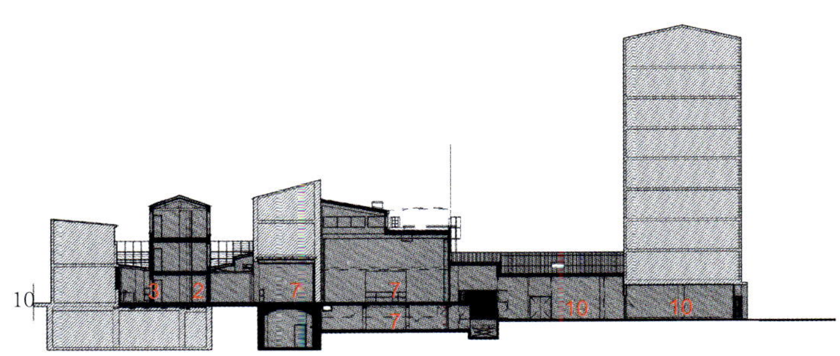

MATISSE MUSEUM

Architect: Beaudouin-Husson
Location: Cateau-Cambrésis
Completion Date: 2002
Photographer: Jean-Marie Monthiers

Architecture and painting follow paths that converge at certain points. For both, there is no difference between the inside and the outside. The space is unitary, it always stays the same, no screen separates it into two, it remains as one.

The Matisse Museum expresses this continuous character of space. It is also an attempt to unite in a single form fragments of buildings and landscapes that, through their history and their situation, are close in space but far away in time: a square, a palace, a school, a park. The aim was to turn these elements into a united whole, a space where each part would be indispensable to the balance of the whole.

The architects sought harmony in the proportions of the museum, giving a musical resonance to the whole. The architecture is based on the superimposition of elements, on the progressive disappearance of what lies behind the things we see. The architecture of a museum is like a machine to slow

2

down time, it forces one to adjust from the accelerated time of everyday life to the more tranquil time of contemplation. The association of two invisible laws of nature makes light and gravity more present. In architecture, light can have weight. If you give weight to light its movement slows down, the light becomes solemn, it settles into a slow thickness. The architecture of the museum is designed as a resonant casing in which this emotion vibrates.

3

4

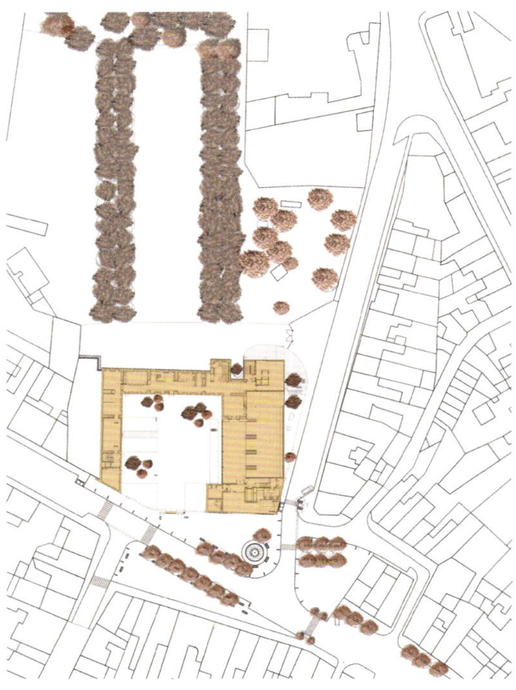

5

6

1. Drawings and sculptures pavilion
2. New wing
3. Cafeteria
4. Matisse room
5. Master plan
6. Sculpture room
7. Section and west façade

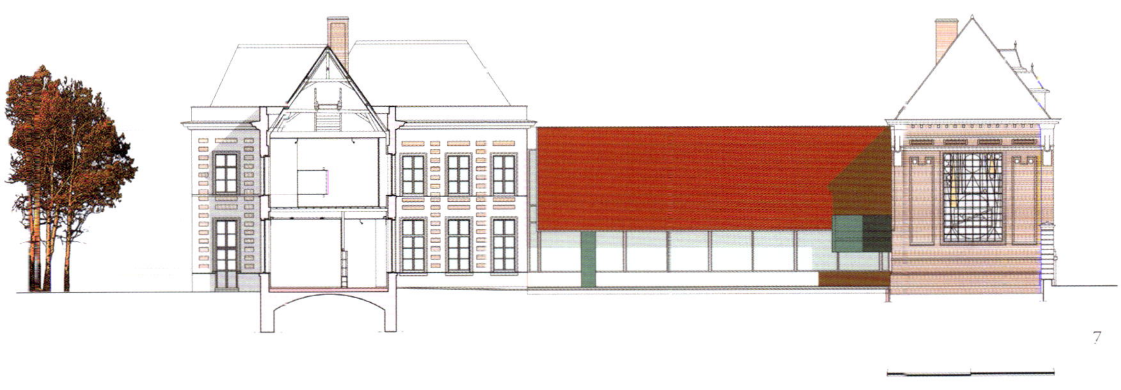

7

8

9

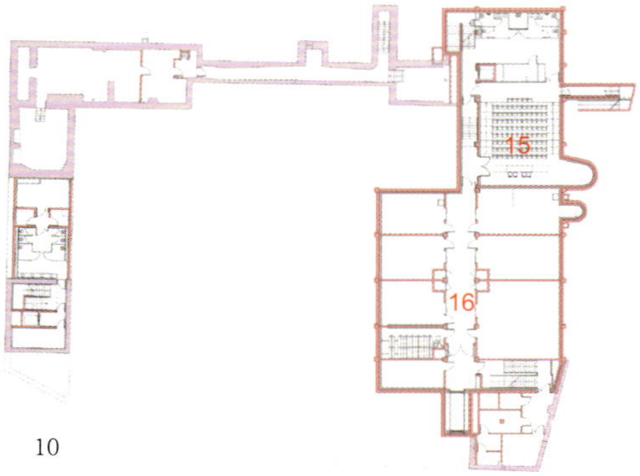

10

11

12

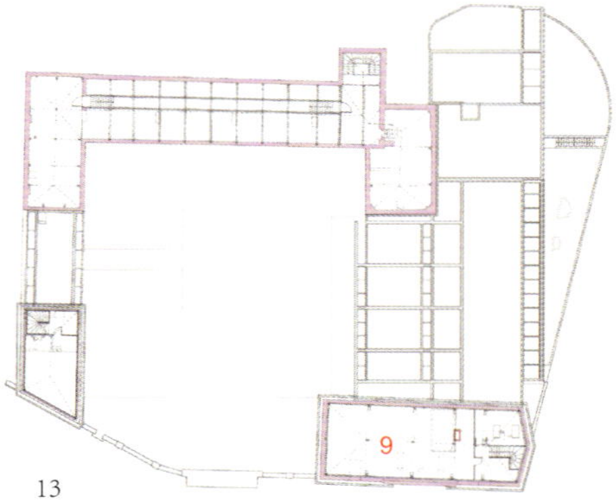

13

8-9&14. Matisse gallery on the 1st floor
10. Basement floor plan
11. Ground floor plan
12. 1st floor plan
13. 2nd floor plan

1. Entrance
2. Courtyard
3. Park
4. Reception / bookshop
5. Temporary exhibitions
6. Cafeteria
7. Drawings room
8. Educational services
9. Administration
10. Herbin rooms
11. Tériade Collection
12. Concrete Art
13. Matisse rooms
14. Sculptures
15. Auditorium
16. Reserves

14

1

LANGUEDOC-ROUSSILLON REGIONAL MUSEUM OF CONTEMPORARY ART

Architect: Pierre-François Moget & Anne Gaubert, Projectiles
Location: Sérignan
Completion Date: 2006
Photographer: Jean-Paul Planchon

In the heart of the Languedoc-Roussillon region, beside the Mediterranean in the small town of Sérignan, the Regional Museum of Contemporary Art (MRAC) is situated in an old wine-makers' warehouse.

The project for transforming it into a museum was entrusted to the architects Pierre-François Moget and Anne Gaubert in 2005-2006. This development provided the region with 2,700m^2 to show temporary exhibitions of its collections and to offer an itinerary through different spaces including the graphic arts room, the video space, the children's workshops and a book and gift shop.

Since 2010, it has been enlarged with a new 500m^2 platform for experimental projects. On the ground floor, large

2

volumes, alternating the more intimate, ceilinged rooms with those whose beams are exposed, are all bathed in natural light. The Projectiles workshop created all the museum furniture including the cabinets in the graphic arts room. A real museum within the museum, the graphic arts room, plunged into half-light, offers the visitor a new experience of perception.

3

4

With his work *Rotation,* the artist Daniel Buren has encircled the museum with a belt of colour applied to all the windows, creating visual effects both on the interior and the exterior. A large ceramic fresco, *Les Femmes Fatales*, by the artist Erró, adorns the exterior façade.

1. Exterior view
2. Erró, *Les Femmes Fatales*, 1995-2006
3. Projections of *Rotation,* installation by Daniel Buren
4. Entrance hall, with a work by Lawrence Weiner on the atrium walls
5. Master plan
6. "Sémiose Éditions" exhibition
7. The museum collection

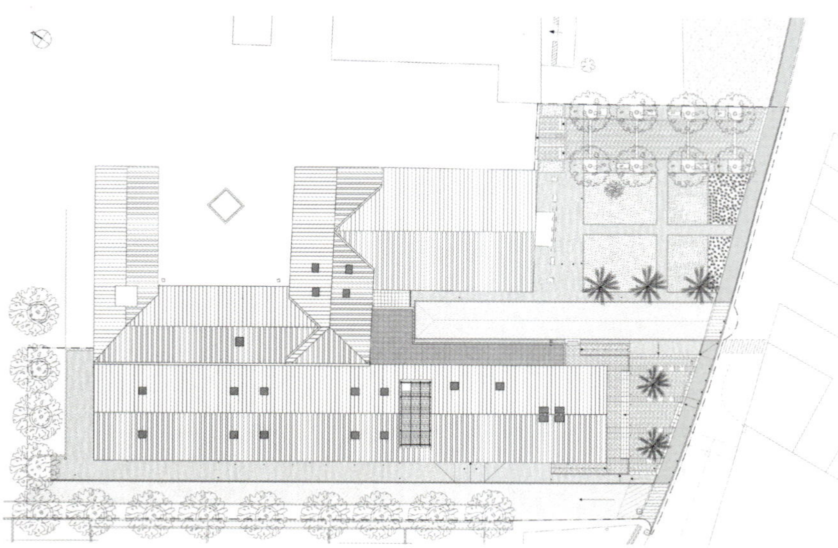

5

Semiose éditions
LA VIE EST UNE
Lourdes
+ Disneyland
= Las Vegas
6

7

8

9

8-10. Graphic art

11

12

13

11. “Géographies du Dessin” exhibition
12&13. Hans Hartung, “Spray” exhibition, 2010
14. Sections

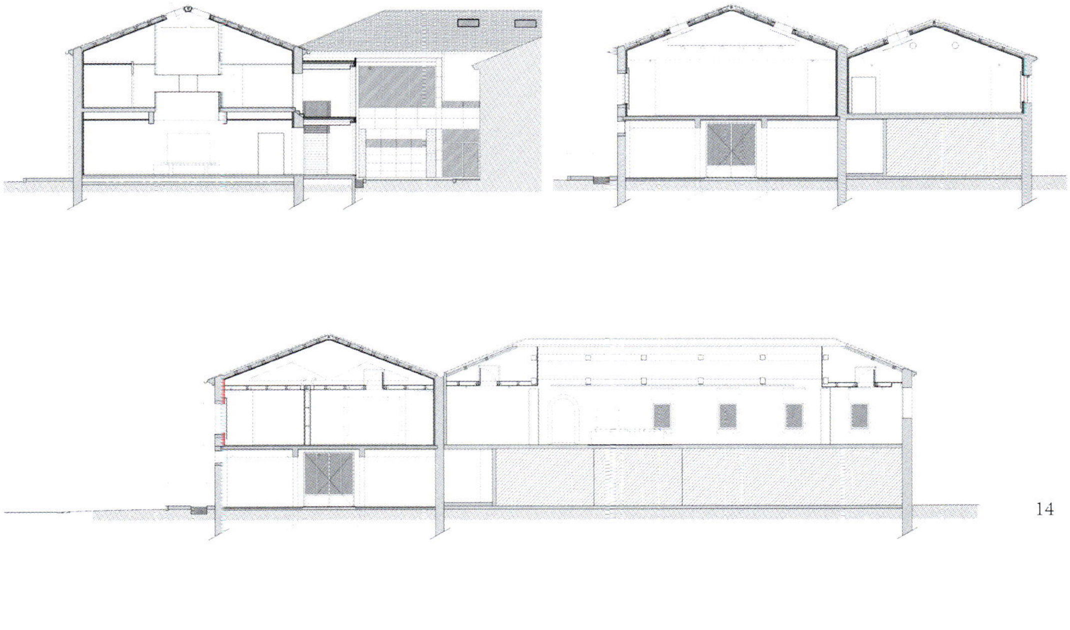

14

JEAN-FRÉDÉRIC OBERLIN MUSEUM

Architect: Frédéric Jung
Location: Waldersbach
Completion Date: 2003
Photographer: Frédéric Jung (pp.140-142), Michel Denancé (pp.143-147)

The Jean-Frédéric Oberlin Museum is dedicated to the work of this 18th-century pastor and educationalist, a man open to the world who was both a witness of his time and an agent for change. Frédéric Jung undertook to convert or renovate the old buildings that date from different periods, from the presbytery (1789) and its common and the Froessel house (1724) to the Sophie Bernard extension (1978). This called for several different types of intervention, according to the intentions of the museum, the problems encountered and the architectural project.

One of the major challenges was to connect the buildings to create a living museum presenting the collections and enabling people to "read" and question Pastor Oberlin's philosophy, through the creation of satellites organised around the presbytery, where the collection is housed. These satellites include the house of children and its educational workshops, the

temporary exhibition rooms, the archive and the thematic gardens.

The presbytery had to be preserved as a museum object in itself. Because there are exhibits from the 18th and the 20th century two forms of presentation and two approaches to the museum's functioning were necessary. They had to be clearly distinguished but linked. The presbytery and the Sophie Bernard extension are the results of these two approaches, one

synchronic, the other diachronic, one housing the collections in their place of origin, the other offering a contemporary reading of the collections – resonances in a consulting room open to the valley, and an observatory surveying the landscape of Ban de la Roche.

1. West façade
2. Museum extension
3. The observatory on the extension
4. The house of children
5. Master plan
6. Children's workshop

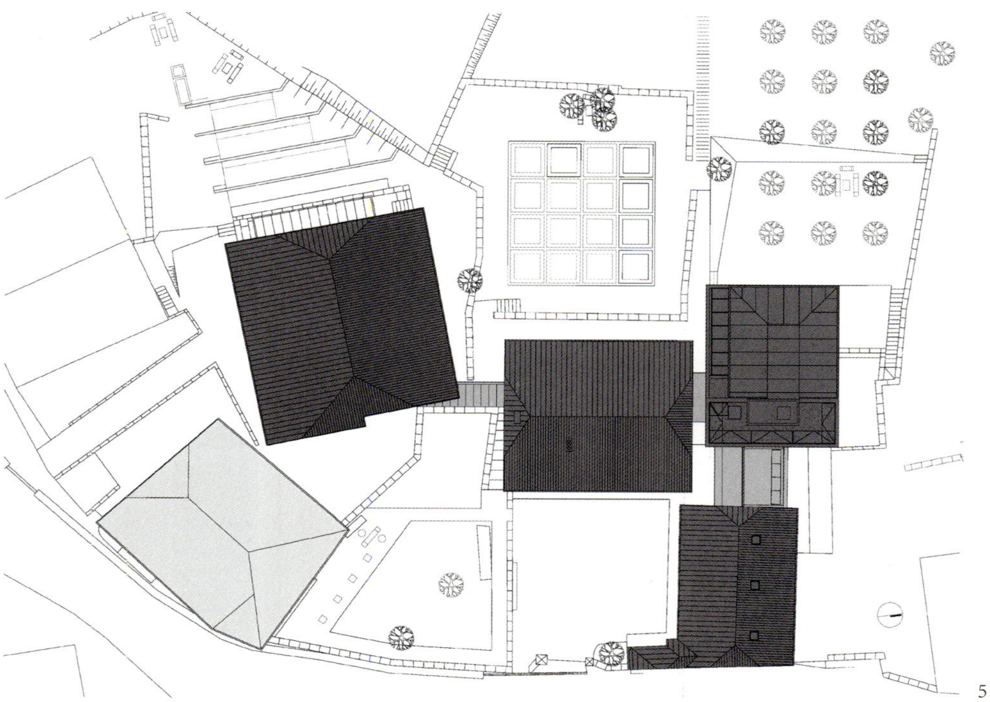

6

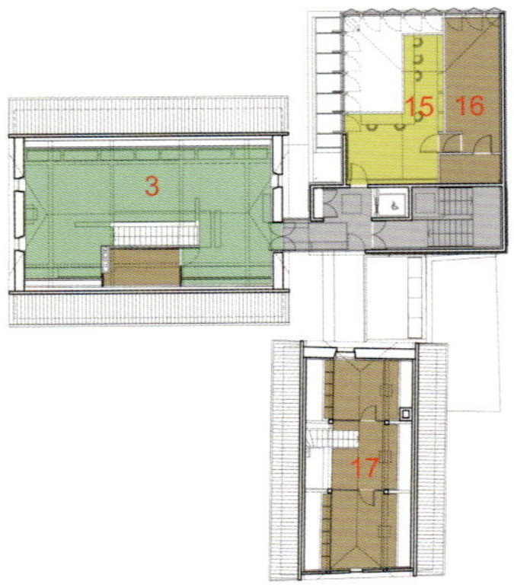

7

Collections
Satellites
Services
Logistics
Circulation

收藏品展览空间
周边活动空间
服务性空间
储藏与管理空间
流线空间

7. 2nd floor plan
8. 1st floor plan
9. Ground floor plan
10. Garden floor plan
11. Section AA
12. Section BB
13&14. The museum collections

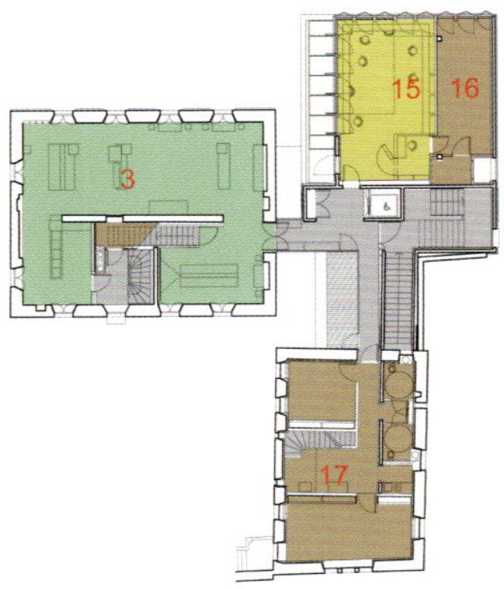

8

1. Entrance hall
2. Bookshop
3. Permanent exhibition
4. Temporary exhibition
5. Workshops
6. Exhibition space for children's work
7. Conference room
8. Discovery room
9. Coat check, restaurant
10. Offices of the activity leaders
11. Educational greenhouse
12. Exhibition terrace
13. Simpletons' garden
14. Children's garden
15. Reading room
16. Reserves
17. Offices

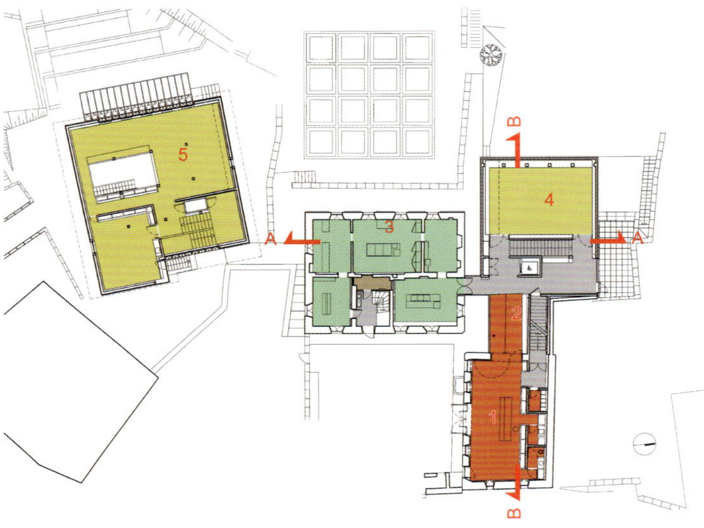

9

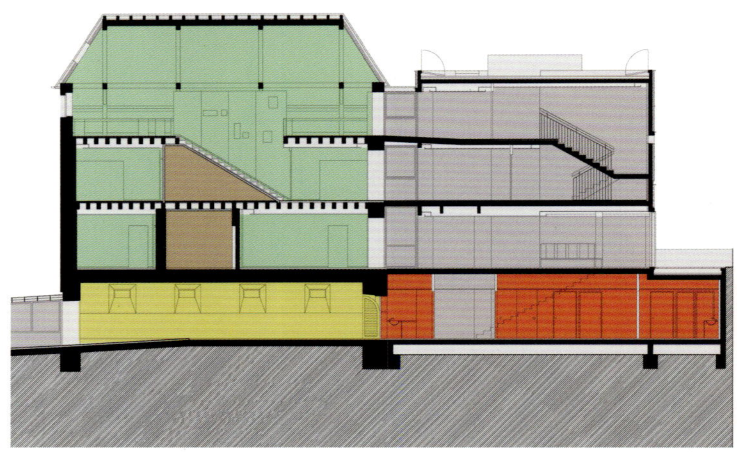

11

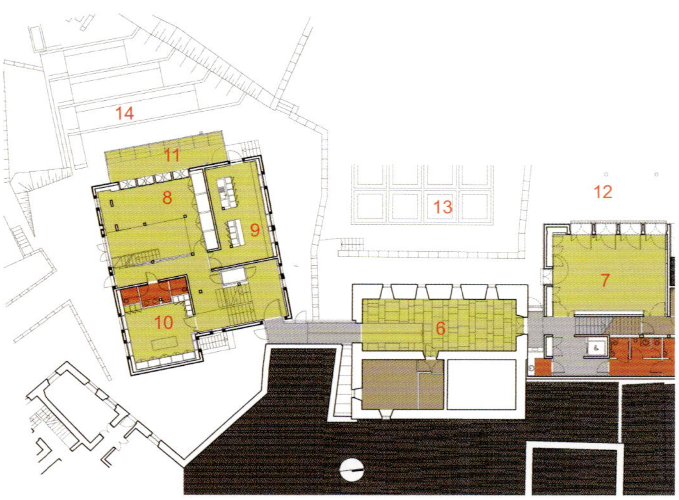

10

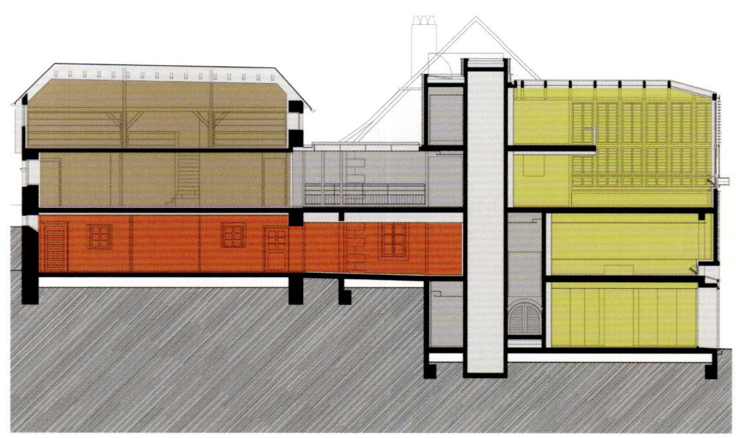

12

13

14

15. The museum collections
16. Link between the presbytery and the extension
17. Temporary exhibition room
18. Reading room

16

17

18

LILLE MODERN ART MUSEUM – LAM

Architect: Manuelle Gautrand
Location: Lille
Completion Date: 2010
Photographer: Max Lerouge

The original museum, designed by Roland Simounet and opened in 1983, was a horizontal structure stretching out lengthways in a lightly undulating park. The west wing housed the administrative offices and the east wing the auditorium and the exhibition rooms. The central section housed the entrance – a glazed gallery which gave onto an interior patio, offering the main breathing space of the museum. In 2000 the building was listed as a Historic Monument.

The donation of a collection of more than 3000 works of Art Brut prompted the museum to embark on a modernisation and extension project. The competition was won by Manuelle Gautrand. Two complex and sensitive challenges are brought together in this project: to extend the work of Roland Simounet, and to invent a place to house this magnificent collection. Manuelle Gautrand did not want to create an independent additional sequence, but rather a connection. The project is built from the starting point of a

1

2

large, gentle form, extending from the west wing of the site to the east. From the south side, visitors discover the new extension at the end of their visit, behind the existing sequences.

The fold in the ground meant that the central portion of the structure had to be narrow. From both sides of this pintucked centre, the volume becomes suppler and comes loose in the form of two fantails enveloping the existing museum. One, in the west, is designated for functions other

3

4

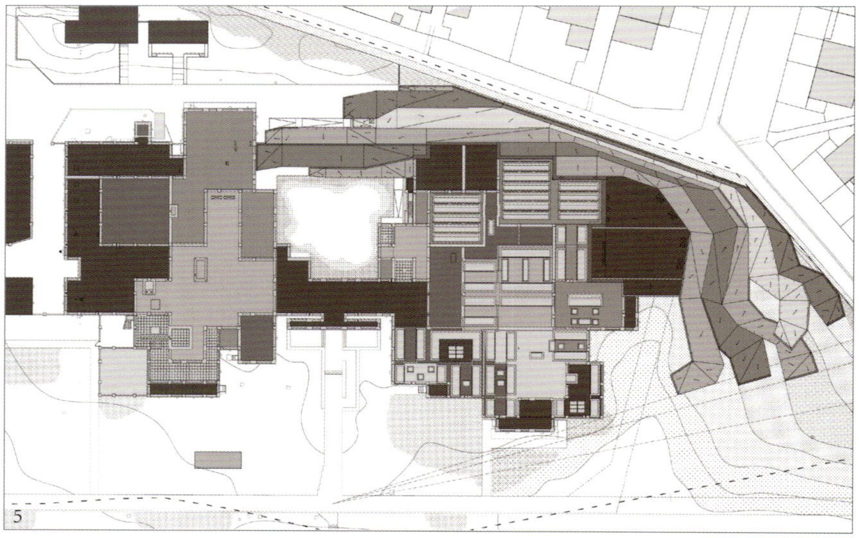

5

6

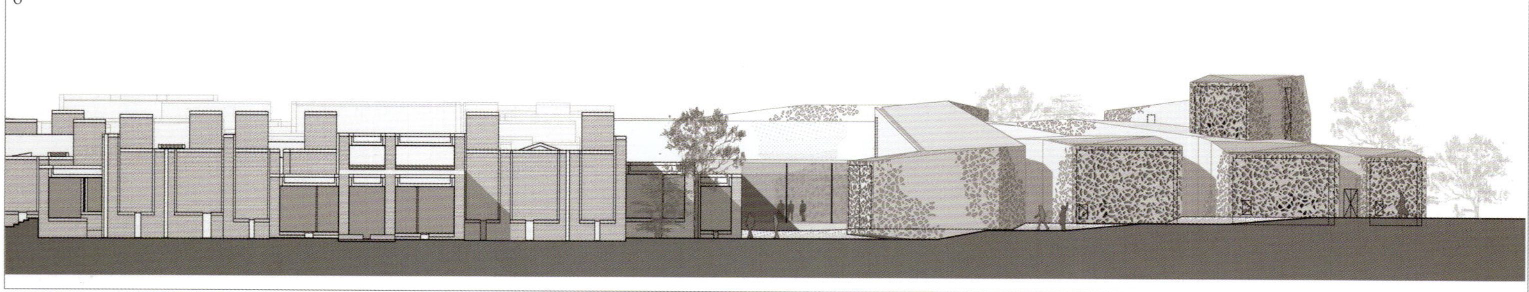

1. View of the existing museum and the extension from the park
2. Extension exterior at night
3. The extension seen from the park
4. Situation plan
5. Master plan
6. South façade
7. The pivot room, leading to the "fingers"

than exhibiting (a technical space for the works, cafeteria, etc.); the other, in the south-east, is devoted to exhibiting the Art Brut collection. These fans are made up of five folds, following the lay of the land, each one housing a different theme from the collection. Where the original architecture is orthogonal, strict and ordered, that of the extension becomes more supple, more organic, expressing the "envelopment" necessary for presenting Art Brut.

In the interior modifications carried out for the existing museum, the reception remains at the geographical centre of the project, leading to the exhibition spaces, the bookshop that runs along the patio, the cafeteria that connects to the auditorium. The storerooms and restoration workshops have been enlarged and modernised. The exhibition spaces have been entirely restructured. In order to bring the security up to date, three almost invisible compartments have been created, while respecting the original architecture. Finally, for the Art Brut spaces, a glazed gallery allowed the architect to extend the original east-west museographic itinerary and prepare the visitor to enter the first room. This forms a fulcrum, opening onto the five Art Brut rooms, which are supple forms that slice into the landscape. Each opening onto the exterior has been designed to create a visual detour, punctuating the visit with escapes into fantasy.

8

9

8. The pivot room, looking towards the existing museum
9. Inside the extension, at the extremity of a "finger"
10. The extension – interior view

11. Purple model of the extension
12. Cross section
13. Ground floor plan
14. The extension – interior view

1. Entrance hall
2. Patio
3. Administrative offices
4. Auditorium
5. Exhibition rooms
6. Functional spaces (technical space, cafeteria...)
7. Exhibition rooms for the Art Brut collection

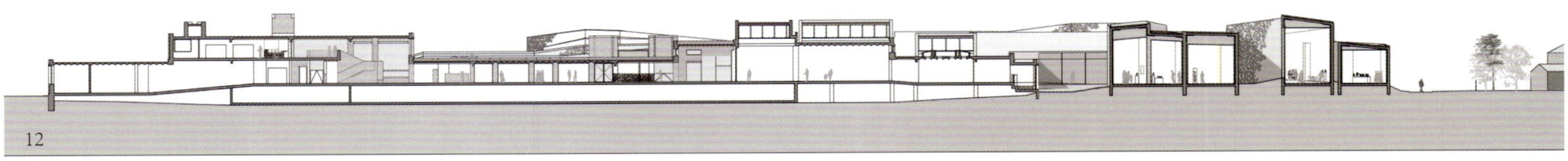

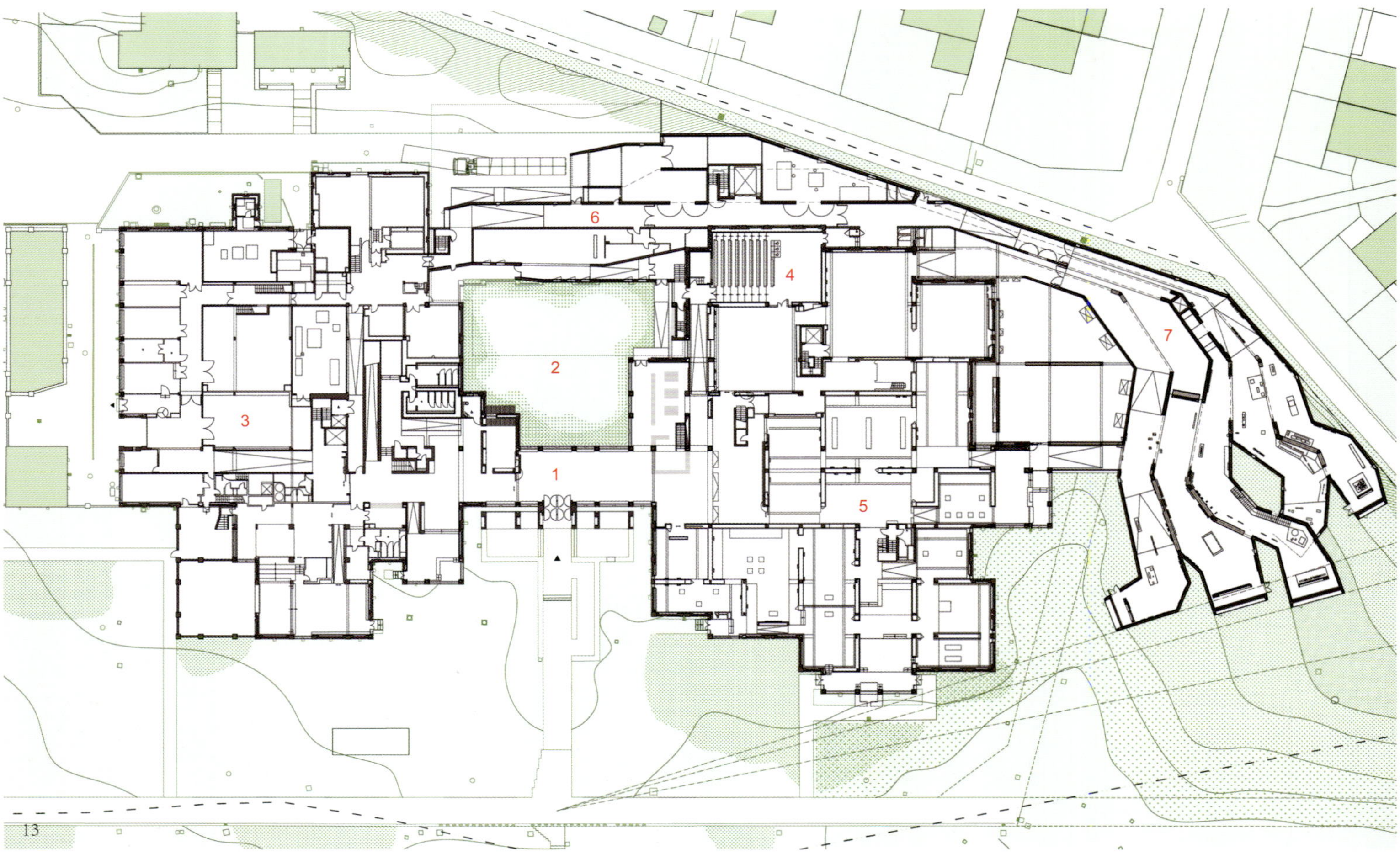

14

15-17. The extension – interior view
18. Interior view of the extension's "moucharaby"

17

18

NANCY MUSEUM OF FINE ARTS

Architect: Beaudouin-Husson
Location: Nancy
Completion Date: 1999
Photographer: Luc Boegly (pp.158-159), Jean-Marie Monthiers (pp.160-163), Olivier-Henri Dancy (p.165)

The extension of the Museum of Fine Arts on Place Stanislas is an abstract work on gravity, light and time. It is composed of three rectangular planes that cannot be seen simultaneously and can only be understood over the course of an exploration of the museum. The architecture calls on our memory of the space.

These three planes have different relationships with gravity. The first is in dark granite placed on the ground; it slides under a second plane of paler stone which appears to be suspended horizontally. The third is white, floating freely in the interior space of the museum. The essence of the project is found in these three surfaces, which establish a metaphorical relationship between the sky and the earth. The museum space moves freely between the exterior and the interior, surrounded by these three elements.

The building is anchored in the history of the site. It is low and horizontal so as not to

1

upset the volumetry of the scuare. It is like a weight that nevertheless removes the effect of gravity, raised above a trarsparent space, like its model, the Pa ais de l'Intendance, a mature masterwork of the architect Emmanuel Héré, who, by the 18th century, had already abandoned formal conventions in favour cf more abstract intentions: horizontality, lightness, transparency.

2

3

4

1. View of the museum from the garden
2. Staircase built in 1936
3. Garden side façade
4. The ramp
5. Master plan

5

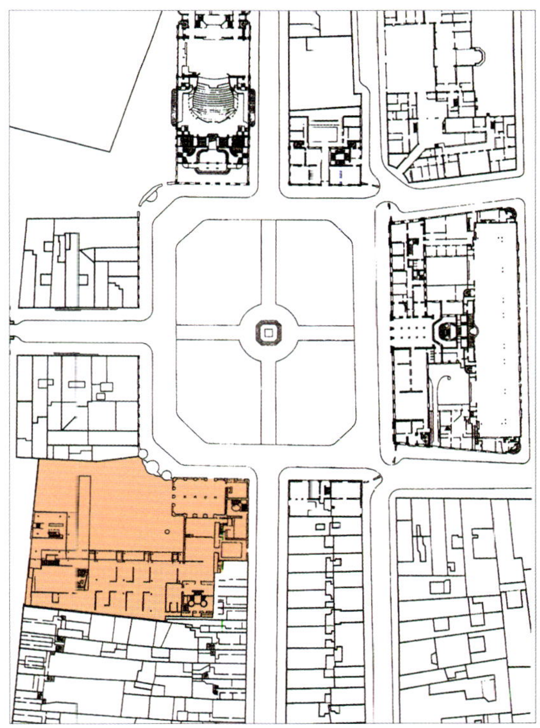

7

8

6. Garden floor
7. Ramp leading to the 1st floor
8. Gallery
9. Longitudinal section

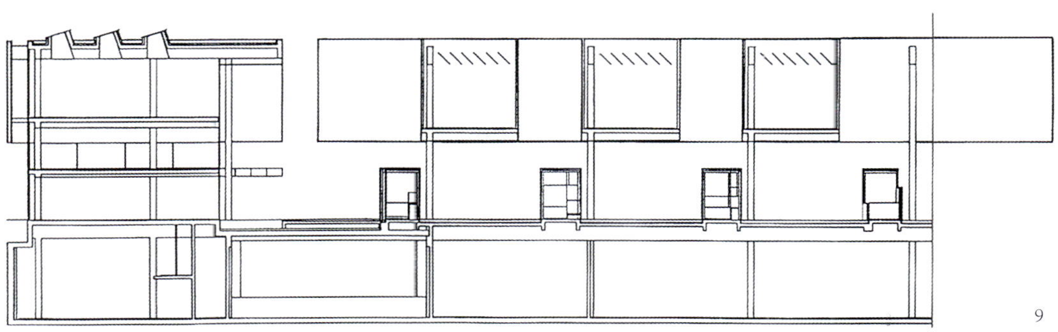

9

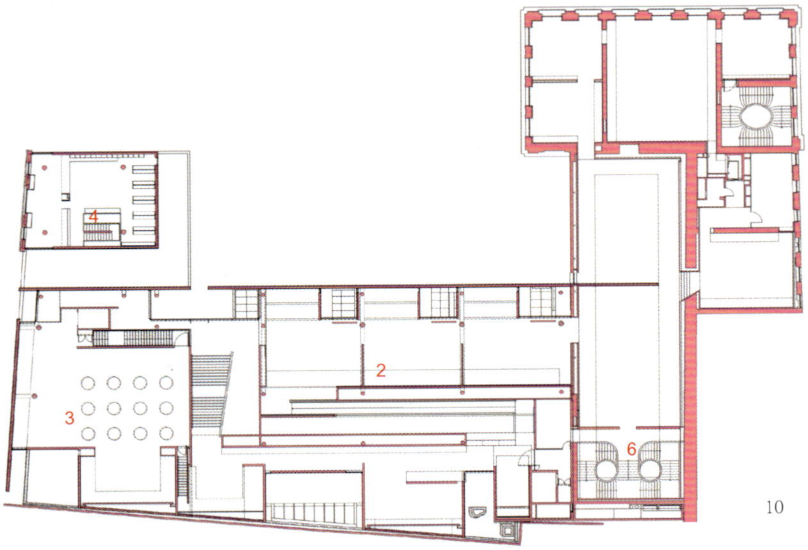

10

10. Basement floor plan
11. Ground floor plan
12. 1st floor plan
13-14. The fortifications and the Daum collections

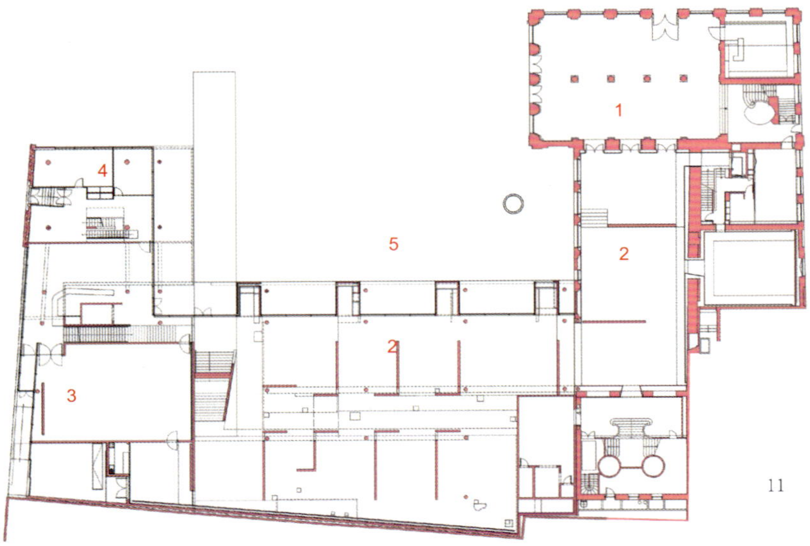

11

1. Peristyle
2. Permanent exhibition rooms
3. Temporary exhibition rooms
4. Administration
5. Garden
6. 1936 staircase
7. Conference room
8. Fortifications and the Daum collections
9. Reserves

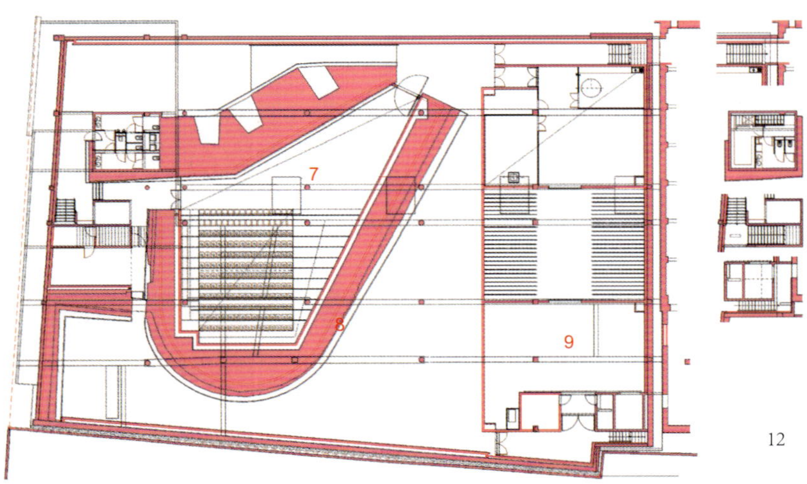

12

13

14

INTERNATIONAL CITY OF LACE AND FASHION

Architect: Moatti-Rivière
Location: Calais
Completion Date: 2009
Photographer: Michel Denancé (pp.166-167), Florian Kleinfenn (pp.168-169), Moatti-Rivière (pp.170-175)

The City extends over 7,500m² and is made up of two main buildings. The first, in the old Boulart factory that dates back to 1870, contains the permanent collections and the administrative offices. The second is the extension (2500m²) for temporary exhibitions. An auditorium seating 200 links the two. The old lace factory is made up of two main blocks with four floors, linked to form a U shape with a large courtyard in the middle. The metallic-framed extension has a Z shape, and forms a rigid box on five faces (roof, floor and three façades – north, south and east) with the sixth open in a double-curve façade. The steel structure allowed for a 17m cantilever.

Moatti et Rivière have designed an usual double-skin façade in tempered glass over the continuous curve of the façade. It is heat-curved and screen-printed on the outer face. The screen-printing

complicated the operation: the motifs had to be adapted to avoid geometrical distortions. The precision of the work and the size of the panels (1.6m x 1.6m) meant they had to be placed and joined with great care. The panels are connected by cleats in moulded stainless-steel with a brushed finish. The printed motif represents the stitches of the Jacquard cards from the Leavers enterprise. A mechanical ventilation between the two skins insulates

2

3

the building, avoids condensation and allows for the surfaces to be cleaned.

The City is entered through the extension, offering a new face to the old factory. The path of the permanent exhibition traces the industrial history of lace in Calais, through five sequences unfolding in rooms distributed over three of the four levels of the old factory. The main staircase, in the centre of the building, has been used to link them scenographically. The third floor is reserved for the administrative offices. The complete gutting and restructuring the Boulart factory has enabled it to welcome the public with a museography freed of all constraints.

1. The new façade
2. The façade at night
3&6. The old factory
4. Master plan
5. Elevation of the façade

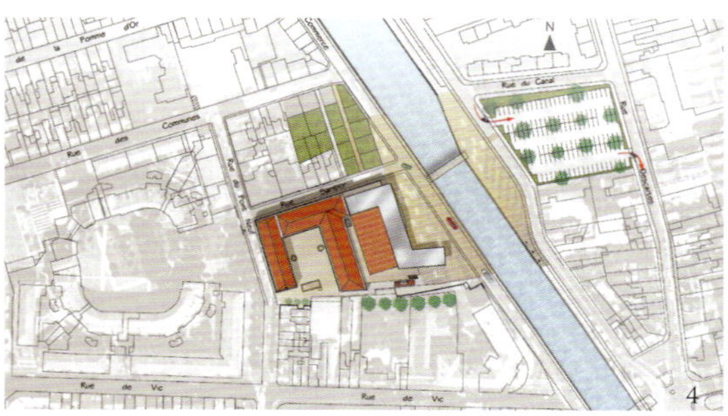

4

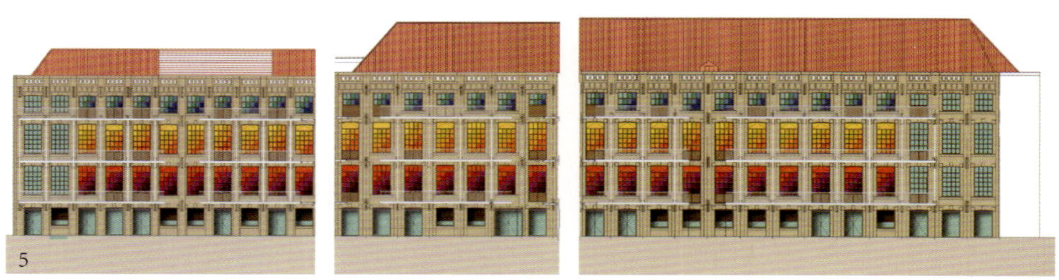

5

6

7

8

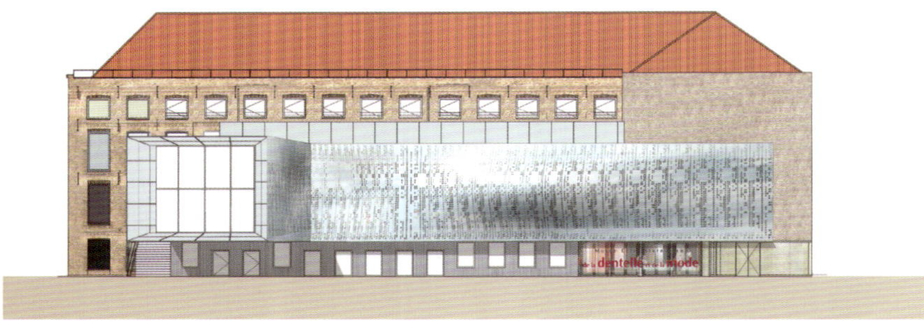
9

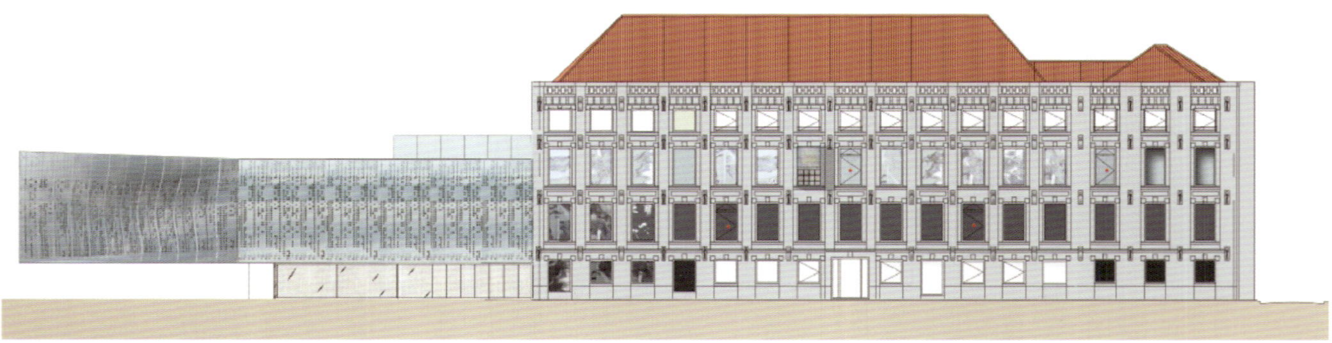
10

11

12

7. The façade at night
8. The façade by day
9. East elevation
10. North elevation
11-12. Detail of the façade

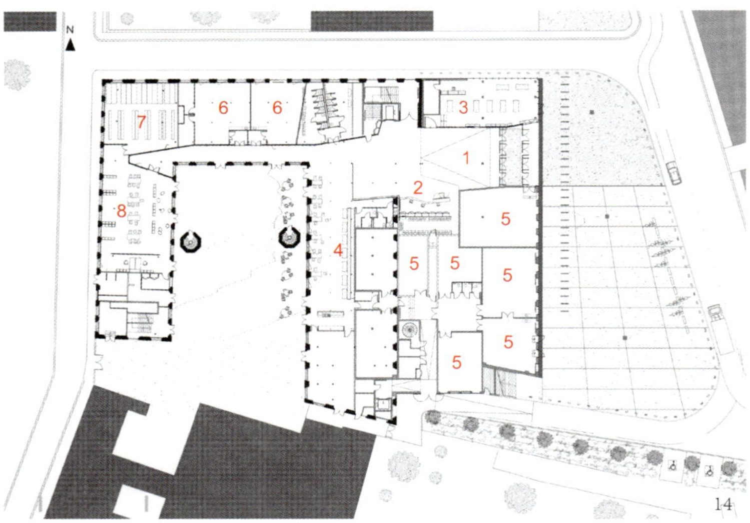

13. Museography, part 1, the origin of lace
14. Ground floor plan
15. Museography, part 2, lace and fashion
16. 1st floor plan
17. 2nd floor plan

1. Entrance hall
2. Reception area
3. Shop
4. Restaurant
5. Restoration workshop
6. Educational space
7. Documentation
8. Library
9. Permanent exhibition entrance
10. Garden
11. Factory
12. Lace today
13. Hall
14. Auditorium
15. Temporary exhibition room
16. Workshop
17. Mirrors gallery
18. Atrium overlooking the temporary exhibitions
19. Atrium to the hall

15

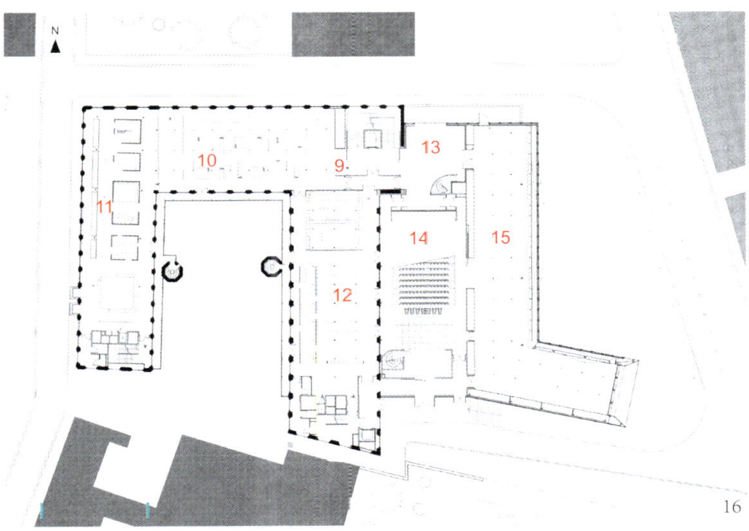

16

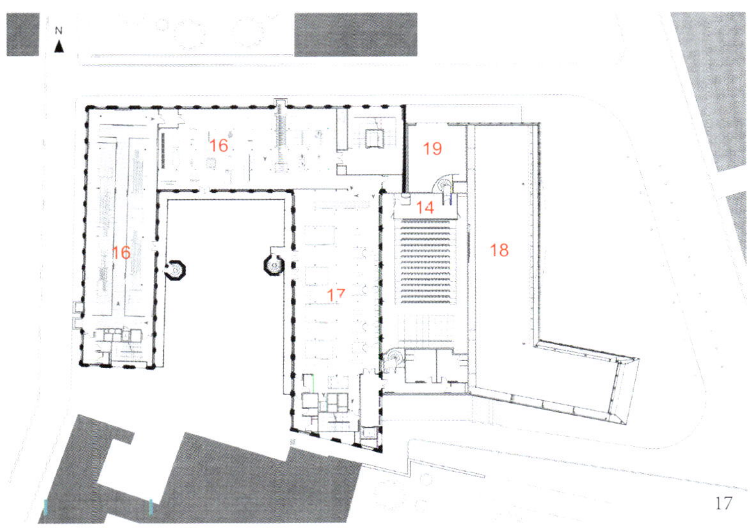

17

18

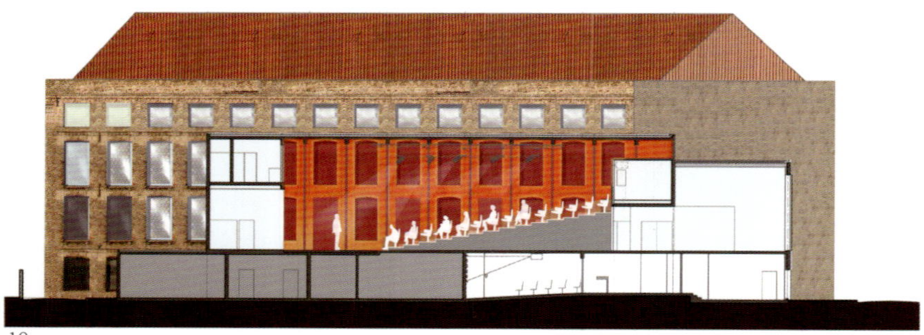

19

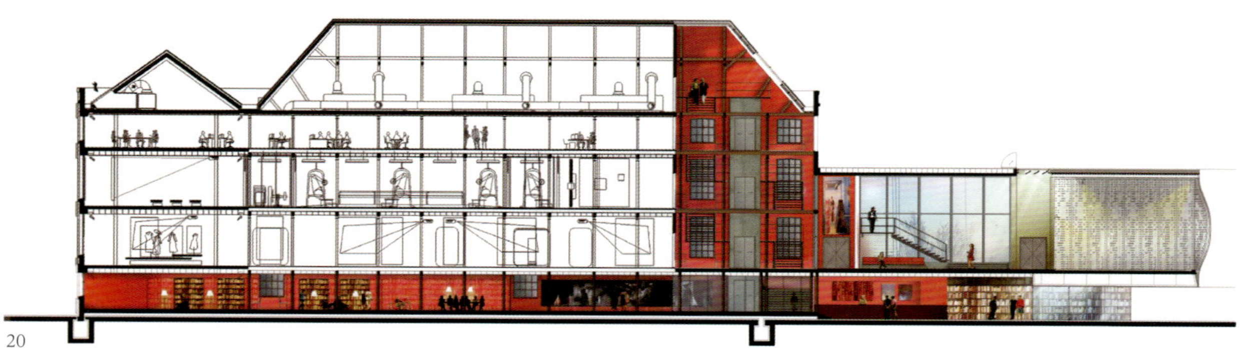

20

18. Museography, part 2, lace and fashion
19. Section of the auditorium
20. Cross section
21. Interior view, detail

21

PRESIDENT JACQUES CHIRAC MUSEUM

Architect: Jean-Michel Wilmotte
Location: Sarran
Completion Date: 2006
Photographer: Fabre (pp.176-178), Gratien (pp.179-180), MPJC (p.181)

In 1998 Jean-Michel Wilmotte won the competition to design the President Jacques Chirac Museum. The construction's insertion into the village of Sarran and the use of the traditional materials of Corrèze architecture ensured a perfect integration of the museum into a protected environment. Two barns formed the departure point for the project. Now restored, they house the restaurant and a small storage locale.

The initial museum was inspired by the proportions and the long volumetry of these two pre-existing buildings, which are typical of the vernacular architecture of the Corrèze. The architects added two buildings, one for the permanent exhibition, the other for temporary exhibitions, covered with a double-slope slate roof. They are linked by a covered gallery that forms the hall of the museum. Granite, slate, oak and chestnut, as well as its division into several units, give it the appearance of

1

a small hamlet and aid the integration of the museum into its environment; steel, concrete and glass anchor it in modernity. The public spaces are vast, open to each other and benefit from direct or indirect natural light in a warm ambiance.

In 2006, the spirit of a contemporary hamlet was completed by two buildings that appear independent but are in fact linked below ground. The first building, which has four floors including two below

2

3

4

1. General view of the museum
2. Footbridge from the library and the esplanade to the museum
3. The museum at night
4. The entrance
5. The museum seen from the park

ground, houses the administrative offices, cultural activities and the restoration and preservation of the collections; the second building, a five-floor tower, houses the library, a space for exhibiting files and storerooms. The tower and the administrative building are linked by a covered footbridge. A wide esplanade, under which are found a large storage reserve that can be visited and an auditorium, link the old building to the new. The architectural approach is homogenous, inspired by the first museum and showing care to integrate into the site through the alternate use of granite, concrete, slate, glass and wood.

6

7

8

6. Reflection of the museum restaurant on the north glass façade
7. Interior of the library
8. Introduction to the museum's permanent exhibition
9. Temporary exhibition room

BRAND NEW
EXPRESSIONS

1

POMPIDOU CENTRE

Architect: Renzo Piano, Richard Rogers
Location: Paris
Completion Date: 1977
Photographer: Renzo Piano Building Workshop

Occupying an entire block and covering approximately 100,000m^2 at the heart of Paris, the Pompidou Centre is devoted to the plastic arts, music and reading. Its architecture, based on a large rectangle at its base, with all its practical functions (air conditioning, water, mobility systems) on the outside, symbolises contact between surfaces or between people indoors or out. Like the Eiffel Tower in its day, the Pompidou Centre sparked passionate debate among the public and politicians at every stage of its design and construction.

The construction work posed numerous technical and logistical problems that were resolved only by great conviction and determination. At the opening, in 1977, the public immediately embraced the Pompidou Centre, its museum of modern art, the square and its neighbourhood. Students and researchers readily adopted its library, and tourists gladly took the trip up its winding, caterpillar-like exterior glass escalator to gain unparalleled views of the neighbourhood and the city.

After 20 years of operation, the museum needed more space, and the library had to be made more accessible. The first major decision of the overhaul was to relocate all of the offices to a neighbouring building. Spaces were thus freed up for the centre's primary activities. The fourth floor houses the museum of modern art, and the fifth is reserved for temporary exhibitions. The library, which is located on the first, second and third floors, has a separate entrance for ease of access. The main ground-floor forum was also modified: a large opening in

the sweep of the main entrance connects the three underground levels (performance rooms), the ground level (entrance, ticket office and information desk) and the two mezzanine levels (boutiques and café). All are linked by elevators and stairways. Aside from cleaning, the only change to the exterior was the introduction of a weather-proof canopy over the main entrance.

1. The building after restoration, night view
2-3. Details of the façade
4. The terraces of the contemporary art museum
5. General view
6. View from the escalator

6

7

8

7&9. The new main lobby, the focal point of all activities and events
8. Cross section
10. Main façade (west) and section of the forecourt with an underground car park

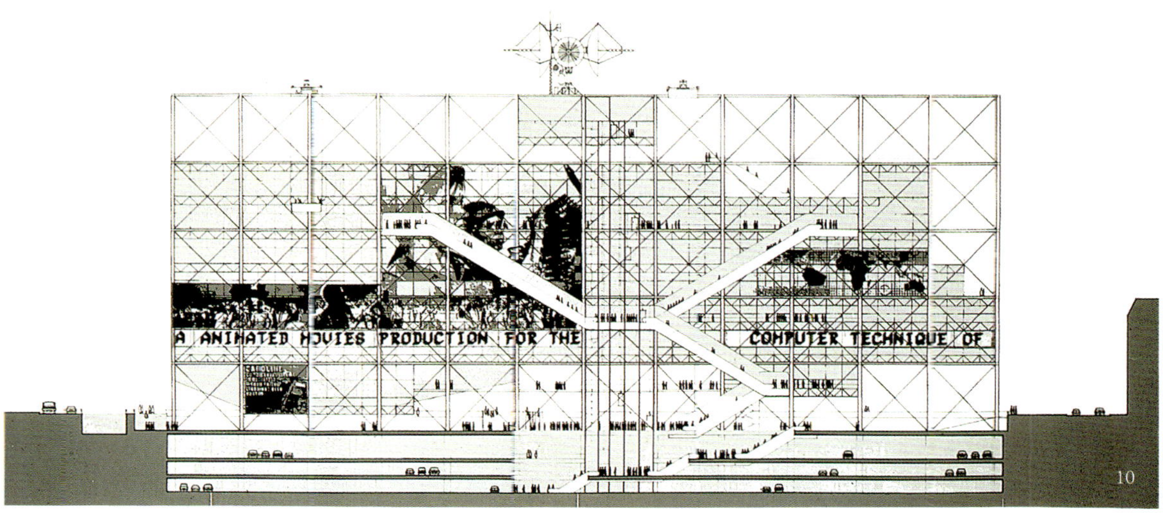

ÉRIC TABARLY CITY OF SAILING

Architect: Jacques Ferrier
Location: Lorient
Completion Date: 2007
Photograph: © jfa / Jacques Ferrier Architectures – photo Luc Boegly (pp.190-191, 193-195), photo Jean-Marie Monthiers (p.192)

A symbol of the revival of the submarine base of Lorient, the Éric Tabarly City of Sailing, covering 6,700m² with 2,500m² devoted to exhibitions, has sprung up in the heart of the old military compound. In contrast to the grounded solidity of the three concrete bunkers, the project offers a shiny metal vessel hanging over the quay. Floating above a transparent ground floor, this sparkling craft is moored to the "tower of the winds", a vertical signal tower placed on a sea arm, around which pontoons are moored.

Covered in iridescent aluminium panels that change colour with the weather, the vessel hangs over the quay to form a spectacular canopy facing the sea. The glazed façade, sheltered by the cantiliver, reveals the activity inside. The reception with its uneven geometry serves as an entrance to the exhibitions and to the auditorium, as well as to the restaurant. The exhibition hangar, accessible from the ground floor, rises in double height to the first floor, with an exhibition room and a space for the maintenance and repair

of boats. The first floor is a wide platform open to the sea, around which exhibition spaces devoted to sailing and yachting are organised. This platform is covered by a hull whose interior surfaces are lined in wood, in reference to naval architecture. A long footbridge extends from the south façade of the building and links the exhibition level with the tower of the winds viewing platform and with the pontoons.

Cap l'Orient is leading the way in sustainable and community-based development, as the

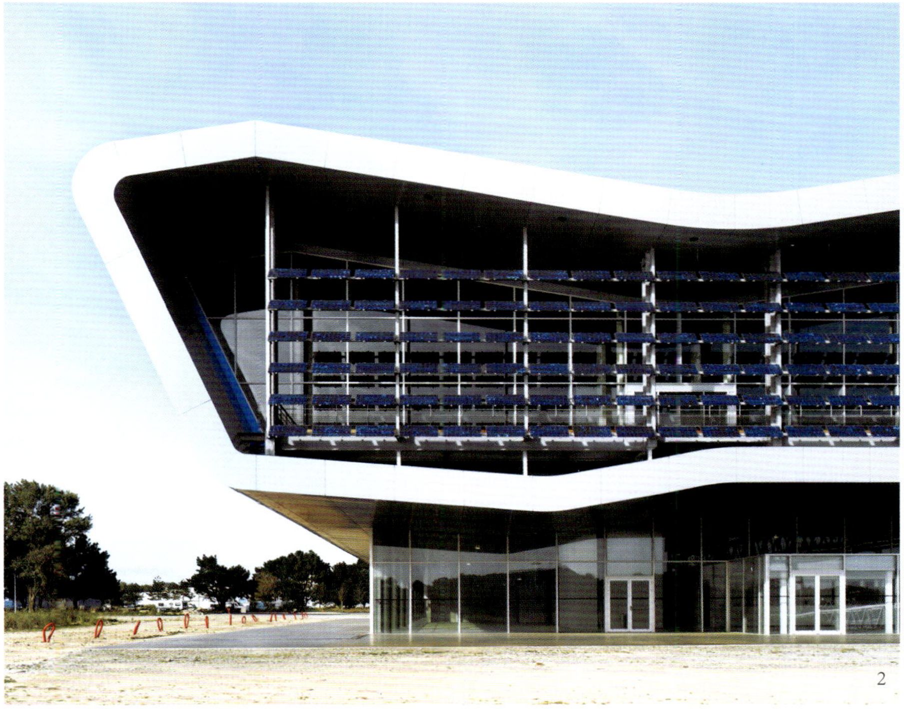

2

3

Éric Tabarly City of Sailing shows. The building was designed according High Environmental Quality (HQE) standards, to reduce its energy consumption as much as possible. Its well-conceived architecture allows it to use solar energy and the natural resources of the site, while its technology ensures low energy use.

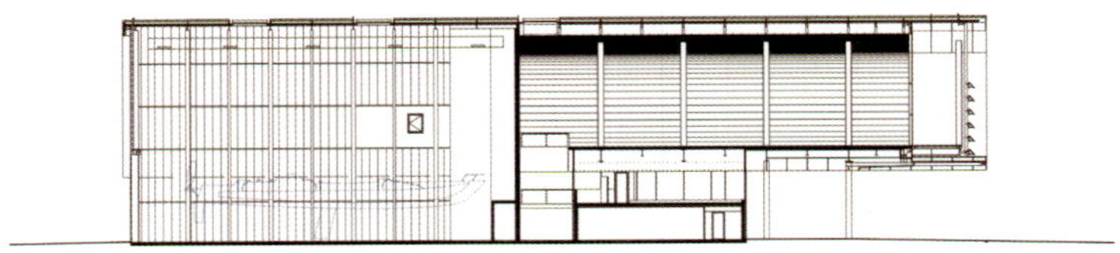

4

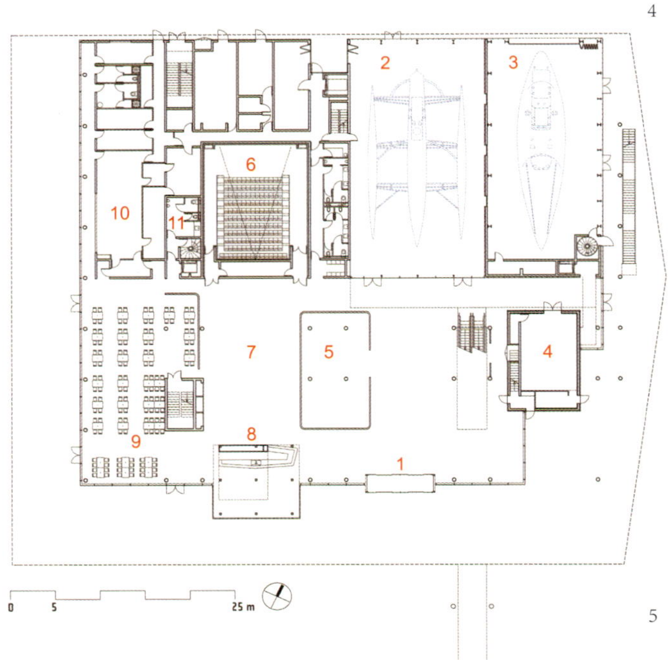

5

1. Entrance
2. Exhibition hangar
3. Repair hangar
4. Boarding lounge
5. Shop
6. Auditorium
7. Sailing News area
8. Bar and storage
9. Restaurant
10. Kitchen
11. Mixed public restrooms

6

7

1. The City, anchored in the water
2. The south façade, covered in photovoltaic panels
3. The Tower of the Winds signal tower
4. Longitudinal section
5. Ground floor plan
6. A boarding quay to get a first taste of sailing
7. Symbol of the renewal of the submarine base of Lorient

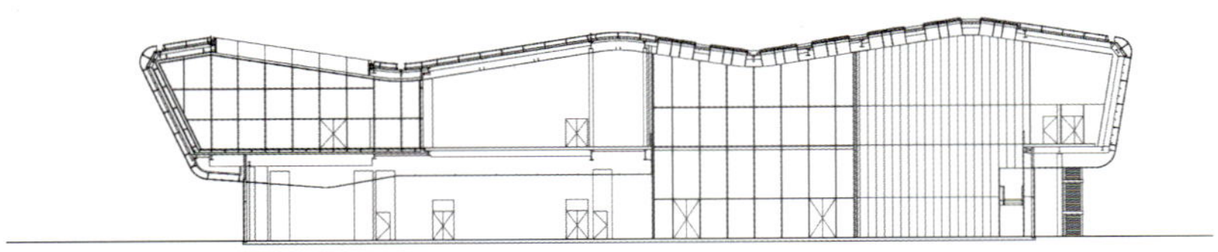

9

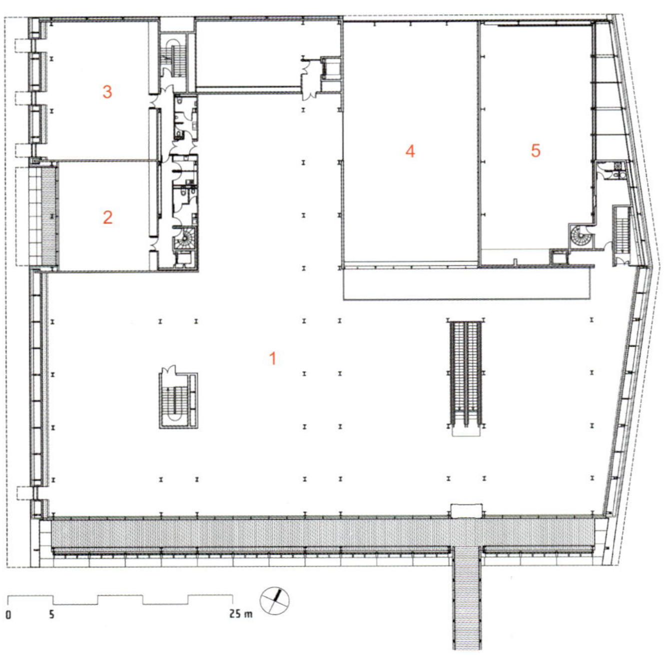

10

8. The first floor, where exhibitions are organised
9. Cross section
10. 1st floor plan
11. The loggia offers a view over the bay

1. Exhibition room
2. Library
3. Offices
4. Atrium over the exhibition hangar
5. Atrium over the repair hangar
6. Crew room

11

CITY OF THE OCEAN

Architect: Steven Holl & Solange Fabião
Location: Biarritz
Completion Date: 2011
Photographer: Laurent Garcia (pp.197 top, 198-205), Emmy Martens (p.196), Balloïde Photo (p.197 bottom)

Designed by the New York architect Steven Holl and his Brazilian colleague Solange Fabião, the City of the Ocean espouses the form of the waves on the Basque coast. Its original architecture, dreamed up by this international duo, is based on the spatial concept "Beneath the sky, beneath the ocean", with a geometry of convex and concave surfaces.

The main building houses a science-through-play area, exhibitions and an auditorium as well as offices. A restaurant with a terrace, a cafeteria and a snack bar that can be entered separately from the exterior offer superb views of the ocean. The roof, on which plants grow through Portuguese limestone cobblestones, makes up a large curved public square, and two glass monoliths echo the two rocky outcrops standing in the ocean that can been seen from Ilbarritz beach.

The City of the Ocean adopts an environmental

2

approach through its perfect integration into the landscape. Situated south of the town, below the château of Ilbarritz, the building is based on the principle of transparency. It is built around an open-air square with the sea for its horizon, a real call to the waves. Its environmental construction also incorporates a self-regulating heating mechanism, a system of rainwater collection via the cobblestone paving and a line of natural vegetation.

3

1-2. City of the Ocean at night
3. Aerial view
4. Exterior close-up view at night
5. Exterior staircase

5

6

6. Detail of the roof terrace
7. East façade
8. Covered courtyard, west façade

9

10

9. Staircase leading to the roof terrace
10. Interior staircase
11. Entrance
12. Footbridge
13. Cafeteria
14. Bathyscaphe
15. Sub-marine base

11

12

13

14

15

1

CARTIER FOUNDATION FOR CONTEMPORARY ART

Architect: Jean Nouvel
Location: Paris
Completion Date: 1994
Photographer: Philippe Ruault

After 10 years in Jouy-en-Josas the Cartier Foundation moved to Boulevard Raspail, Paris in 1994. Here, Jean Nouvel created an ethereal structure of glass and metal whose transparency elongates the perspective of the boulevard. A magnificent Lebanon cedar planted in 1823 by Chateaubriand is echoed by a vertical garden above the entrance, created by the tropical botanical specialist Patrick Blanc in 1998. The garden and the architecture marry in this space without merging into one.

The ground floor is entirely "open" onto the garden, offering an extraordinary volume with its eight-metre ceiling height. Jean Nouvel sought a quasi-dematerialisation of the building, multiplying the possibilities in a flexible, free and dynamic space. Six floors are placed on top of this, of which three are

2

devoted to exhibitions. The changing appearance of the Foundation ‑or each new exhibition thus calls out to ɔassers-by.

"It's all about an architecture of lightness, windows and finely hatched steel. An architecture that blurs the tangible limits of the building and creates a poetic of mist and vanishing where the reading of a solid volume is redundant. When virtuality

3

4

attacks reality, architecture, more than ever, must have the courage to take on an image of contradiction," says Jean Nouvel, crystallising the essence of the building in a few lines.

1. Entrance
2. Exhibition space
3. Garden
4. Car park entrance
5. Offices

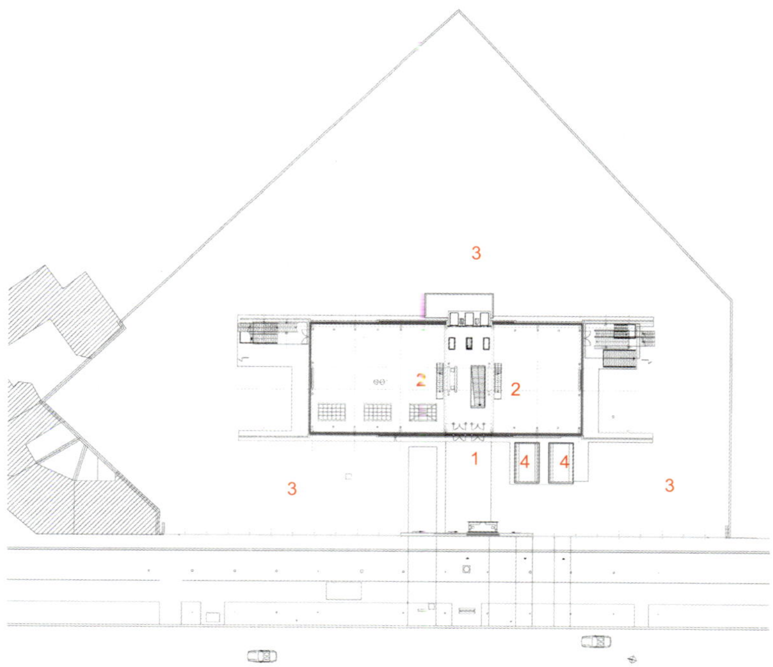

5

6

1&3. The façade on Boulevard Raspail
2. Garden, César exhibition
4&6. Interior, César exhibition
5. Ground floor plan
7. Office floor plan

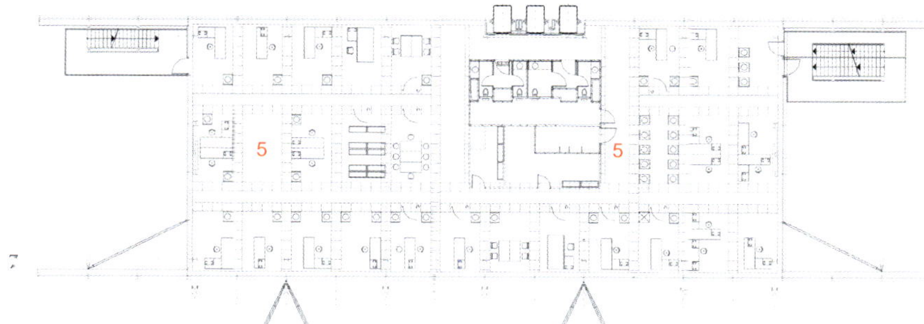

9

8. View from Boulevard Raspail
9. César exhibition
10. Cross section

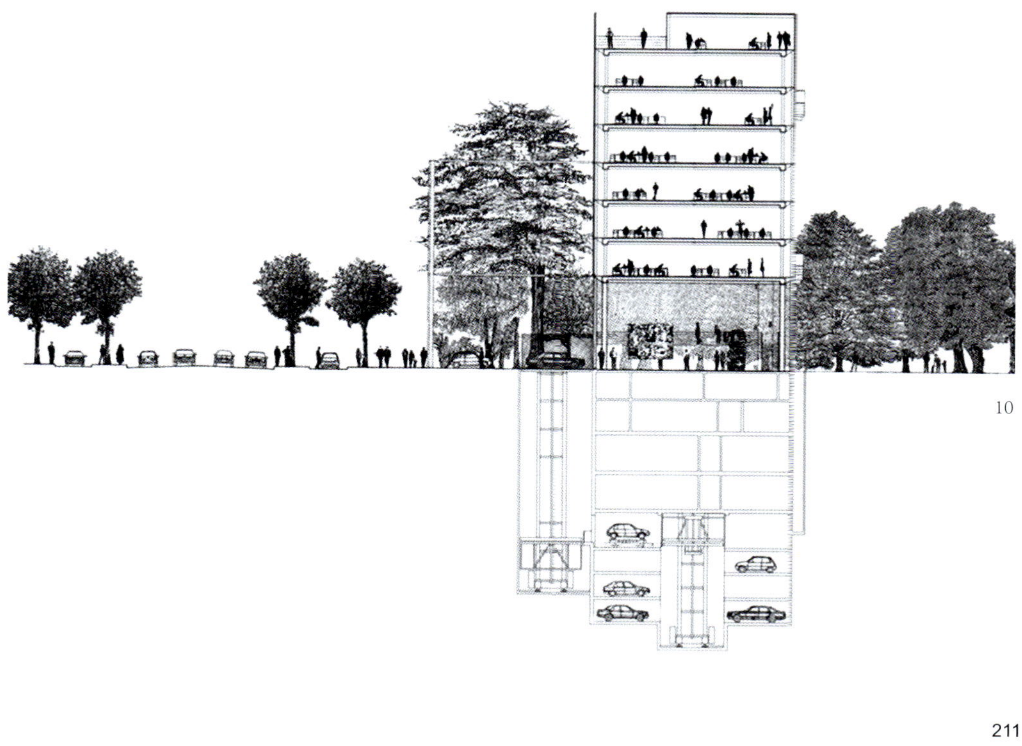

10

MEAUX COUNTRY MUSEUM OF THE GREAT WAR

Architect: Christophe Lab
Location: Meaux
Completion Date: 2011
Photographer: Philippe Ruault

The building of the Meaux Country Museum of the Great War is a brutal form, symbolising the effect of the mobilisation of forces on humankind and on the landscape. This allusive form disrupts the geography, concentrating the energy of war. The reference to the tortuous field of battle, the uprooted ground, is not literal but impregnates the imagination.

A sheltered forecourt leads to the entrance of the museum. It is a covered space, a transition between the exterior and the interior. Its light grey paving is a vast silent map, representing the north-east quarter of France and reflecting a soft light. It can receive large projections showing the movements of troops at different points in the war. Crossing the forecourt to the entrance hall, the visitor's path is illuminated and punctuated by pools of light shed by luminous openings like

1

enormous "spotlights" overhead. Looking up they are intrigued by elements of the museum displays on the first floor partially visible through these glass openings.

A staircase with deep treads and shallow risers takes the visitor to the reception's upper level. It climbs around the shop, which the visitor perceives from different angles before reaching the ticket desk and then the exhibition itself. Neutral

2

3

mannequins appear to walk out of display cases 14 and 18, dissolving the glass screens in order to limit their significance and offering a spectacular run up to a "heightened" reality. Here, sound, moving light projections and partial mirrors doubling the crowd effect evoke the experience of war and throw the spectator in among the mannequins.

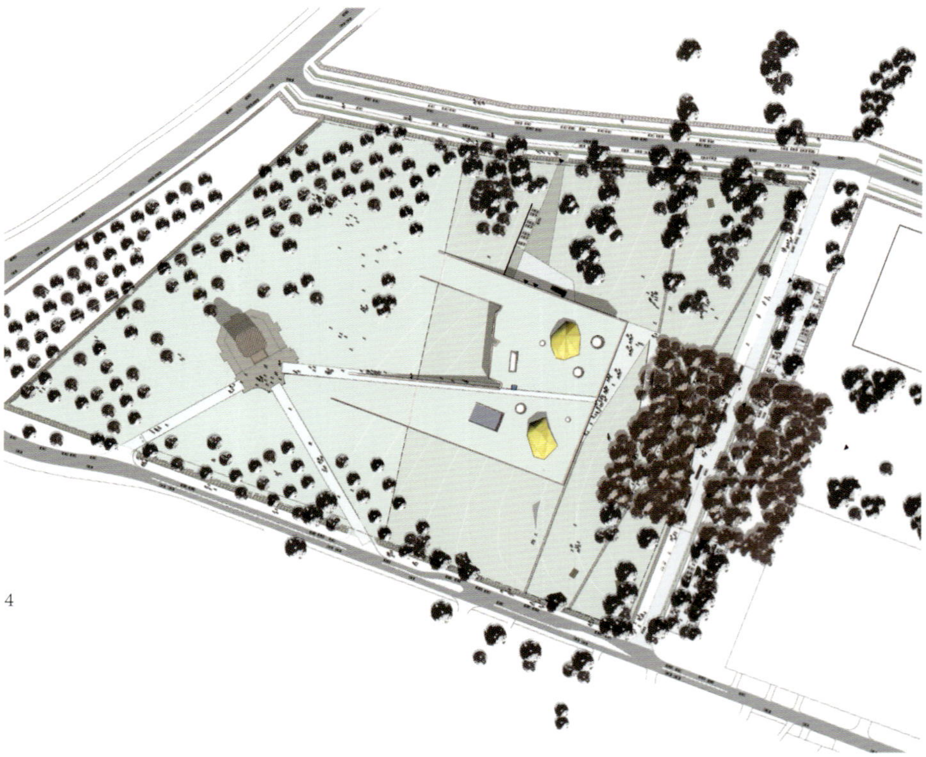

4

5

1. Façade on Route de Varredes
2. Trench suspended from beneath the building
3. Main façades and forecourt
4. Master plan
5. Approach from the forecourt

6. Access to the upper reception area
7. Crossroads of the central hub: the arrival and exit staircases
8. Arrival at the upper reception area, shop and ticket office

8

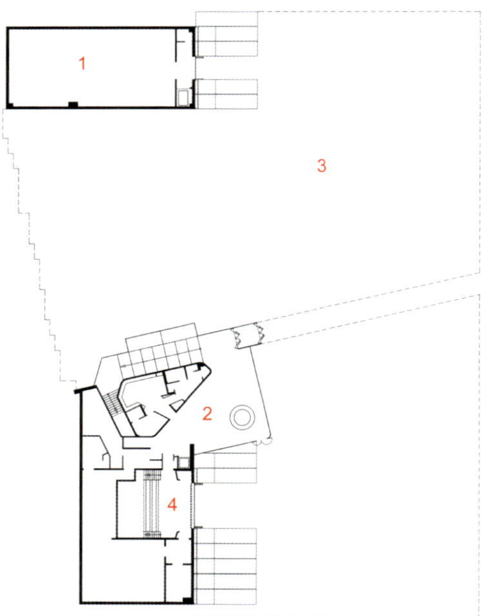

10

11

1. Lower reserves
2. Reception and snack bar
3. Forecourt
4. Auditorium
5. Upper reserves
6. Administration
7. Reception and shop
8. Educational workshops
9. Temporary exhibitions
10. Central nave
11. Thematic exhibitions

12

9. Upper reception area
10. Lower ground floor plan
11. Upper ground floor plan
12. Shop and ticket office
13. Cross section AA
14. Cross section BB

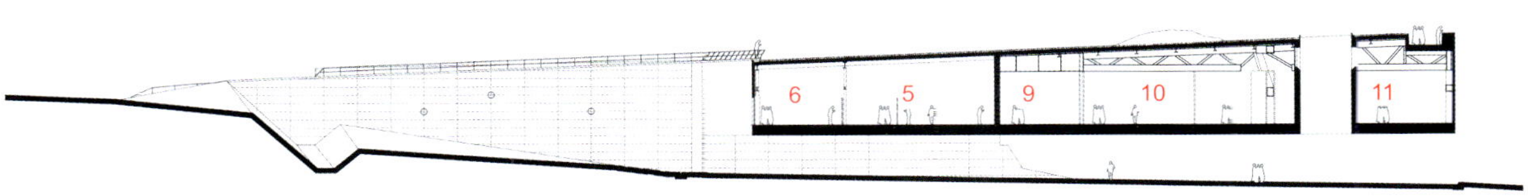

13

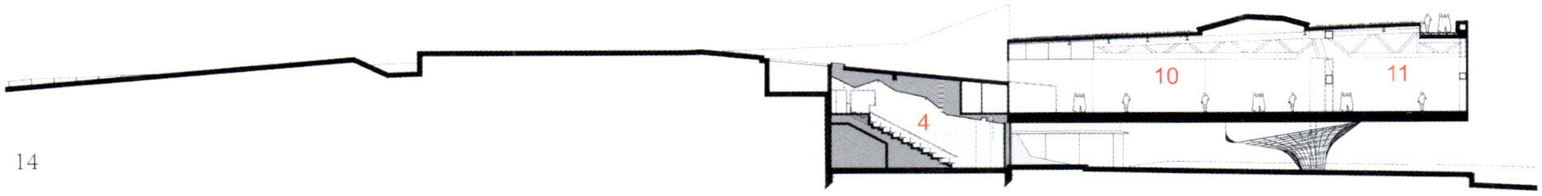

14

15

16

15. Introductory room with a fresco created by Jacques Tardi
16. "From school to the dugout" area
17. Marne 18 display case, from which a "neutral" mannequin emerges
18. German trench

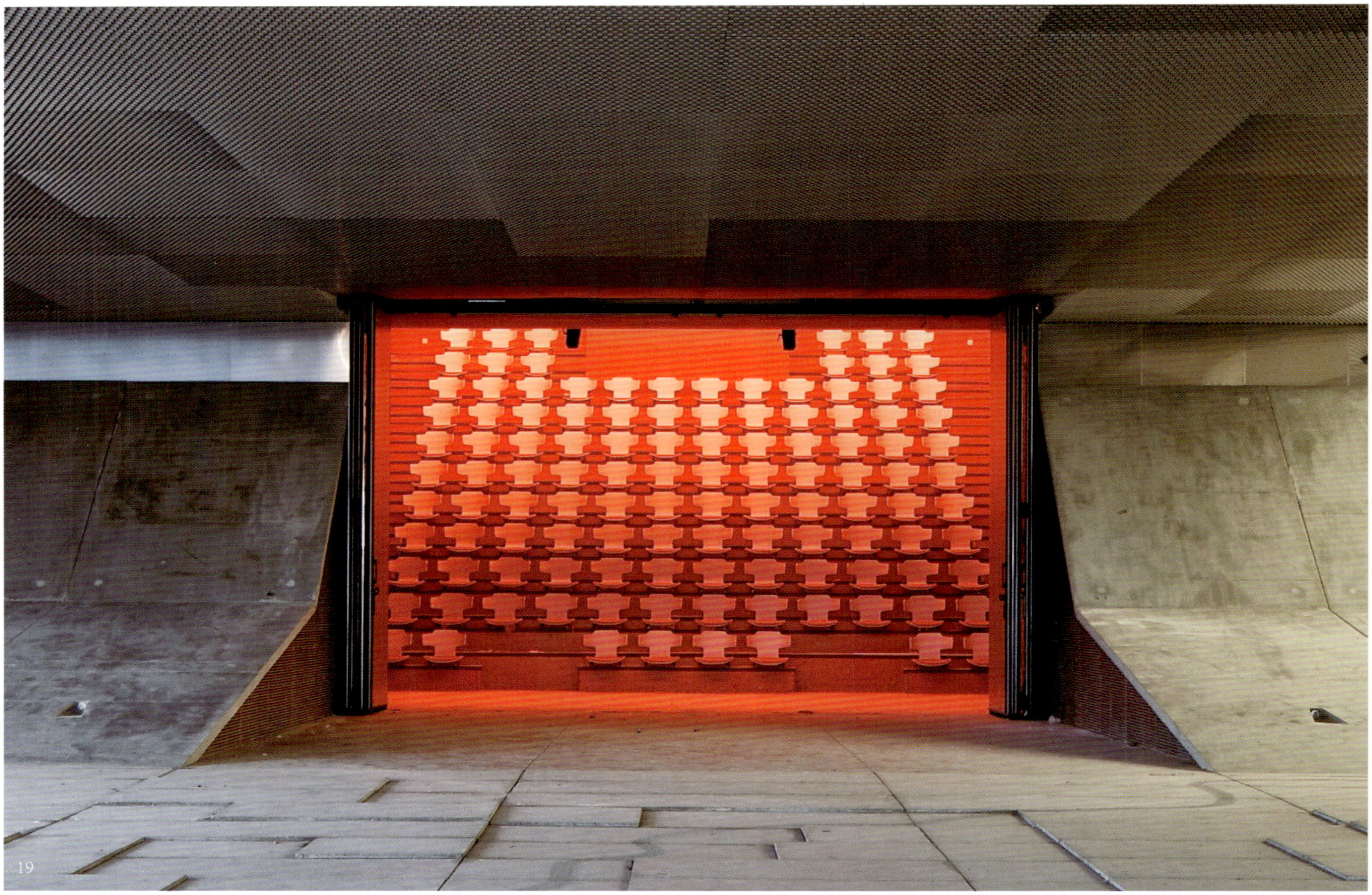

19

20

21

19-20. Auditorium seen from the forecourt
21. Forecourt seen from the auditorium
22. Auditorium section, backstage open to the forecourt

22

INSTITUTE OF THE ARAB WORLD

Architect: Jean Nouvel, Pierre Soria, Gilbert Lezenes, Architecture Studio
Location: Paris
Completion Date: 1987
Photographer: Philippe Ruault

The Institute of the Arab World was opened in 1987, the fruit of an agreement between France and 19 Arab countries, later joined by three more, to encourage a greater understanding of the contemporary Arab world and Arab-Muslim culture. On the banks of the Seine, facing the Ile Saint-Louis and adjoining Jussieu University, it combines an imaginative synthesis of architectural ideas from the Arab world and the West.

The spirit of Arab culture is particularly evoked in the diaphragms placed on the south façade, 240 moucharabiehs that open and close according to the outside light, thus creating a play of light and shadows inside the institute. Light has great importance here, as Jean Nouvel explains: "I started to consider the question of light at the Institute of the Arab World. The theme of light is seen on the south wall, composed only of photographic diaphragms, in the

organisation of the staircases, the flow of contours, superimpositions, reflections and shadows." The north façade is "a literal mirror of western culture", reflecting, but also reproducing, the landscape of Paris through a series of lines, of signs capturing the spirit of Paris, an echo of the buildings on the opposite banks.

The entrance to the auditorium, below ground, is pure fantasy: the space seems infinite, while the repetition of massive,

3

5

4

6

strong columns recalls the hypostyle rooms of Arab buildings. The tower of books, the patio and the interior courtyard also show the positive results of Jean Nouvel's questioning of western culture, which, having distanced itself from all clichés, finds in this building a strong and shared identity.

1. View from the Seine
2. South façade
3. North façade, detail
4. West façade, interior of the tower of books
5. Patio, detail
6&8. South façade, interior
7. Axonometry of the museum side
9. Ground floor plan

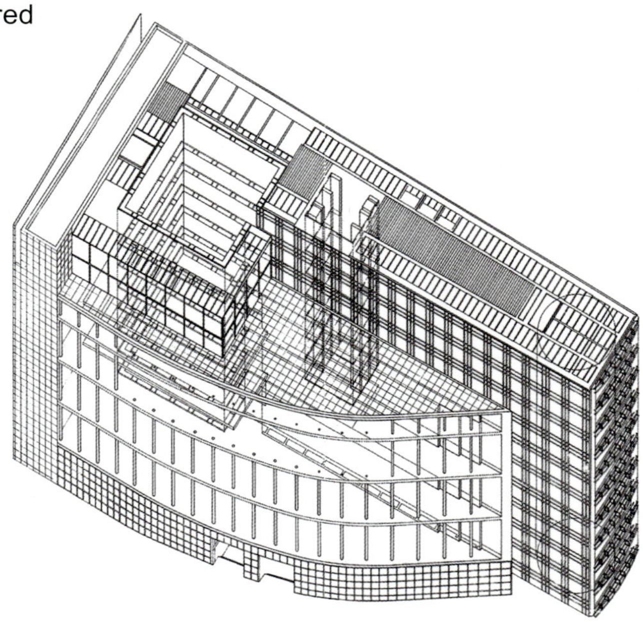

7

8

1. Forecourt
2. Entrance
3. Entrance hall

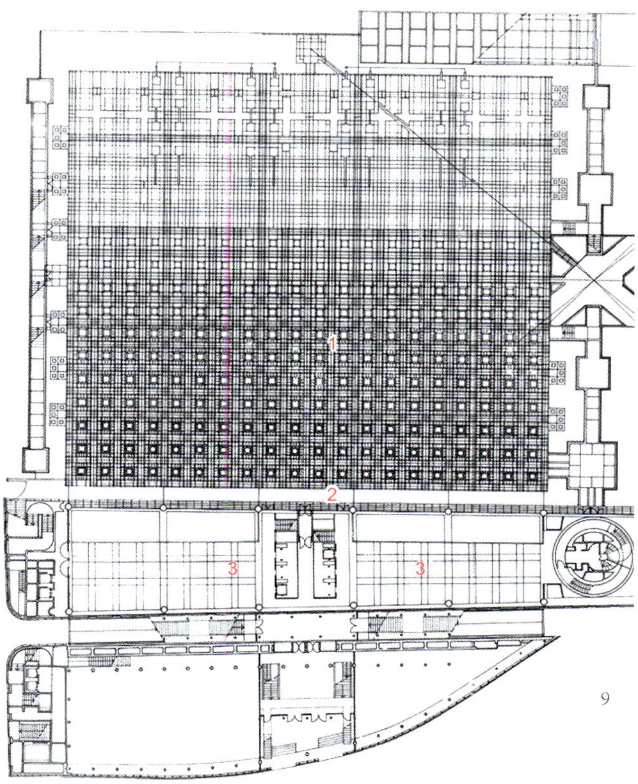

9

10

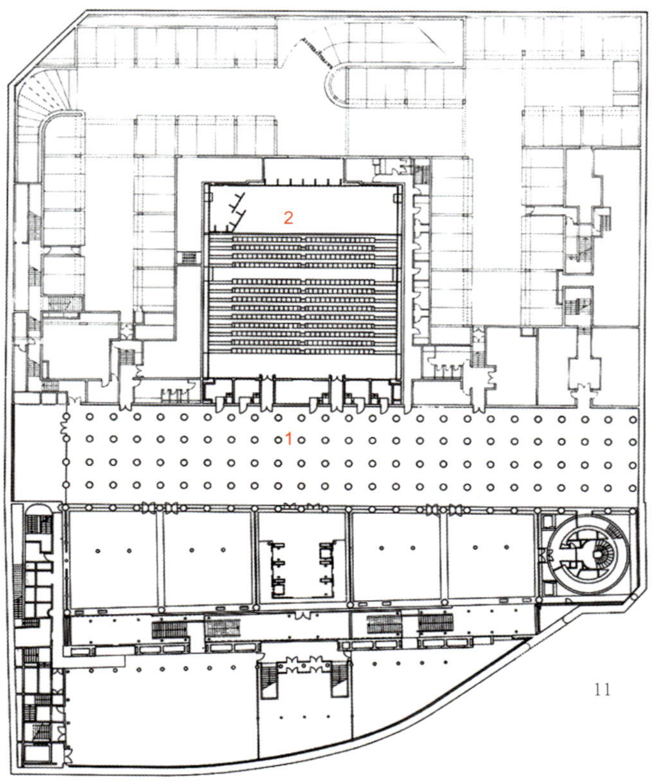

11

10. Smoking room
11. Basement floor plan
12. Staircase / south façade
13. 5th floor plan
14. 6th floor plan
15. 7th floor plan
16. 9th floor plan

1. Hypostyle room
2. Auditorium
3. Museum entrance
4. Museum
5. Museum atrium
6. Offices
7. Library
8. Library atrium
9. High council room
10. Restaurant
11. Terrace

12

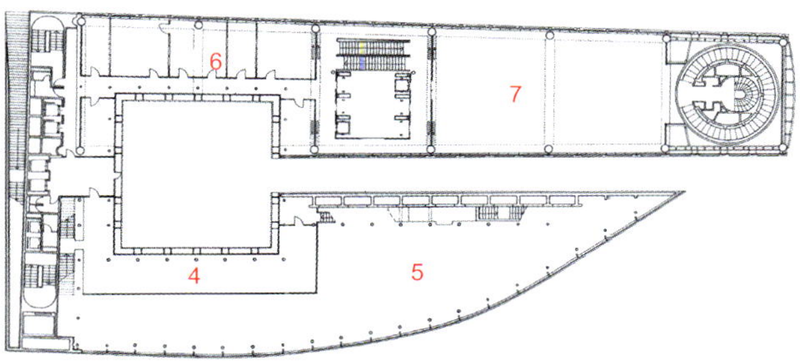

13

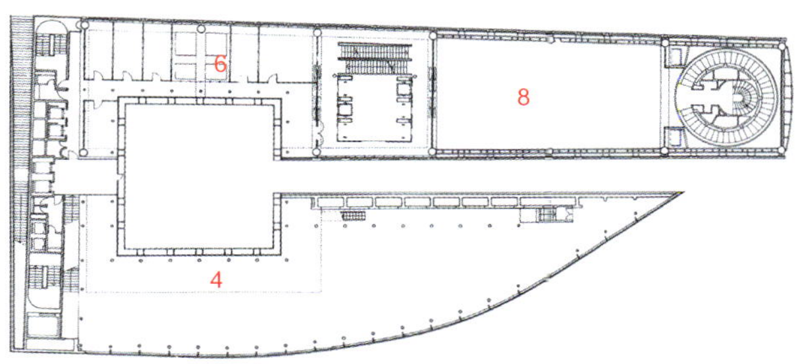

14

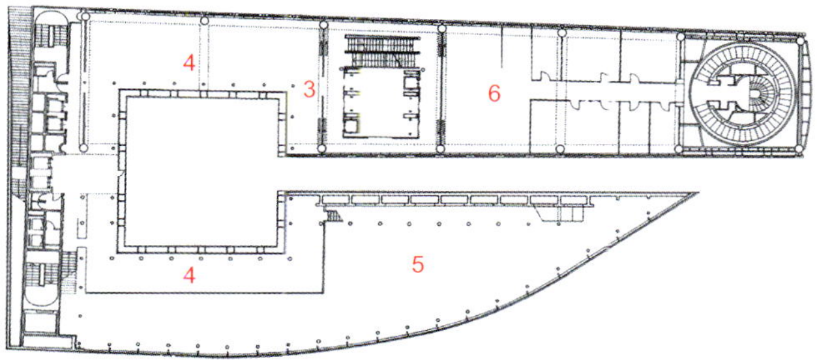

15

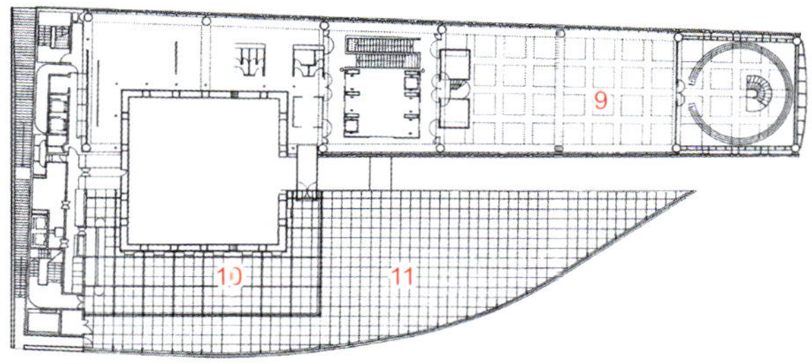

16

MOBILE ART PAVILION

Architect: Zaha Hadid
Location: Paris
Completion Date: 2011
Photographer: Francois Lacour, courtesy of Institut du Monde Arabe
Drawings: Zaha Hadid Architects

After being shown in Hong Kong, Tokyo and New York, the Mobile Art Pavilion designed by Zaha Hadid was donated to the Institute of the Arab World in Paris by Chanel, where it will form a permanent exhibition venue. Its first exhibition, running from 29 April to 30 October 2011, was on the work of Zaha Hadid herself, offering a three-fold entry into her world: through the building, the exhibition design and the projects exhibited. The aim was, she says, to evoke "a kind of strangeness and newness that is comparable to the experience of going to a new country".

The pavilion illustrates Hadid's use of digital imaging technology to break free of the geometric constraints of the industrial age. Its organic form has evolved from the spiraling shapes found in nature. This system of organisation and growth, expanding towards its circumference, gives the pavilion generous public areas at its entrance with a 125m^2 terrace. Through the parametric distortion of a torus, a constant variety of exhibition spaces are

1

created around its circumference, whilst at its centre, a large 60m^2 courtyard with natural lighting provides an area for visitors to meet and reflect on the exhibition. This arrangement also allows visitors to see each other moving through the space, facilitating the viewing of art as a collective experience.

The organic fibre reinforced plastic shell is created with a succession of reducing arched steel segments. As the pavilion has traveled over three continents, this

2

3

segmentation allows the structure to be easily transported. The partitioning seams become a strong formal feature of the exterior façade, whilst creating a spatial rhythm of perspective views within the interior exhibition spaces.

In creating the Mobile Art Pavilion, Zaha Hadid has developed the fluid geometries of natural systems into a continuum of fluent and dynamic space – where oppositions between exterior and interior, light and dark, natural and artificial landscapes are synthesised. Lines of energy converge within the Pavilion, constantly redefining the quality of each exhibition space whilst guiding movement through the exhibition.

1. Night-view Perspective of Mobile Art Pavilion in front of the Institute of the Arab Word (Institut du Monde Arabe – IMA)
2. Birdseye Perspective of the Mobile Art Pavilion by night illuminated via RGB machine
3. Birdseye Perspective of the Mobile Art Pavilion by day
4. Roof plan
5. Ground floor plan

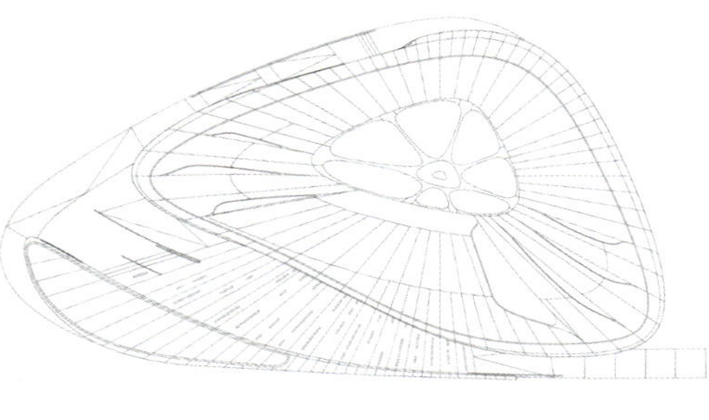

4

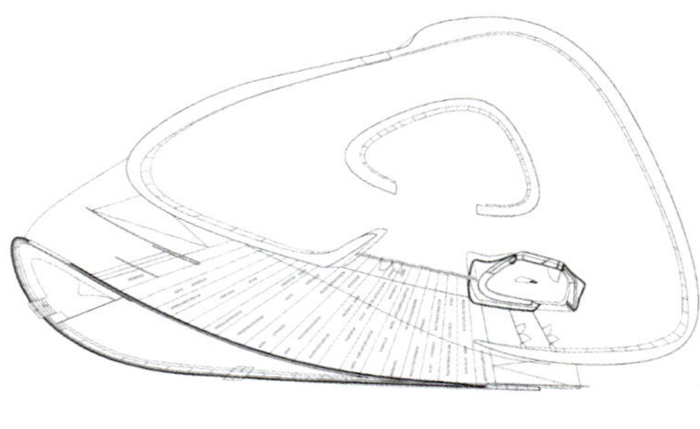

5

6

6. Eyelevel perspective of Mobile Art pavilion in front of the IMA
7. Front Elevation
8. Back Elevation
9. Right Elevation
10. Left Elevation

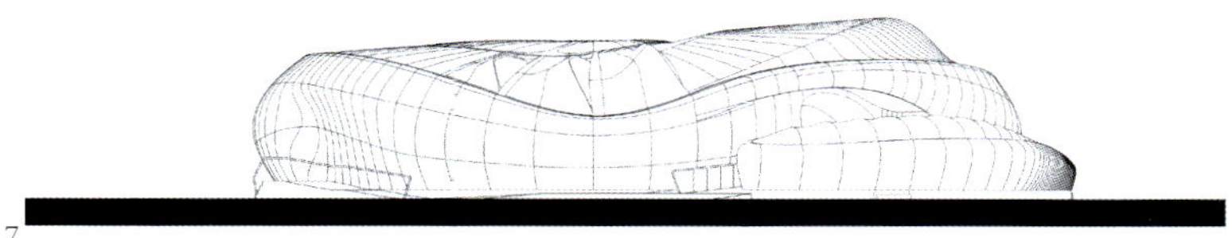

7

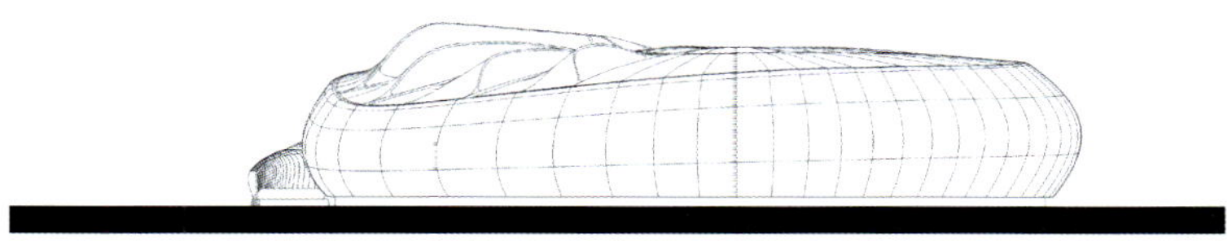

8

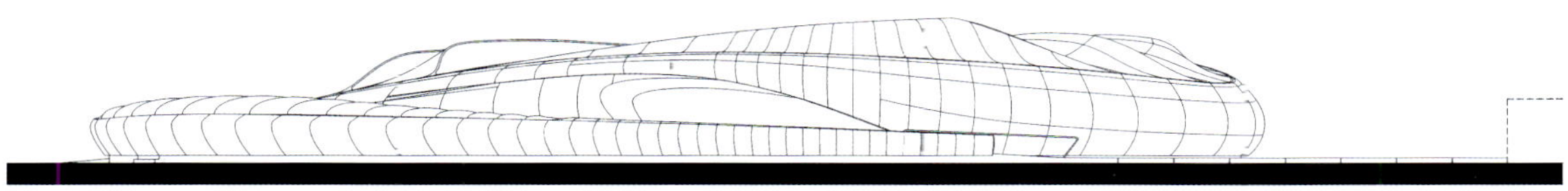

9

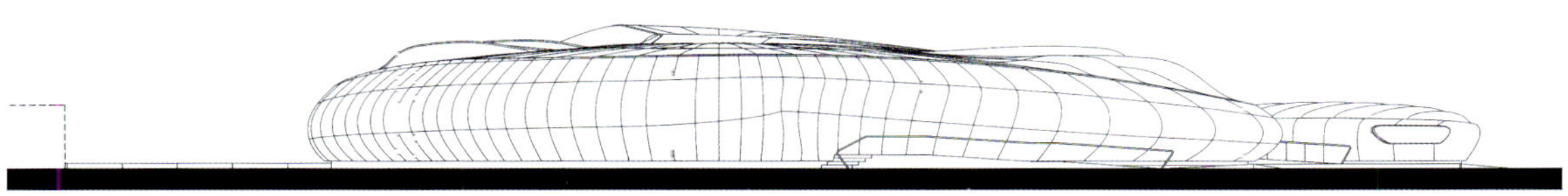

10

11

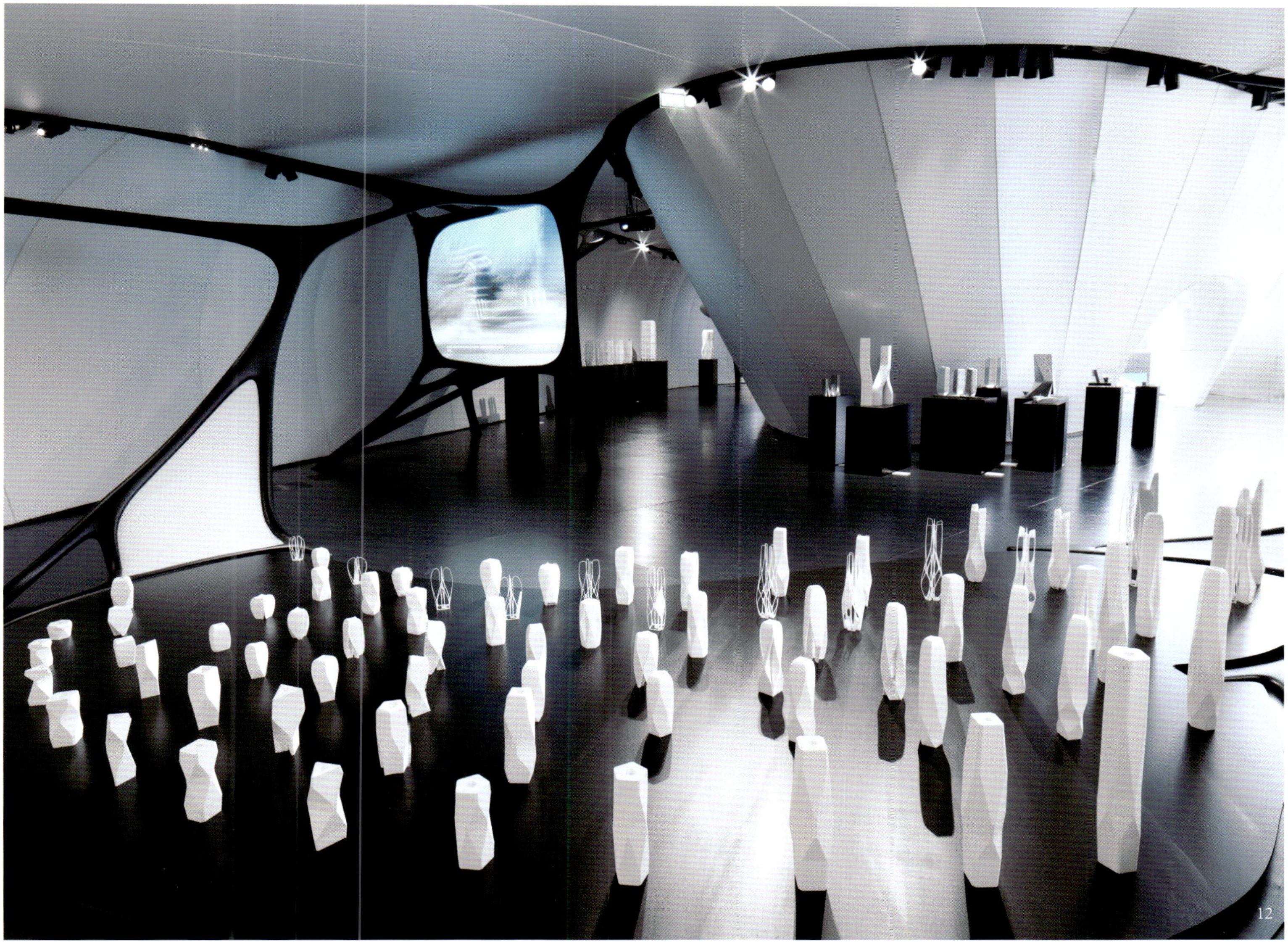

11. Interior View of exhibition Installation "Zaha Hadid – une architecture" with 3-dimensional scenographic structure housing large projection screens
12. Interior view towards the courtyard with Towerfield of Beijing Central Business District Competition in the foreground and silver models in the background

13

14

13. Interior view with Lunar Relief mounted in front of textile skin and the Slovakian Bratislava City Center Model and Animation as well as the Moroccan Rabat Tower exhibited on black plinths
14. Detail Lunar Relief
15. Interior view of 3-dimensional cellular structure made from CNC milled polyurethane foam painted in matt black with a car paint system and stretch fabric suspended from cells as projection devices
16. The pavilion roof topography was modeled on a spherical geometry using a radial grid
17. The inner walls of the Pavilion are made from a stretch fabric that was developed through a series of cutting patterns

15

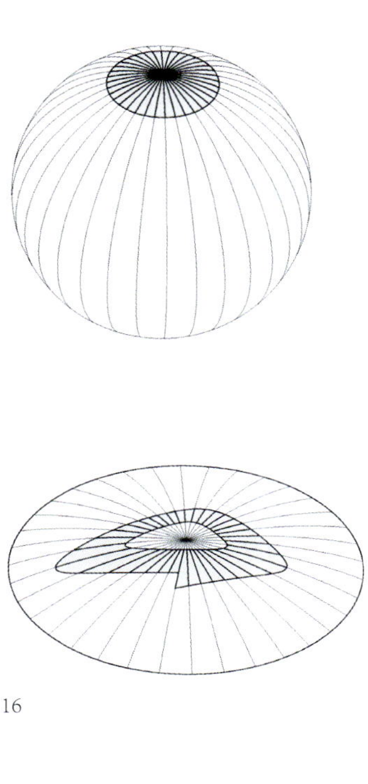

16

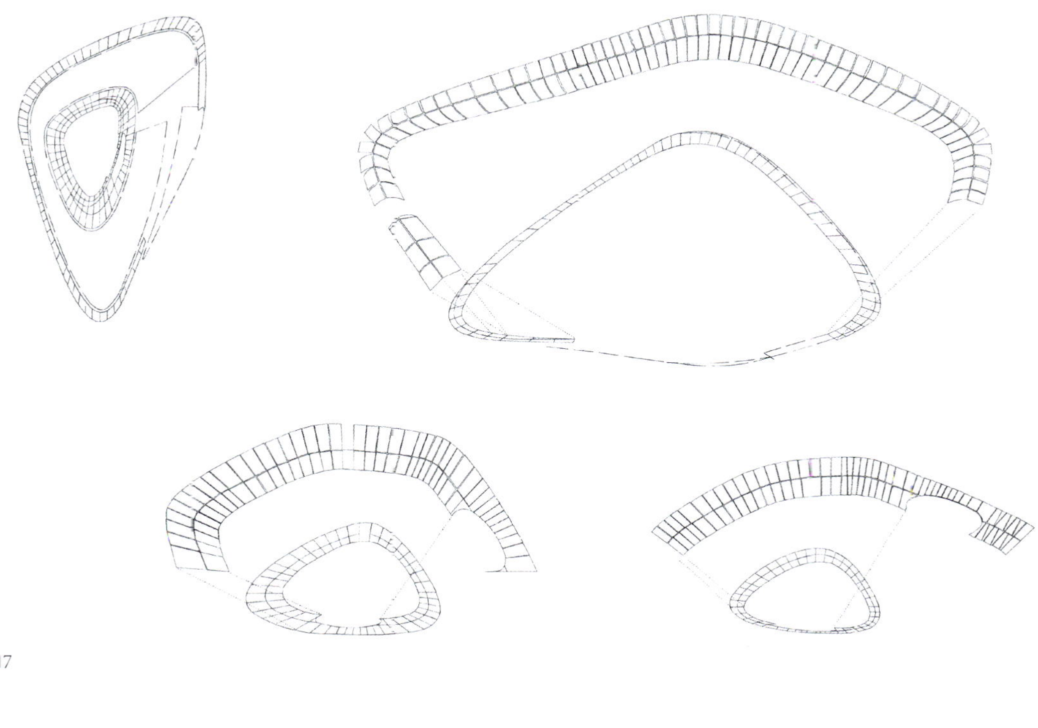

17

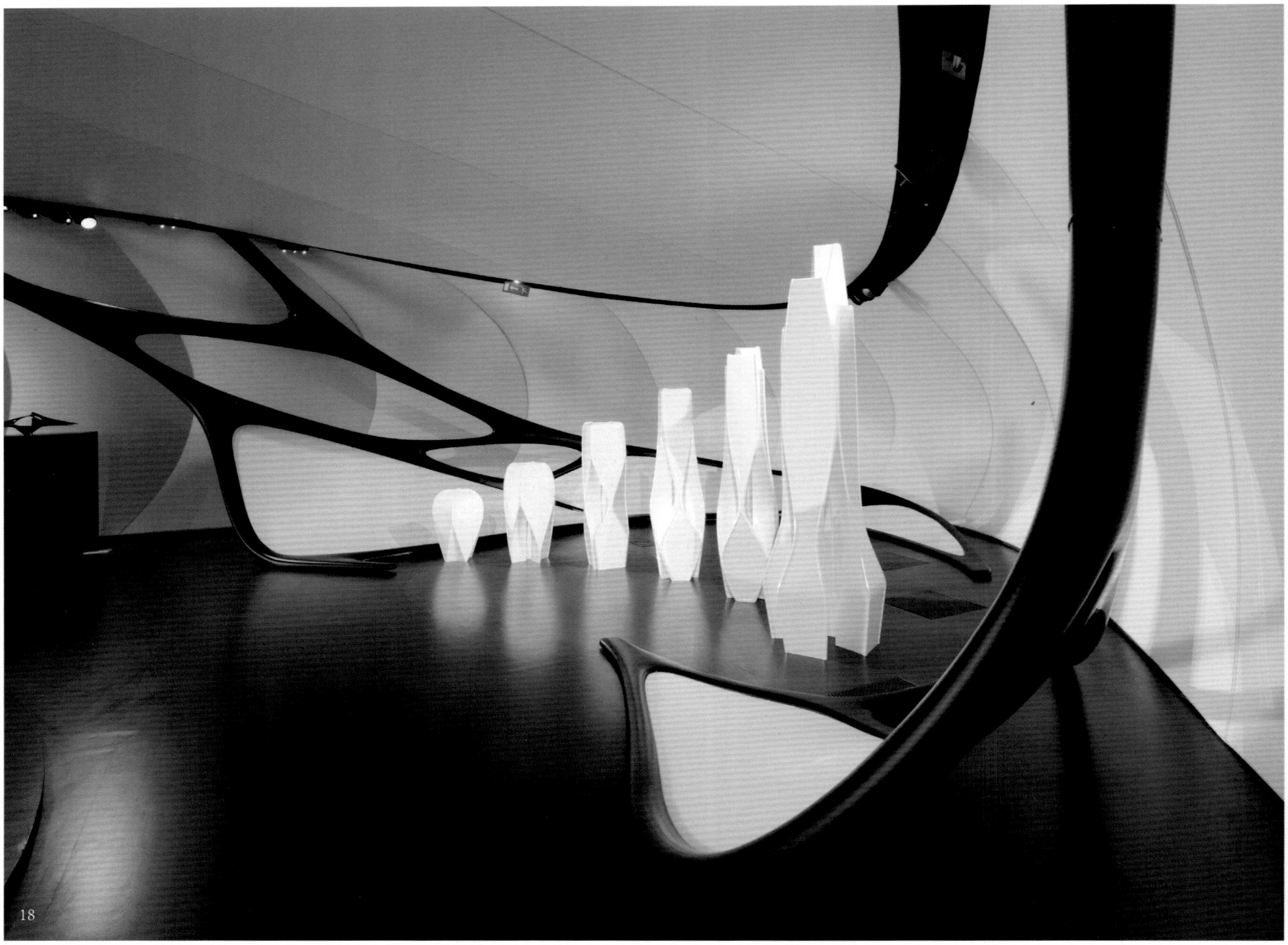

18

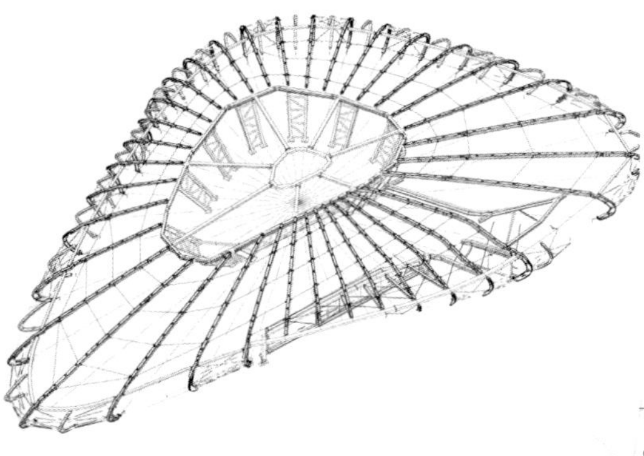

19

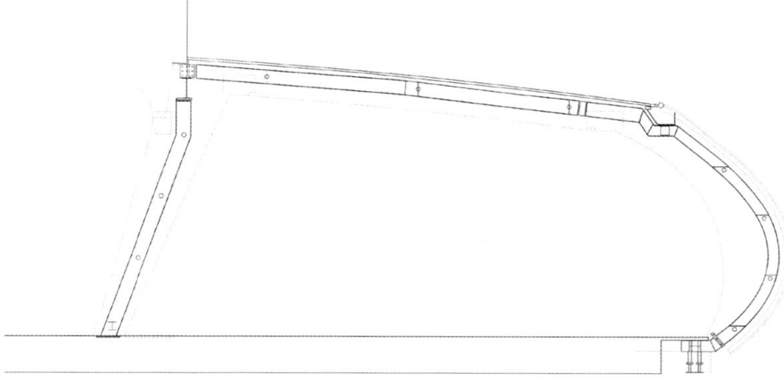

20

18. Detail of scenographic elements enveloping 6 large scale Tower models CNC milled from foam
19. Radial structural arches composing the primary steel structure of the pavilion
20. Dimensioned radial section of an arch composed of a series of bend I-Beams
21. Detail of the Abu Dhabi performing Arts Center embedded within the fluid environment of the pavilion and its scenographic design
22. Detail of Silver Painting -Barcelona Tower- floating in front of textile internal skin
23. Detail of Silver Models and projection screen

21

22

23

JEAN COCTEAU MUSEUM

Architect: Rudy Ricciotti
Location: Menton
Completion Date: 2011
Photographer: Olivier Amsellem

Winner of an international competition launched by the town of Menton in 2008, Rudy Ricciotti's project will house the Séverin Wunderman donation in its entirety in a 2,700m² space. The site is not neutral and the project entails strengthening the town out towards the sea, creating a bedrock to ensure that it will sit on the existing "urban canvas". The building forms part of the urban framework but the quay on which it is situated had to be reclaimed for pedestrians. In the distance the cloudy vision of the arcades, an image from old postcards, reminds us of Menton when it was a fashionable seaside resort.

The museum does not try to hide the sea, but is rather a plinth and architectural narrative, forging a new link with the original, elegant era of Menton where the great stylistic movements of the 1900s were played out. The building must convey the freedom of its romanticism: it is there because it could not be elsewhere. It has its place just as the covered market has

2

its place. It is an urban form that helps to repair a fragment of this neighbourhood, to convey the fact that this now urban space was once just an embankment on the sea. The building must let itself be discovered. Should it not retain a mystery? The mystery of its constructive truth, of its stasis? The museum accepts its appearance, intrigues through its transparency, attracts by what it lets us glimpse. The architecture summons up the elusive and complex world of Jean Cocteau.

3

4

5

1-2. The black and white aesthetic is linked to the works of Jean Cocteau
3. The museum has sweeping views of the exterior
4. The arcades, evoking memories from old postcards
5. Master plan
6. Transition space between interior and exterior

6

7

8

9

7-9. Interior views: the play of shadows creates sublime effects
10. A museum as a mirror of the artist and his work

Dreaming up this museum was like imagining an architectural principle that could take the contrast between light and darkness and make it into a sublime play of shadows. The architectural approach, and above all the aesthetic of black and white, convey the dream-world, the mystery and the complexity of the works of Jean Cocteau. A museum as a mirror of the artist and his work. Which means refusing the dictature of a tyrannical modernity and considering story, dreaming and design as a possible opening for architecture.

11

12

13

14

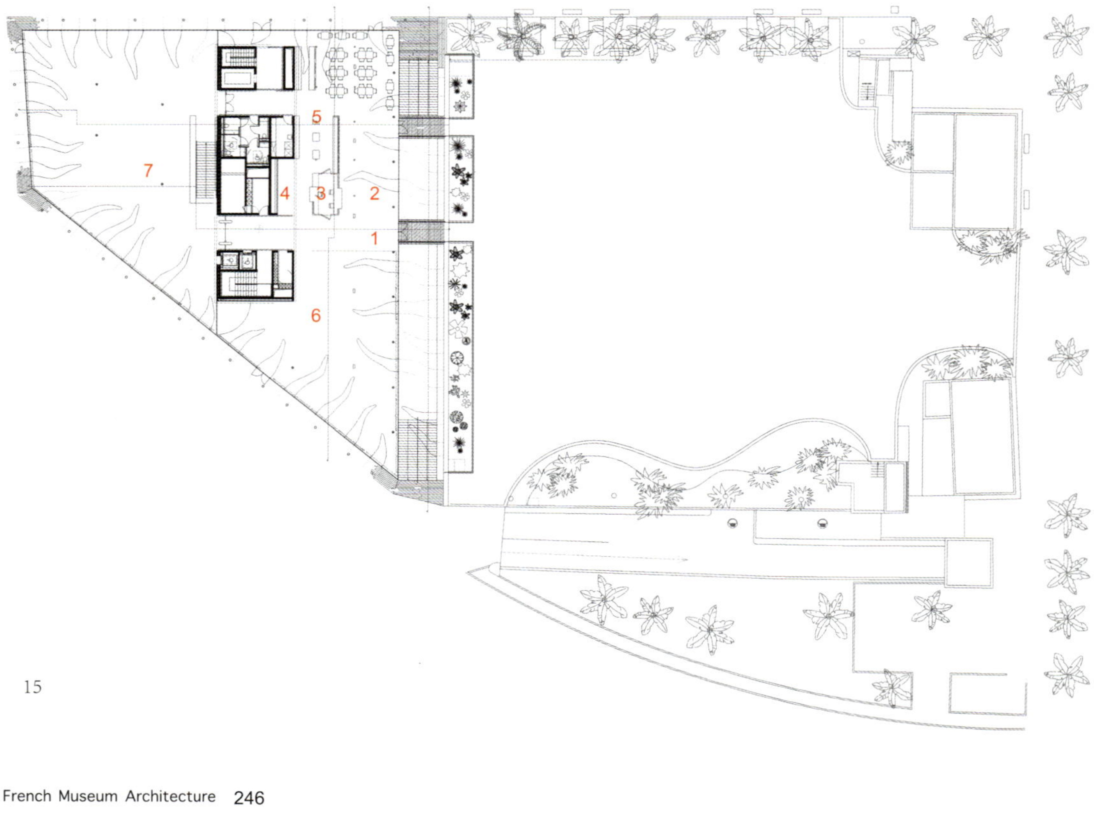

15

1. Entrance
2. Hall
3. Reception
4. Bookshop
5. Café
6. Temporary exhibition
7. Permanent exhibition
8. Reserve
9. Museographical workshop
10. Maintenance and Upkeep Workshop
11. Graphic arts space
12. Documentation
13. Offices
14. Educational workshop
15. Car park

16

11-14. The importance of contrast between light and shade
15. Ground floor plan
16. The architectural device of the arcades has been revisited in an entirely contemporary spirit
17. 1st floor plan

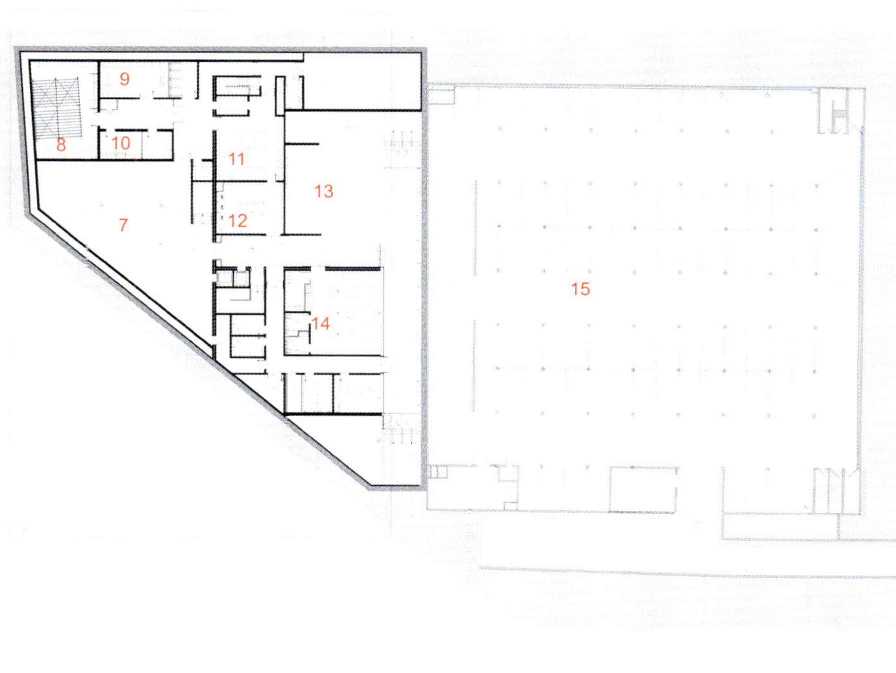

17

VAL-DE-MARNE MUSEUM OF CONTEMPORARY ART

Architect: Jacques Ripault
Location: Vitry-sur-Seine
Completion Date: 2005
Photographer: Pauline Turmel (pp.248-249), Patrick Muller (pp.250-251), Jean-Marie Monthiers (pp.253-257)

The Val-de-Marne Departmental Museum of Contemporary Art, known as the Mac Val, gathers together the collection of paintings, sculptures and drawings by contemporary artists that have been acquired by the department of Val-de-Marne since 1982. The museum aims to make art and culture available to everyone, to create a place for learning, familiarisation and knowledge, but also a place for feeling and finding peace.

With an architecture that revolves around the works, the artists and the public, this museum offers an opportunity for self-development and fulfilment.

The Mac Val is entered at street level via a longitudinal gallery, with a pathway that leads to the garden. Moving from east to west, the visitor encounters the amphitheatre, the restaurant and its terrace. In the centre, near to the entrance

hall, is found a bookshop and on the upper floor a library. In the west wing a wide, light-filled corridor opens onto large rooms lit via skylights in grooves running the length of the ceiling. In the south wing, a hall free of structures uses light reflectors. The museum was designed not to appear monumental, imposing or spectacular at first sight. It offers a linear geometry, and contrasting planes and transparencies that dilate or draw in the spaces.

3

Light is the raw material, it carves up the volumes, slips between two planes, reflects itself between two partitions and marks contrasts over the course of the visit. The aesthetic is not one of stacking but of stretching out, with a construction of horizontal and vertical planes alternating with the light, which display paintings and sculptures and strengthen the lines of the public space. Through the contrasts of sand-coloured concrete and the dark wenge wood floors, this museum is essentially black and white; it is the works themselves that bring free forms and colours.

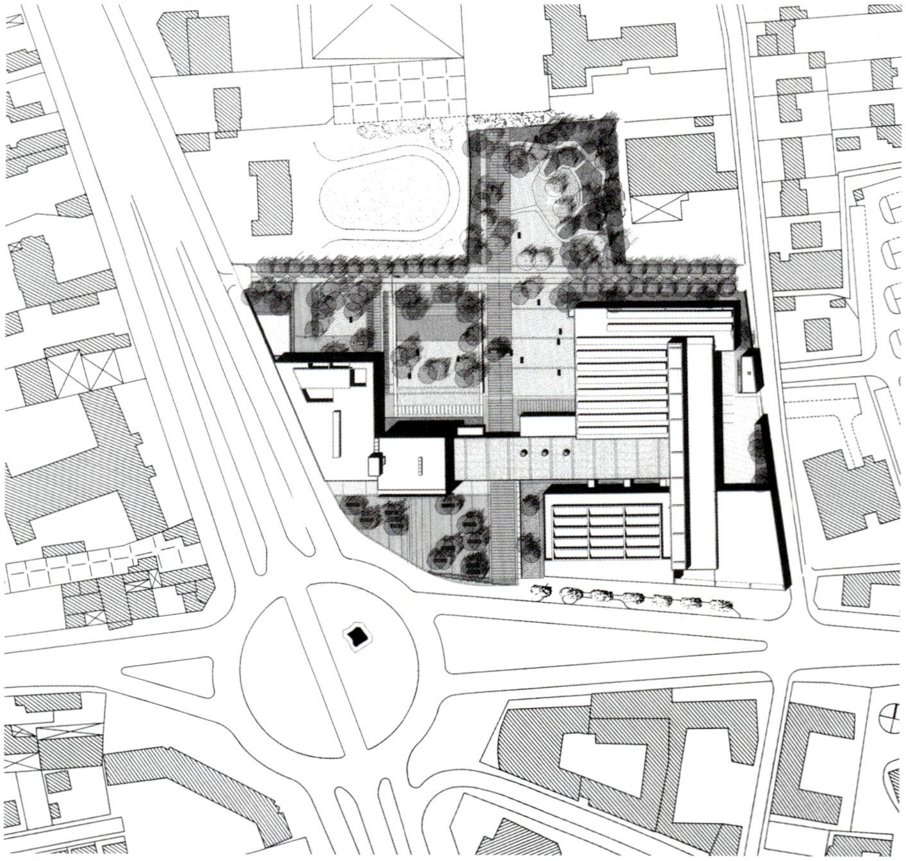
4

5

1. Overall view in its context
2. Grand gallery enfilade
3. Horizontal planes of the entrance
4. Master plan
5. Restaurant and artists' studios
6. Section

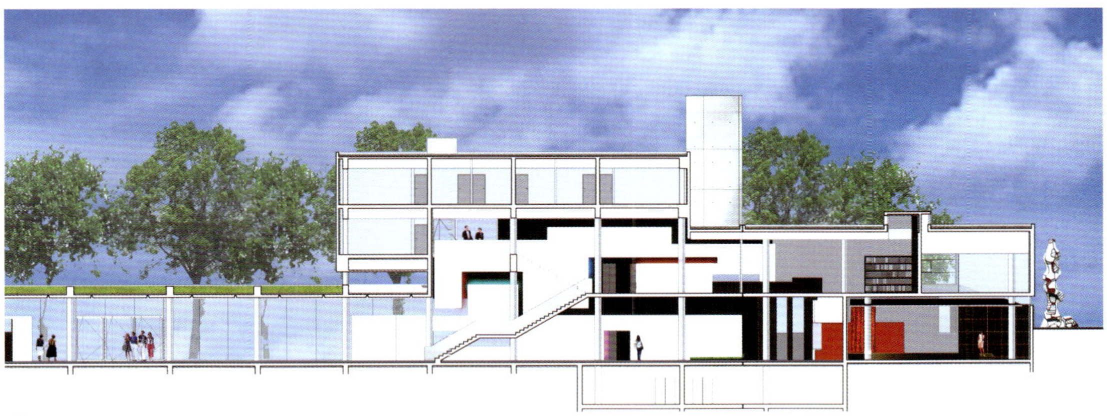

6

7. Ground floor plan
8. Mezzanine plan
9. 1st and 2nd floor plan
10. General diagram
11. Frontal view
12. The forecourt

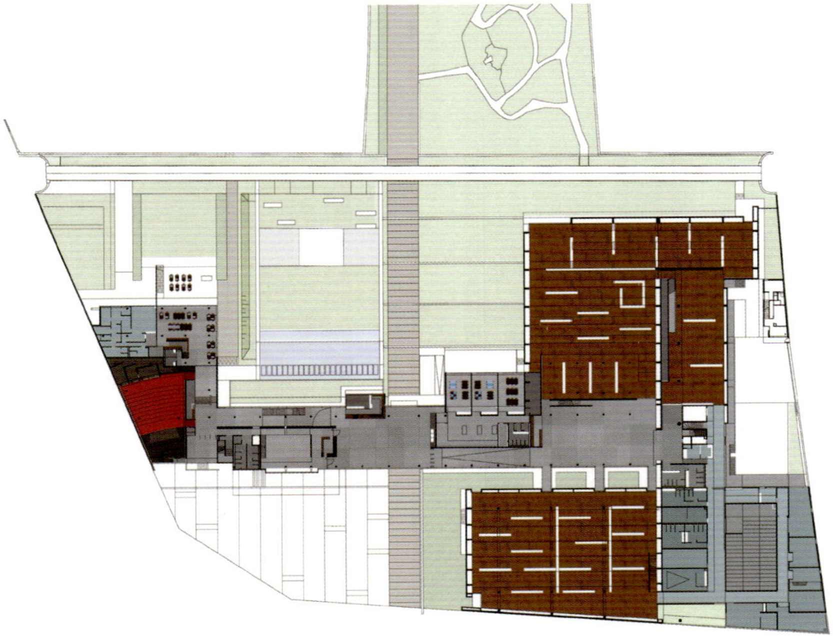

7

1. Educational spaces
2. Permanent exhibitions
3. Temporary exhibitions
4. Reserve – Restaurant
5. Auditorium – Research centre
6. Bookshops – Administration

A. Museum forecourt
B. Sculpture garden
C. Restaurant terrace
D. Delivery area

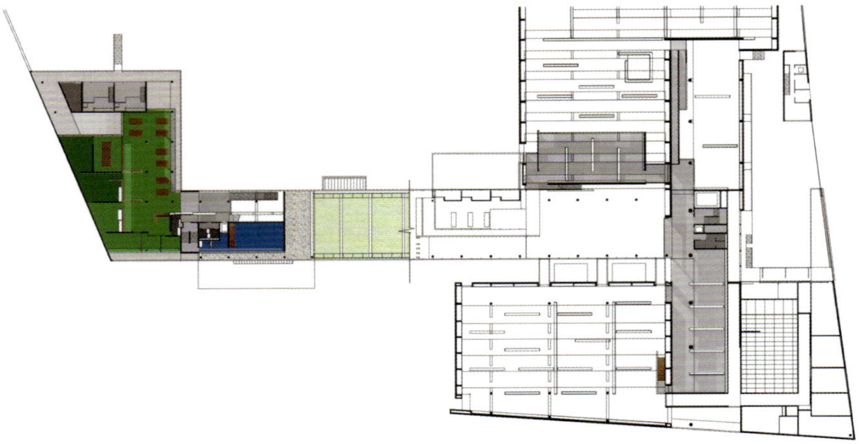

8

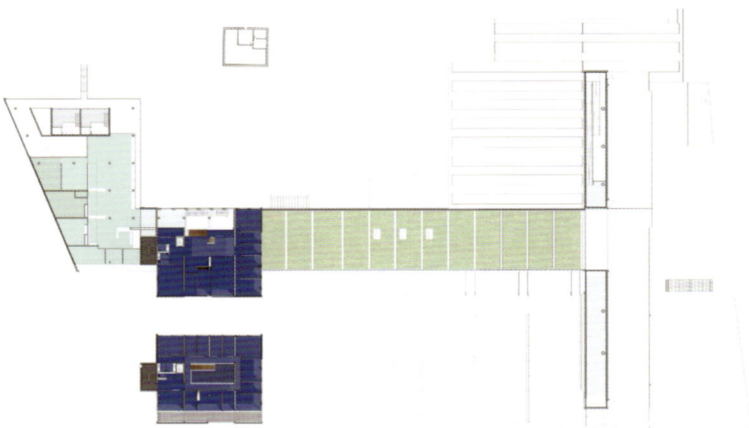

9

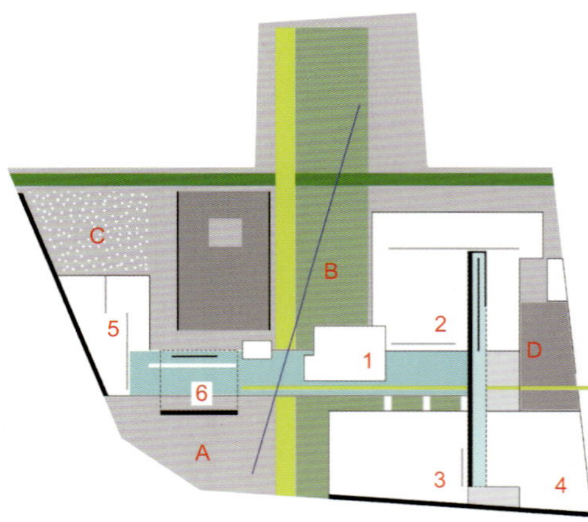

10

11

12

13

13. Hall leading to the exhibition rooms – installation by Varini
14. Exhibition space section

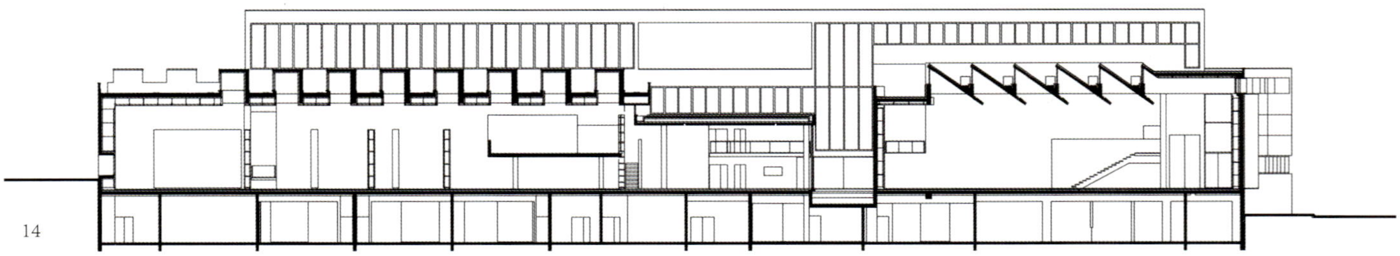

14

15

15. Exhibition room with 9 metre ceiling height
16. Section/perspective of the permanent exhibition room
17. Section/perspective of the temporary exhibition room

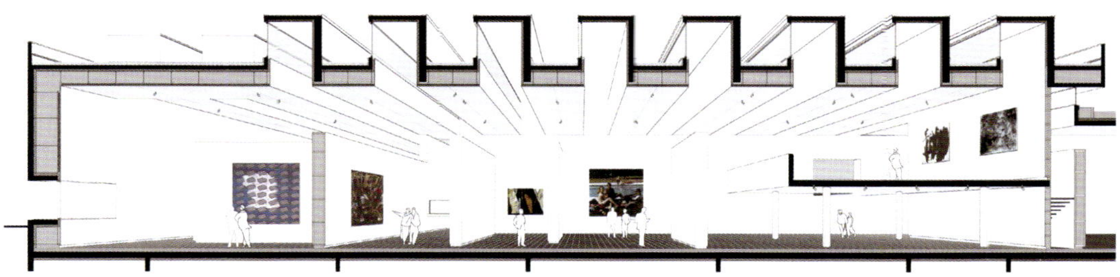

16

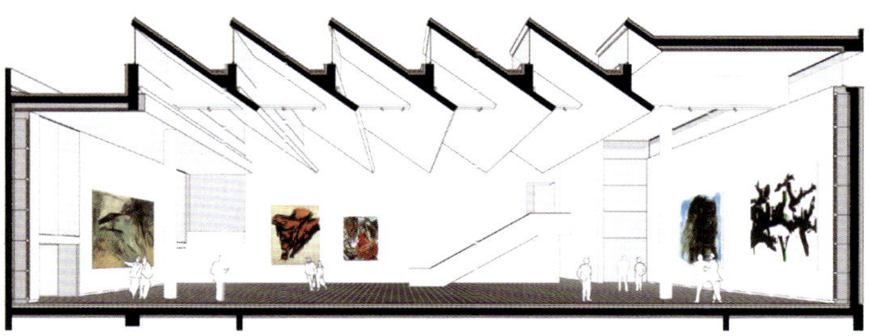

17

18

19

20

18. View of the exhibition rooms
19. Permanent exhibition room
20. Bookshop
21. Permanent exhibition rooms on the mezzanine
22. Temporary exhibition room

MALRAUX MUSEUM

Architect: Beaudouin-Husson
Location: Le Havre
Completion Date: 1999
Photographer: Jean-Marie Monthiers

This museum in Le Havre was one of the pioneering buildings of the early 1960s that marked an evolution in the history of architecture. Its architects, Guy Lagneau, Jean Dimitrijevic and Michel Weill, talented students of Perret, all became successful after its completion. The project's influence was not immediate, and yet the ideas of Lagneau and his engineer Jean Prouvé have continued to exert their influence to this day.

Beaudouin-Husson Architects were commissioned to transform the museum, and did so with the encouragement and help of Guy Lagneau and his partners, Jean Dimitrijevic and Michel Weill. One of the solutions used to preserve the double-height volume was to gather all the peripheral spaces (library, conference room, etc.) in the two first spans of the building, using the untapped space in the eaves. The flexibility of the original design was partly preserved in the spatial relationship between the temporary exhibition room and the large volume of

1

the permanent collections.

The degree of fluidity is subtly adapted to suit collections that range from modern to old master paintings. Bit by bit one is led into the more intimate spaces. The ceiling follows suit: glazed in the nave and around the outer edges of the building, it becomes opaque above the mezzanine to gain height in the free volumes of the eaves. To filter the natural light, glass sun screens pivot vertically throughout the day in the double skin of the west façade. In the east

2

4

5

façade, the floor stops abruptly to create a double-height space that totally frees up the mezzanne. In this luminous void, a rail 25 metres long, suspended from the structure, seems to float in mid air. These two levels of exhibition spaces are linked by a ramp strengthening and echoing the visual continuity between the museum and the sea.

1. Night exterior view
2. General interior view
3. North façade
4. Ground floor
5. Library
6. The ramp

7

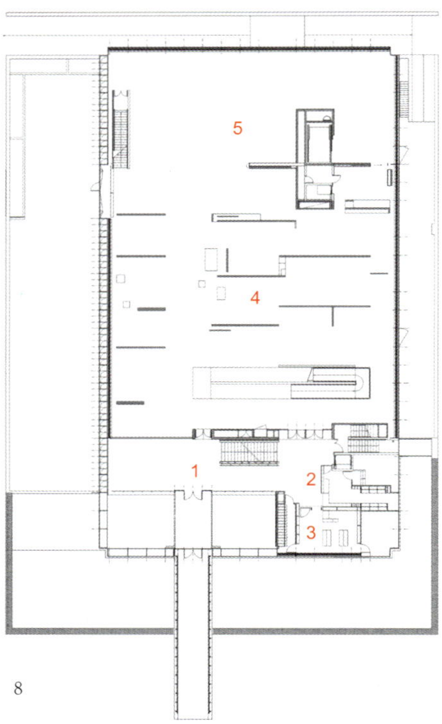

8

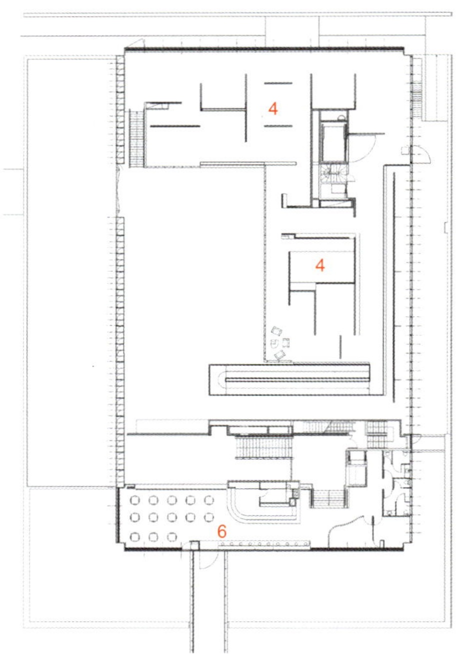

9

7. The ramp
8. Entrance level plan
9. Mezzanine plan
10. Suspended gallery
11. Upper level gallery

1. Entrance
2. Reception
3. Bookshop
4. Permanent exhibition room
5. Temporary exhibition room
6. Café

10

11

STRASBOURG MUSEUM OF MODERN AND CONTEMPORARY ART

Architect: Ateliers AFA
– Adrien Fainsilber & Associés
Location: Strasbourg
Completion Date: 1998
Photographer: Edith Rodeghiero

Stretching along the River Ill, the Museum of Modern and Contemporary Art (MAMC), embraces Strasbourg and reconstructs the urban landscape through its link with several strong features: the river, the Saint-Jean commandery, the Vauban dam and the administrative headquarters of the Bas-Rhin department on the opposite bank. Its relationship with the water, light and the historic city have strongly influenced the organisation of the site.

The museum is spread over three floors, one of which is partially a mezzanine. The wide central nave forms the backbone of the museum, hosting the welcome desks and opening onto the different public areas. As a nod to tradition, the contrast in materials and textures – glass, pink granite and smooth, white concrete resin panels – evokes traditional Strasbourg architecture with its white plaster surfaces outlined in pink sandstone.

Adjacent to the entrance on the ground floor, the modern art room and a gallery housing the works of Gustave Doré run the length of the riverside wing. The modern art room devoted to the sculptures of Jean Arp is the showpiece of the museum. The Doré gallery fits the works that it houses. It is 12 metres high and lit by a skylight, with a lower ceilinged area for drawings and sculptures. On the opposite side of the nave, a temporary

3

exhibition room is both high ceilinged and adaptable through its moveable partitions, so it can respond to the most unexpected demands of contemporary. On the first floor, four exhibition rooms fill the length of the building. And on the roof, with the restaurant, Mimmo Paladino's horse sculpture can be seen from afar, heralding the presence of the museum in the city.

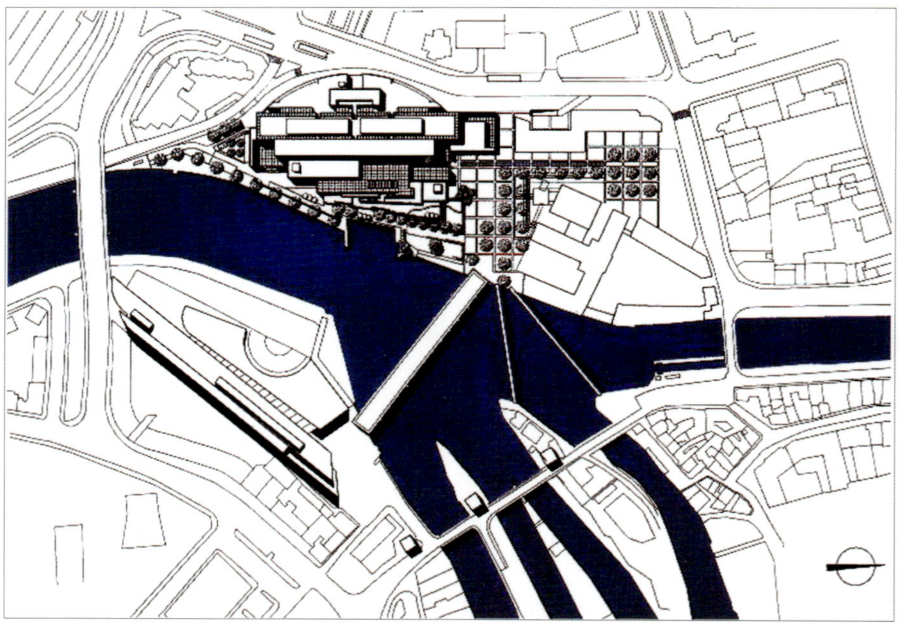

4

1. View from the Ill
2. Exterior view
3. The glass façade
4. Master plan
5. Panoramic terrace
6. Entrance detail

7

8

7. Escalator and footbridge in the nave
8. Detail of the staircase
9. Cross section
10. Nave interior
11. Framed view of La Petite France

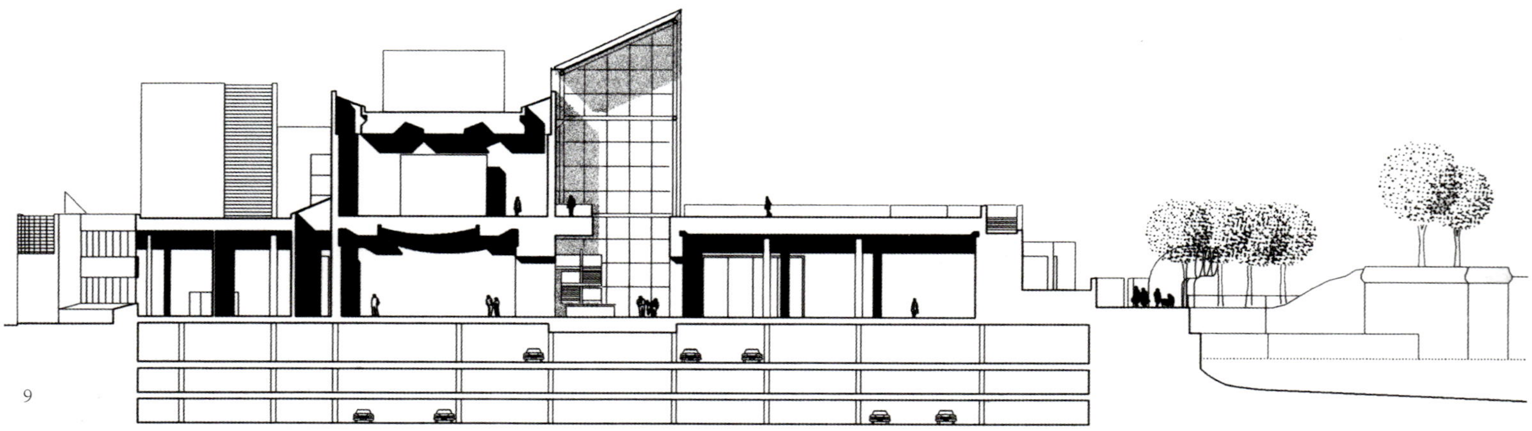

9

10

11

12. 1st floor plan
13. Mezzanine plan
14. Ground floor plan
15. Launch party in the nave

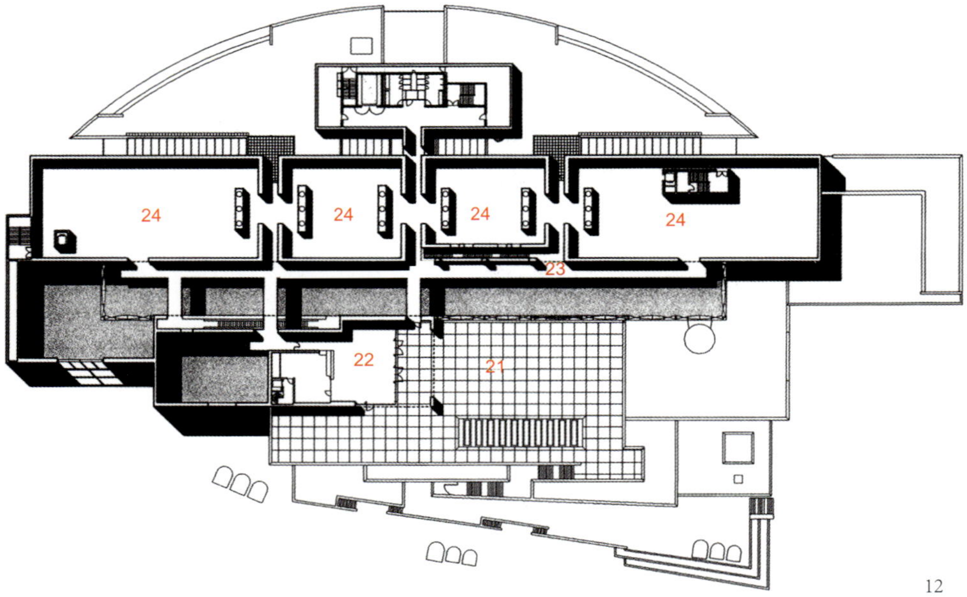

12

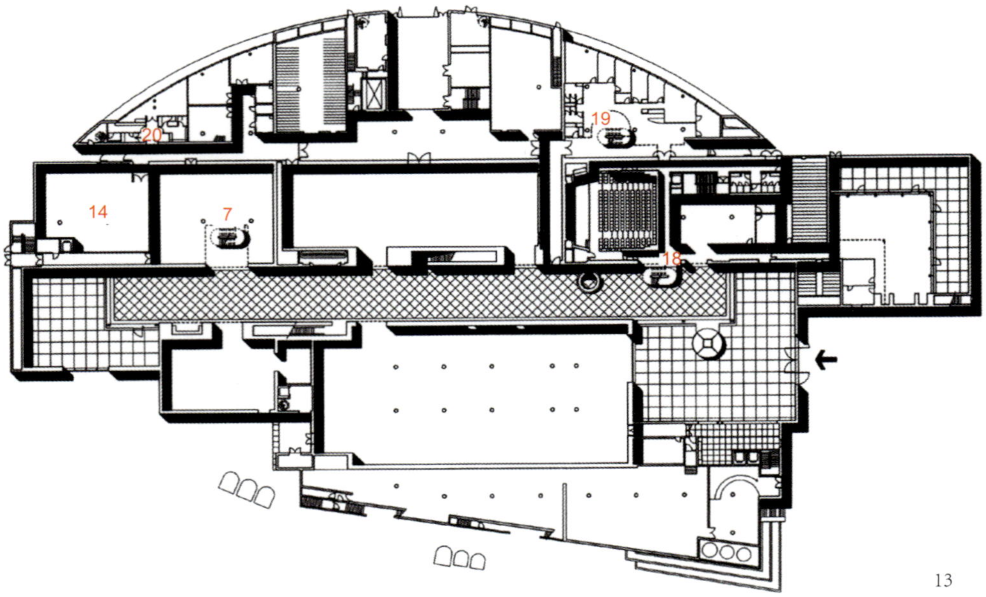

13

1. Entrance courtyard
2. Nave
3. Coat check
4. Historic and modern room
5. Doré gallery
6. Sculpture garden
7. Graphic art rooms
8. Temporary exhibitions
9. Auditorium
10. Bookshop
11. Library
12. Library garden
13. Administration
14. Reserves
15. Transit zone
16. Delivery area
17. Workshops
18. Educational service
19. Conservation
20. Guest apartment
21. Panoramic terrace
22. Restaurant
23. Corridor
24. Contemporary art rooms

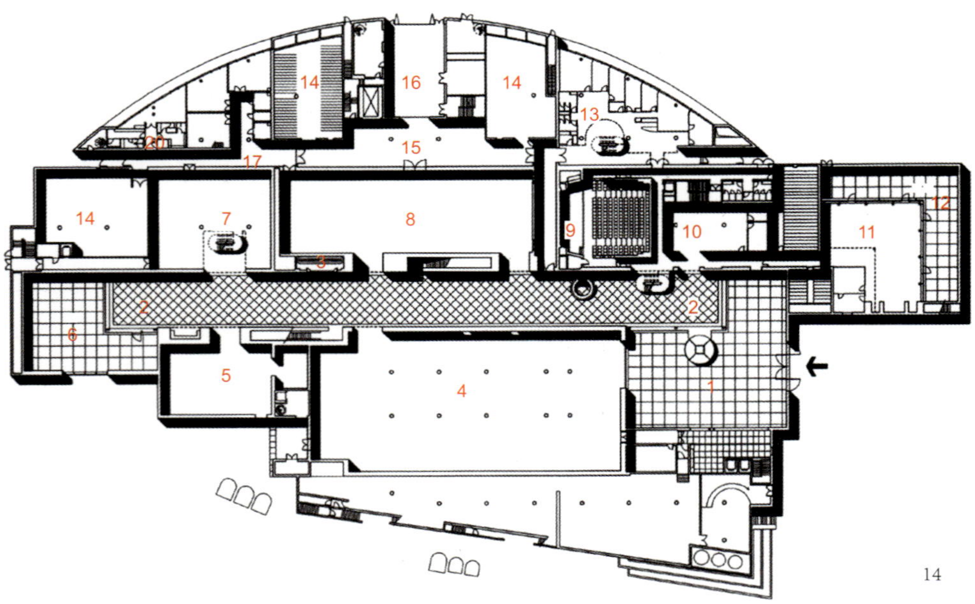

14

15

17

18

16. The nave and the corridor
17. Exhibition room
18. Detail of the administration staircase

1

QUAI BRANLY MUSEUM

Architect: Jean Nouvel,
with Gilles Clément (Landscape),
Patrick Blanc (Vertical garden),
Yann Kersalé (Light installation)
Location: Paris
Completion Date: 2006
Photographer: Philippe Ruault (pp.274-279), Roland Halbe (pp.281-283)

The Quai Branly Museum is a meditation on the other and elsewhere. The space that houses the objects is neither religious nor sacred. Jean Nouvel wanted to surround them with mystery, to give them back their own life. Rejecting western rationality, he preferred to create them a home where they would be together, conversing with each other, or withdrawn into their existence alone. Instead of a clear museum approach, which shines light on the works in white and neutral rooms, in glass cases, he preferred appearance and disappearance. No magic or illusion: Jean Nouvel opted for allusion.

A single floor was proposed, an open gallery. The collections are grouped by continent, but the geography that results is an imaginary map, a long gallery measuring more than 200 metres. To welcome the objects it was necessary to lose one's bearings, to disorientate. This place is the foyer of a home. Half-light dominates, necessary for conservation and for this work of adaptation. The

light is diffuse, through latticework. The materials are soft, tactile, ductile, without impediments on their surfaces. Motifs appear at the same time as they hide. The floors are not uniform or flat: walking, balance, are in play to accompany the exploration. The colours are warm, dark, deep and absorb the light.

Bearings are needed, however: long and narrow, the gallery is between two façades that the daylight makes vibrate differently. On the Seine side, the motifs of forests

4

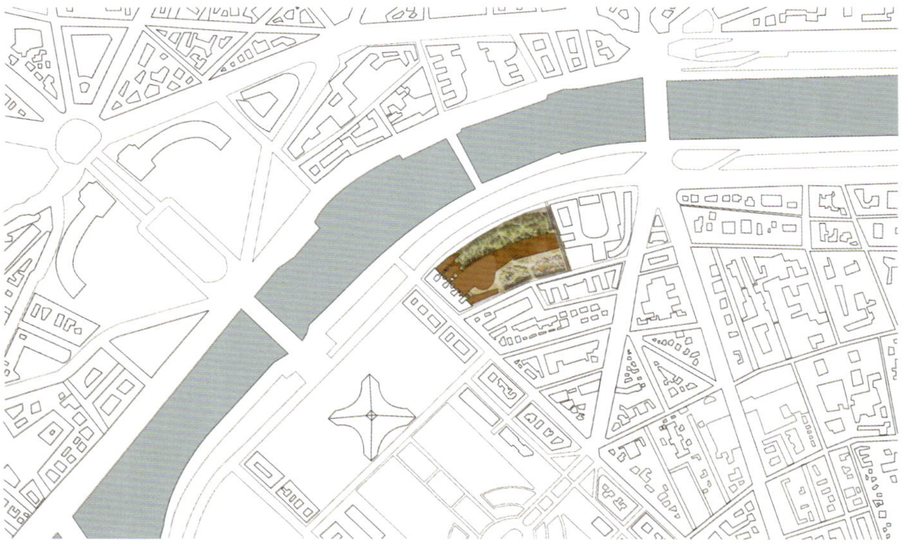

5

soften the north light (a film in the thickness of the glass panes reflects it towards the exterior) and on the building housing the administration a façade was designed with the botanist Patrick Blanc. On the south side, very filtering glass is behind panels that play like the slats of a blind. A geometric break allows for the framing of the Eiffel Tower. Thus, the museum is not enclosed within its walls, but enshrined by the thickness of its façades that filter its relationship with the outside world.

1. Façade on Quai Branly
2. Branly and Auvent buildings, administration
3. North façade, garden
4. South façade of the museum
5. Master plan
6. Collections floor

7

8

9

7. Collections floor, north façade
8-9. Collections floor, south façade
10. Collections floor
11. Ground floor plan

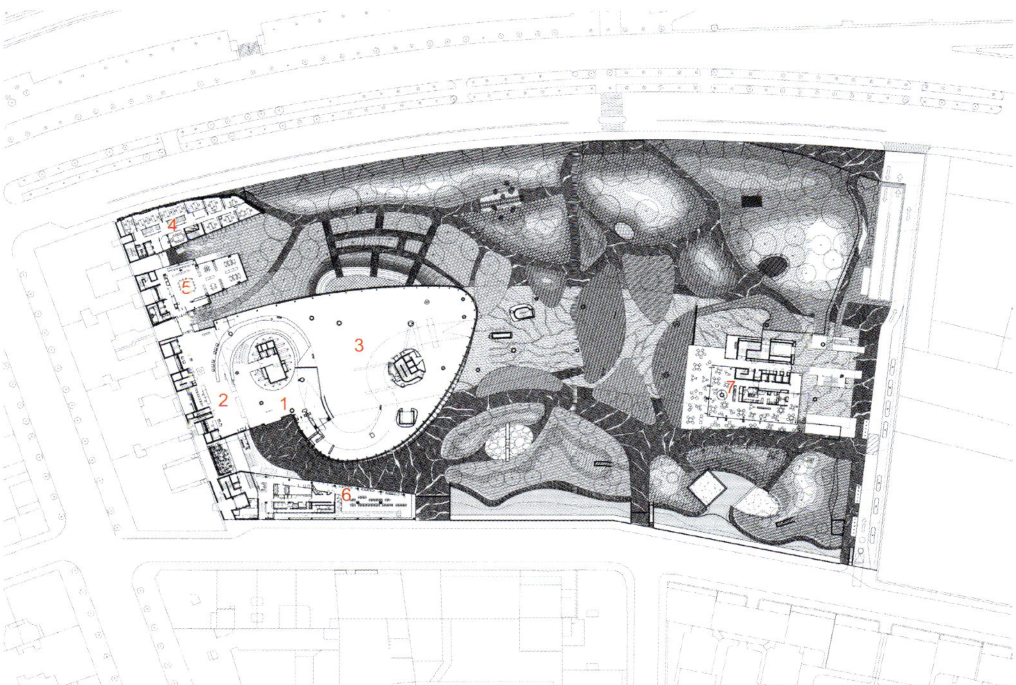

1. Entrance hall
2. Ticket desks
3. Temporary exhibitions
4. Administration
5. Kerchache room
6. Bookshop
7. Cafeteria

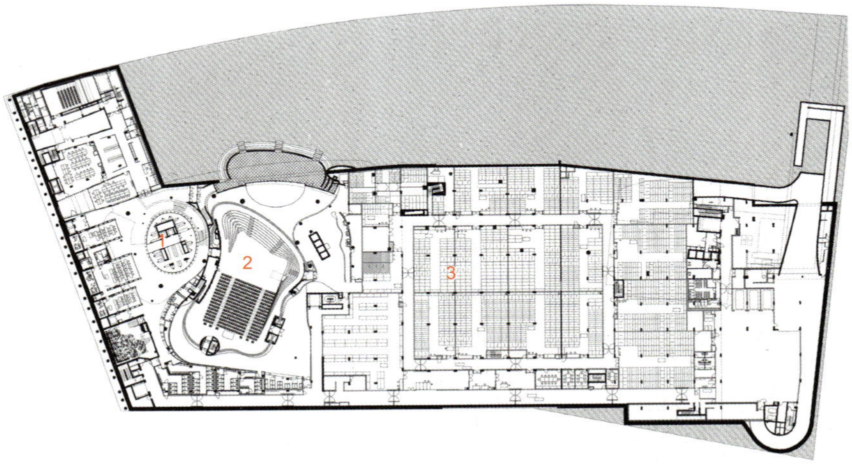

12

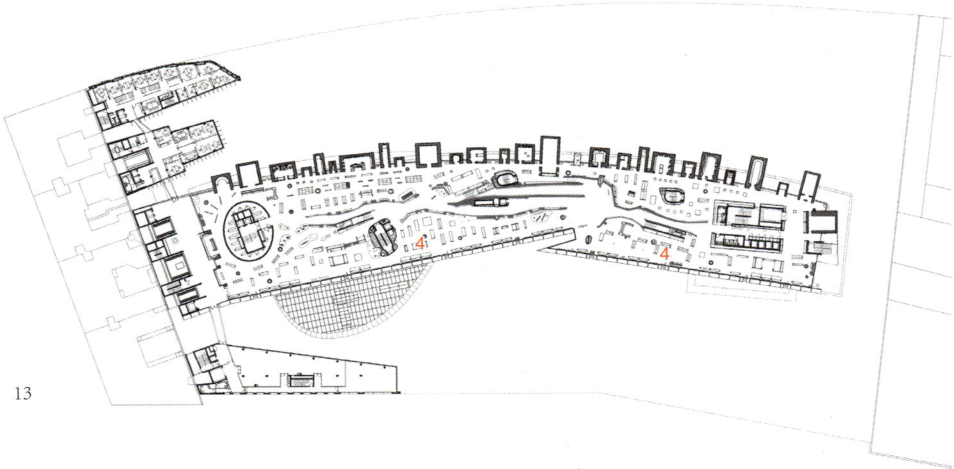

13

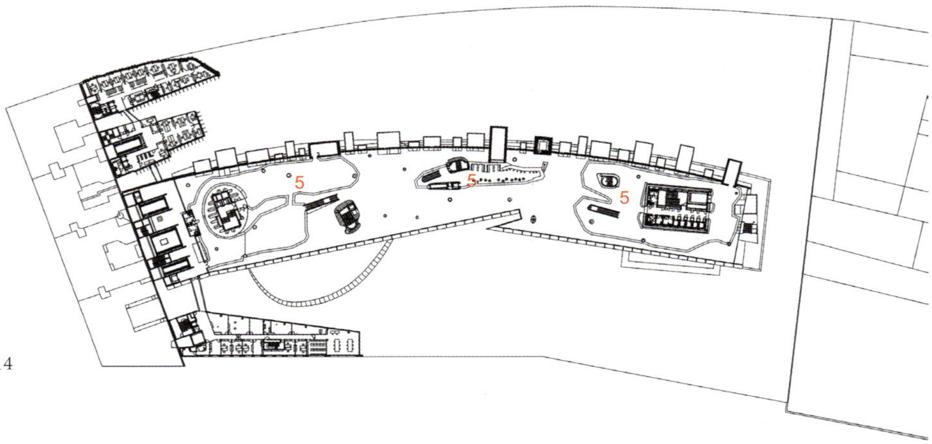

14

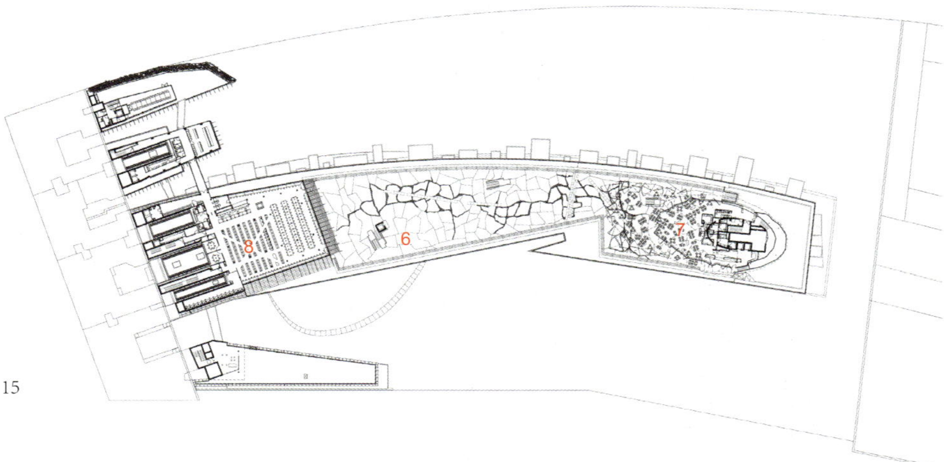

15

12. Basement floor plan
13. 1st floor plan
14. 2nd floor plan
15. 3rd floor plan
16. Mezzanines

1. Instruments tower
2. Auditorium
3. Reserves
4. Collections floor
5. Mezzanines
6. Terrace
7. Restaurant
8. Mediatheque

16

17

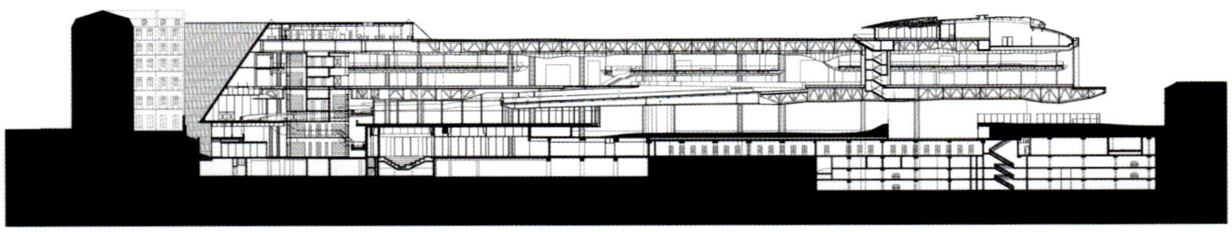

18

17. Collections floor
18. Longitudinal section of the museum (BB)
19. Collections floor, the serpent
20. Cross section of the Branly, Auvent and Université buildings (AA)
21. Cross section of the restaurant, museum and car park (CC)
22. Cross section of the atrium, auditorium, ramp and museum (DD)

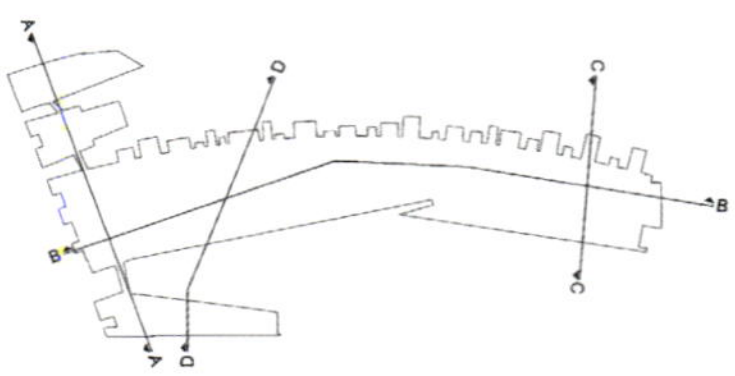

19

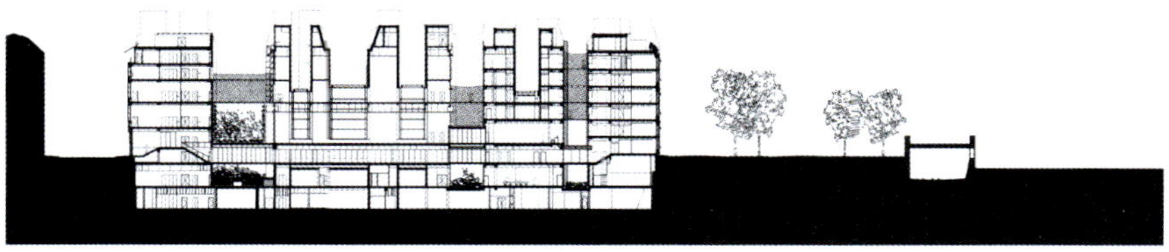

20

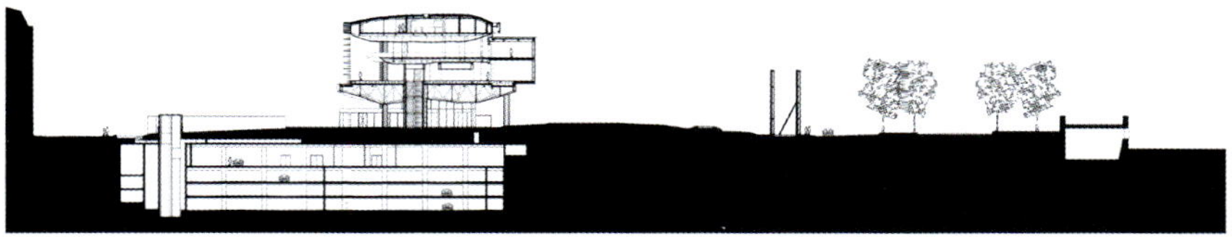

21

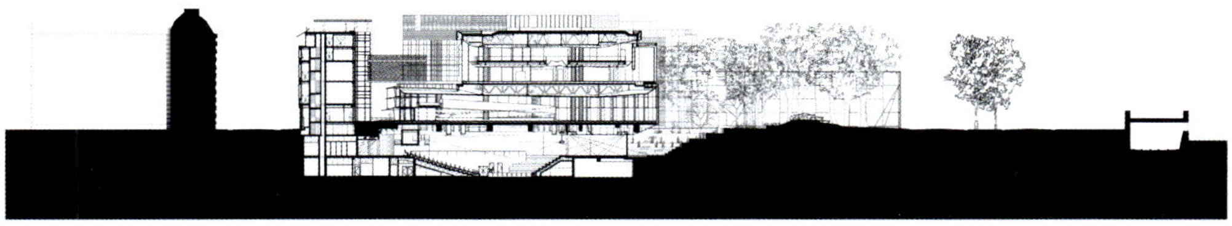

22

WÜRTH MUSEUM

Architect: Jacques & Clément Vergély
Location: Erstein
Completion Date: 2008
Photographer: Erick Saillet

The Reinhold Würth collection was to be housed on the same industrial site as the Würth-France headquarters. To express the extreme variety of the collection and its contrast with the functionality of the head office, a diversification and neutrality of the spaces was called for. Two perfectly identical, parallel parallelepipeds separated by a welcome space form the morphology of the building.

The choice of rough concrete was obvious. The two monoliths had to express the unadorned abstraction of the two built bodies and their protecting symbolism through the use of a single material. The proximity of the head office imposed a confrontation that enhances both buildings, the glass façades of the head office finding a pertinent counterpoint in the opacity and courseness of the rough concrete. The functional sequences are very easy to read. In the east all the services offered to the public are gathered on two levels,

1

while the west houses the delivery and maintenance areas, and the reserves. In the centre are the rooms devoted to artistic expression. In the north an exterior, uncovered space opens up, in which sculptures may be placed.

Separated by the music rooms, the exhibition spaces have deliberately contrasting dimensions. The three rooms have common characteristics in terms of materials: a polished concrete floor, walls made up of wood and plaster

2

3

4

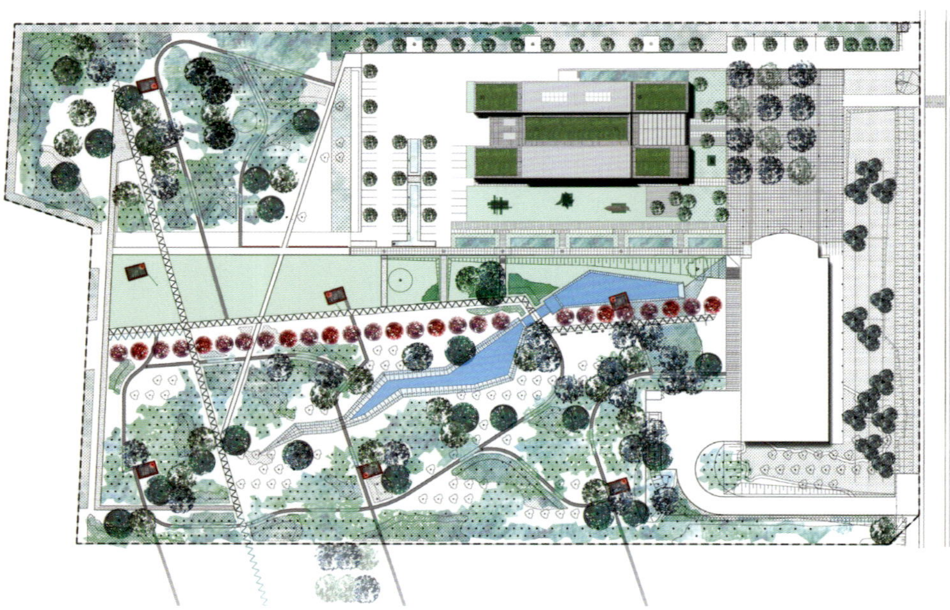

5

combinations that allow for easy hanging fittings, a false ceiling integrating the air conditioning system. The walls and the ceiling are white. The major common characteristic of these exhibition spaces resides, in the end, in their unusual use of natural light.

6

1. South façade of the museum from the Würth France head office building
2. South façade of the museum and the park
3-4. South façade of the museum
5. Master plan
6. South façade of the museum, the covered gallery and the park – play of reflections

7

8

9

7. Museum entrance, east façade overlooking the forecourt, night view
8. South façade of the museum and the park, night view
9. Forecourt with a sculpture by Bernard Venet, 220° Arc x 5, 2002, Collection Würth, Inv. 10552
10. Cross section

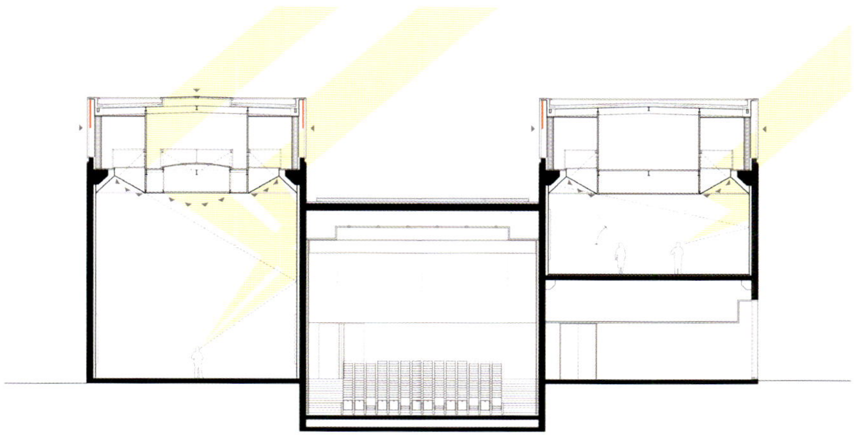

10

1. Entrance hall
2. Reception and shop
3. Café des Arts
4. North main exhibition room
5. Auditorium
6. Conservation offices
7. Dressing room
8. Reserves
9. Educational room
10. Library
11. Würth room
12. South main exhibition room
13. South small exhibition room
14. Patio
15. Technical area

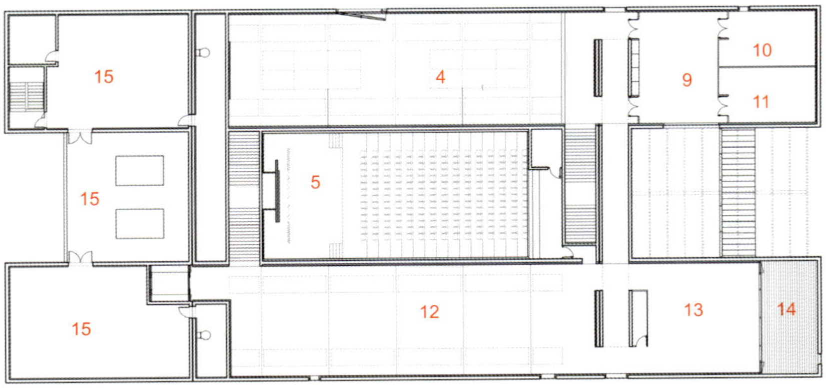

11

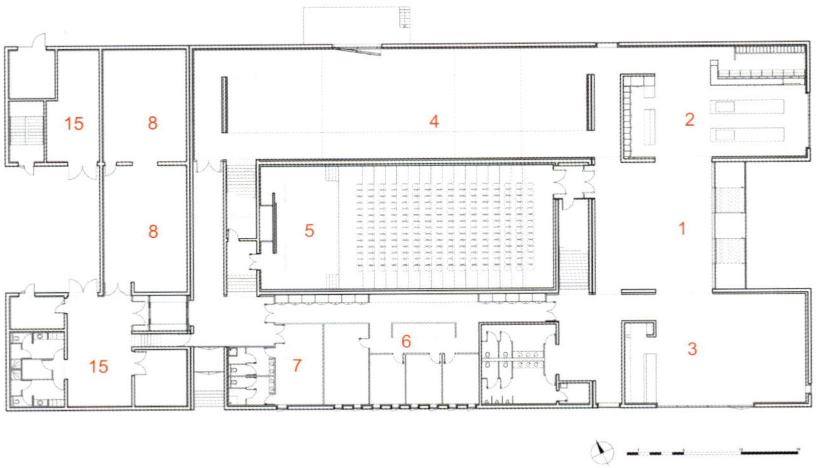

12

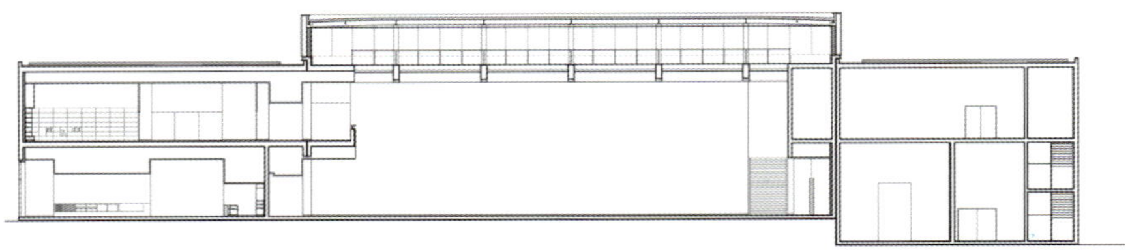

13

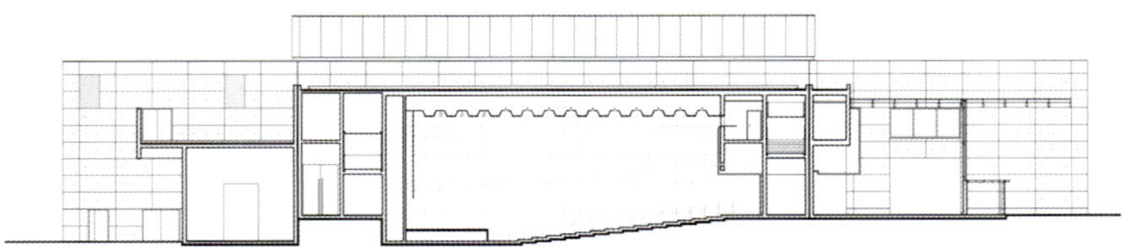

14

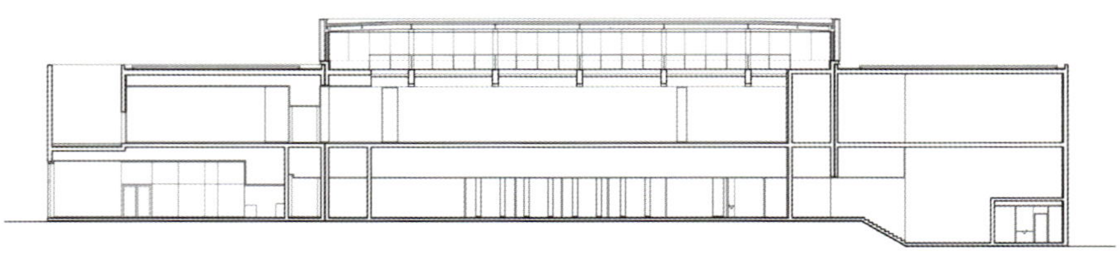

15

11. 1st floor plan
12. Ground floor plan
13. Longitudinal section of the north exhibition room
14. Longitudinal section of the auditorium
15. Longitudinal section of the south exhibition room
16. Entrance hall and museum shop
17. Museum shop
18-19. Café des Arts

16

17

18

19

20. South small exhibition room and patio
21. Patio
22. North main exhibition room
23. North main exhibition room and mezzanine
24. Museum auditorium

22

23

24

VESUNNA GALLO-ROMAN SITE-MUSEUM

Architect: Jean Nouvel
Location: Périgueux
Completion Date: 2003
Photographer: Philippe Ruault

In Périgueux, the site-museum designed by Jean Nouvel preserves and exhibits the remains of a large Gallo-Roman residence, the Vesona mansion (Domus de Vésone). The daily life of ancient times is presented through archaeological collections going back to the 1st to 3rd centuries A.D. Jean Nouvel introduced the project in this way: "We must reveal and protect this site. With nobility. With tact. With clarity, using the sensitivity and culture of our age, through an architecture that will have the awe-inspiring privilege of coming face to face with the ghosts of antiquity."

The visitor first enters a long building known as the "thick wall" running along the west side of the site and forming a screen that directs the gaze towards the Vesona Tower. This building groups the reception, a shop, one section of

1

the "museum" circuit and the technical services. Two floors designed as mezzanines overlook the remains of the mansion.

The museum's main attraction, the mansion reveals the scope of the remains of the ancient city. Everything is organised around it. The heart of the mansion, with the garden, a peristyle and the rooms arranged off it, is protected by

2

3

a "large sheltered courtyard" covered with a huge metal umbrella held up by 9-metre pillars. The covering juts out several metres, protecting the museum from direct sunlight. Inside, the visitor can walk among the remains on wooden decking placed on a metallic structure.

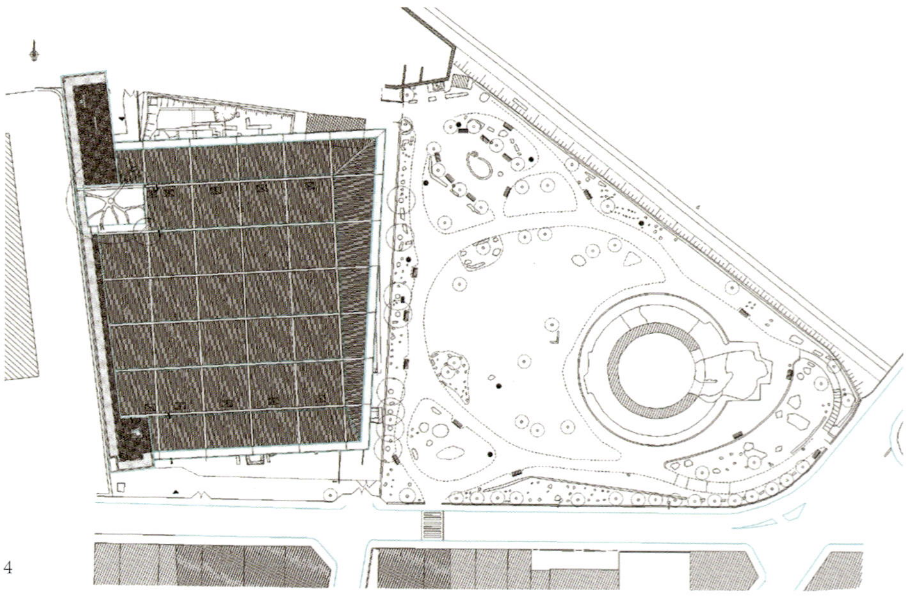

4

1. North façade overlooking the park
2. North façade at night
3. Museum entrance
4. Master plan
5. North façade, M. Taillefer's house

6

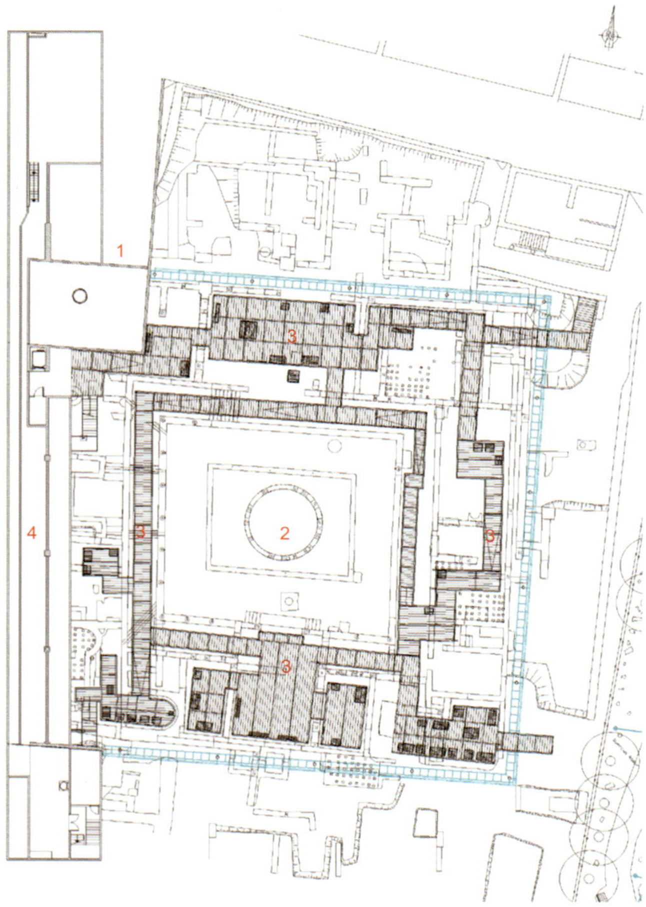

7

6. Est façade, view into the museum's interior with the mezzanines in the background
7. Domus floor plan
8-9. Museum, Domus floor

1. Entrance
2. The domus, remains of a large Gallo-Roman residence
3. Wooden decking placed on a metallic structure
4. The “thick wall”, mezzanines grouping the reception, a shop, one section of the “museum” circuit and the technical services

8

9

10

11

10-12. Museum, Domus floor

12

BLIESBRUCK-REINHEIM GALLO-ROMAN BATHS

Architect: Frédéric Jung
Location: Bliesbruck
Completion Date: 1993
Photographer: Hervé Abbadie

This museum-style project for covering the Gallo-Roman Baths forms a first stage in a larger scheme for protecting the archaeological digs of the European Archaeological Park of Bliesbruck-Reinheim. The construction avoids any restitution or dangerous pastiche. No part of the structure is planted within the confines of the remains.

It merely signifies the former solidity of this major ancient edifice, bordering one of the city's most important public squares, through the positioning of the porticos supporting this vast copper covering. It is a "museographic machinery" that reveals the site and allows us to read the remains. The museography simply indicates "how to look". The objective is to provide the means of deciphering the different significations of the ruins and to understand the aims and methods

1

of archaeology. The museum signs are designed to help the visitor interpret what he sees and feels, by providing information that stimulates observation.

The idea is to encourage visitors to walk around the site via a series of footbridges raised above the general levelling of the remains, at approximately the height of the original floors, in order to remove the ambiguity of accessing the

3

4

1. North façade
2. West façade
3. Side view of the auditorium
4. South façade
5. General plan

remains at the level of the basements and hypocausts and to give a synthetic vision of the arrangement of the rooms and their functioning. This approach naturally protects the remains. The internal museography offers suspended, light and mobile partitions (Venetian-blind style screens) suggesting how the spaces would have been dispersed in antiquity according to today's archaeological theory, which may yet be contradicted by work still to come.

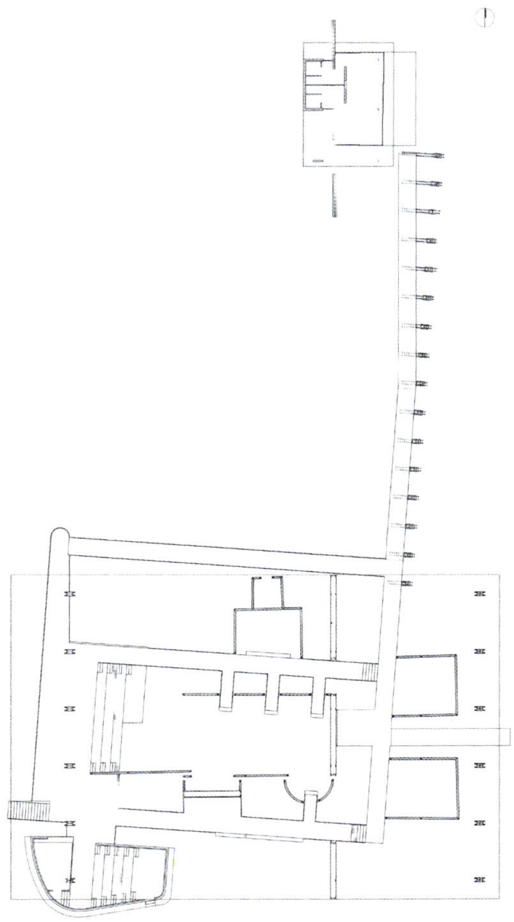

5

6. Remains of the latrines
7. Approach bridge
8. System of viewing platforms suspended above the Gallo-Roman remains

Archeological remains:
1. Ovens and baths
2. Caldarium (hot bath)
3. Tepidarium (warm bath)
4. Frigidarium (cold bath)

Suspended museographical system:
5. Footbridges
6. Auditorium
7. Control room
8. Platforms overlooking the baths
9. Suspended screens (volumetric reconstruction)
10. Protective glass screen
11. Mobile glass screen
12. Thick wall integrating sliding doors (between the public spaces and public facilities)
13. Display case

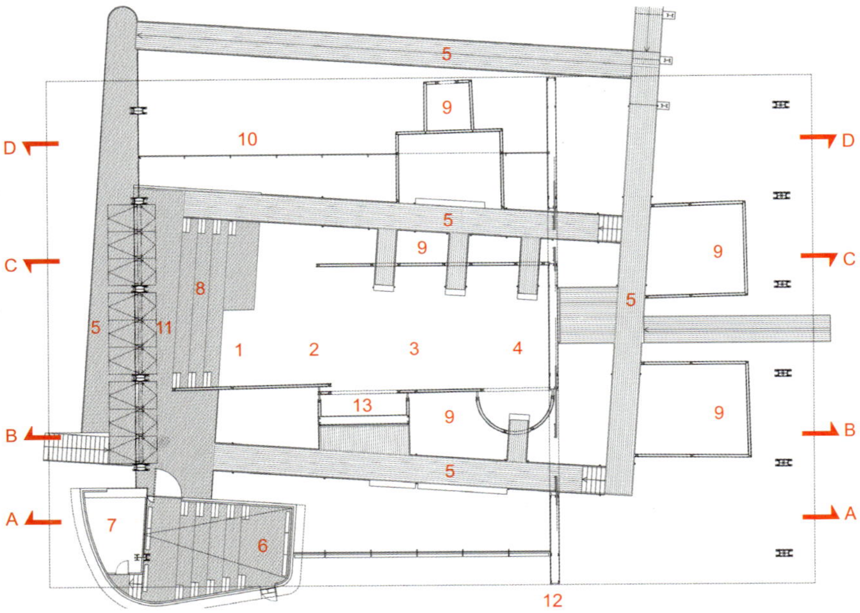

9

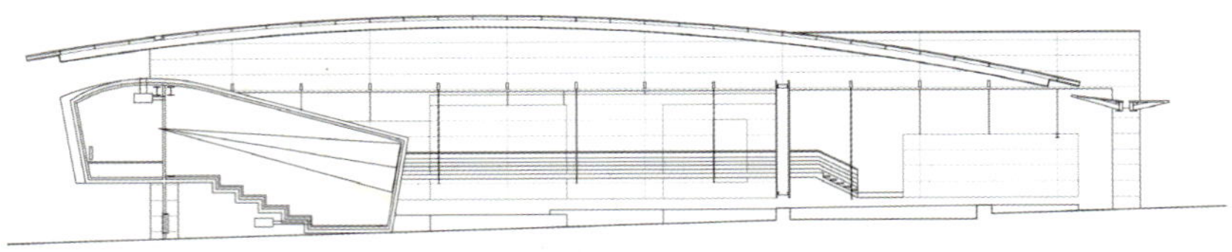

10

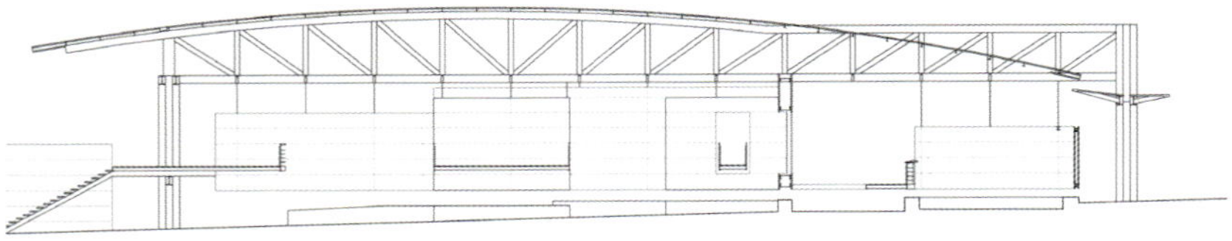

11

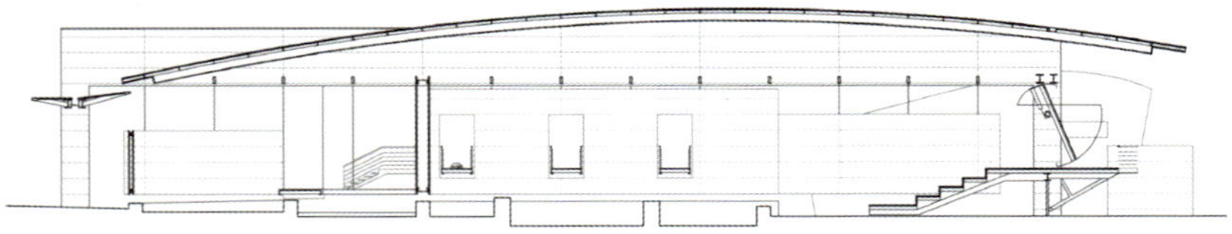

12

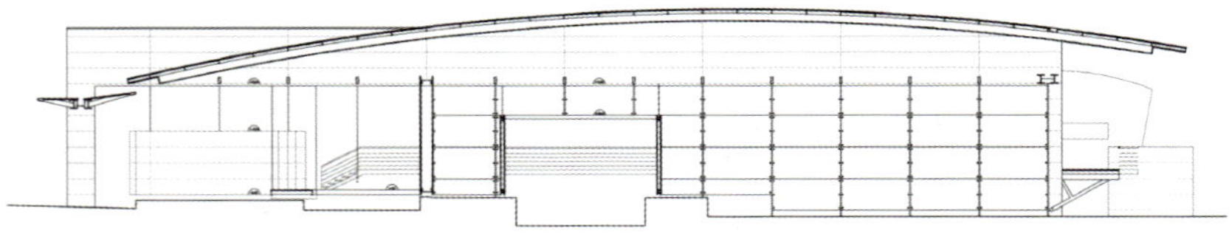

13

9. Plan
10. Section AA
11. Section BB
12. Section CC
13. Section DD
14. Viewing platform over the frigidarium

14

FUTURE PROJECTS

CONFLUENCES MUSEUM

Architect: Coop Himmelb(l)au
Location: Lyon
Completion Date: 2014
Visual documents: Coop Himmelb(l)au

On the southern tip of the Presqu'île of Lyon, at the confluence of the Saône and the Rhône, the Confluences Museum is a museum of science and of society. The questions of the future will be decided through the transitional fields of technology, biology and ethics, which form the central theme of the museum.

Conveying the knowledge of our age in a direct and interactive way, it is not only a museum but also a resource for the city. The architecture is both functional and ethereal, creating a hybrid of a museum and urban leisure space, a place that combines education and relaxation, and a connection between the city and culture. Partly inspired by its site, providing an interface between the river and the city, it is composed of two complexly connected architectural units: crystal and cloud. They symbolise the known and the unknown, the clarity of the familiar environment of today and the uncertainty of tomorrow. The entrance is from the town side in the north, the crystal rising towards the built

1

environment and calling cut to it. Raised on 8-metre stilts, the cloud seems to float above the Confluent gardens on the south side – a soft space of hidden streams and countless transitions. It is clad in a metallic envelope that reflects colours and light and captures the echoes of sky and city, water and greenery.

The spatial arrangement of the museum is designed to stimulate the public s curiosity about the present and the future, the known and the still unknown. Ramps and

2

3

surfaces merge the inside and the outside, resulting in a dynamic sequence of spatial events. This movement continues inside. Closed black boxes and free exhibition areas alternate, making use of the double room height over two levels. The architecture is as changeable as the exhibitions it holds, creating an urban event that is perpetually reinventing itself.

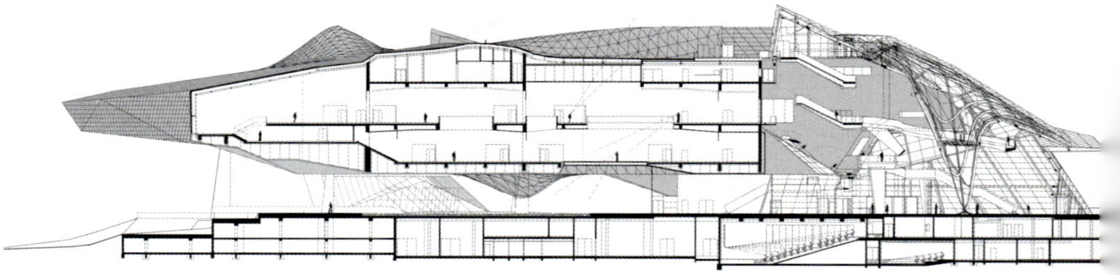

5

4

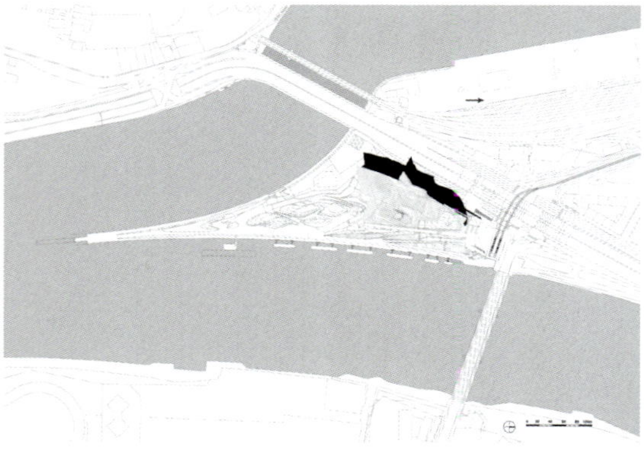

6

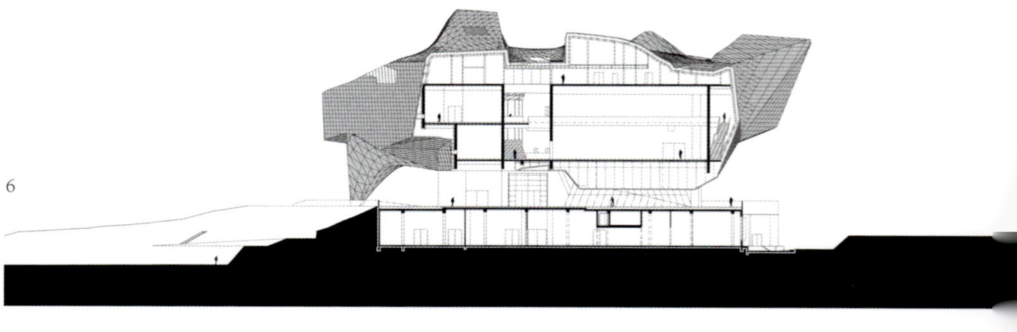

7

1. Confluences Museum – the Crystal Cloud of Knowledge
2. Underneath the Cloud
3. Front view: the Crystal
4. Master plan
5. Longitudinal section
6. Cross section
7. Main entrance
8. Building elements

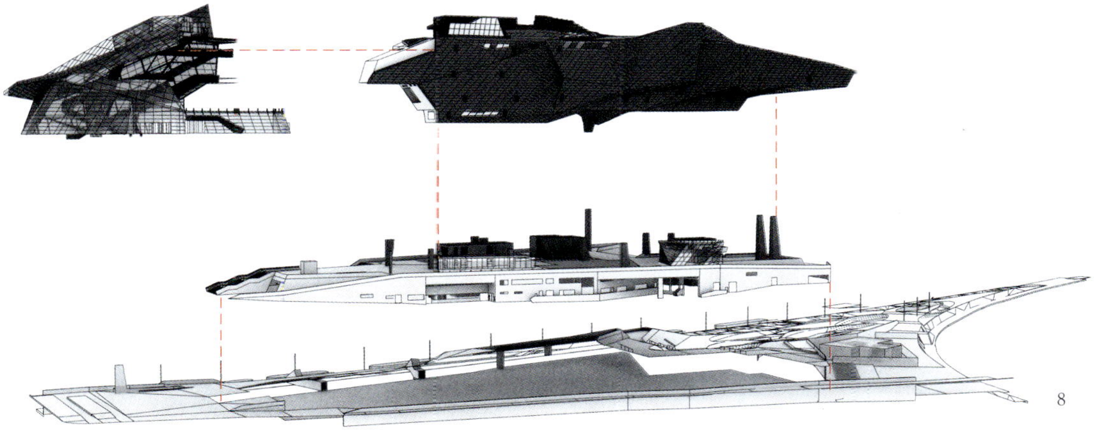

8

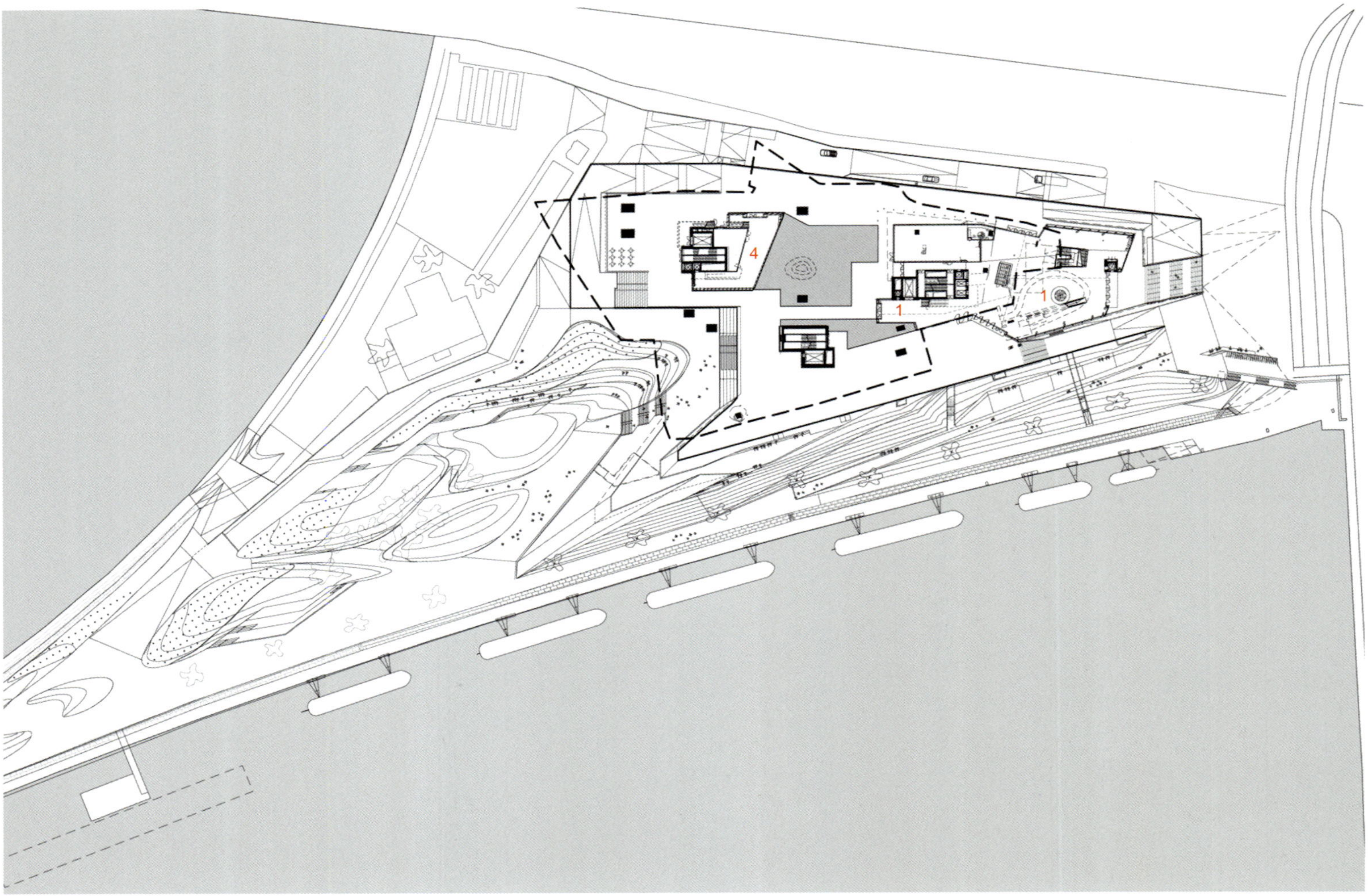

9

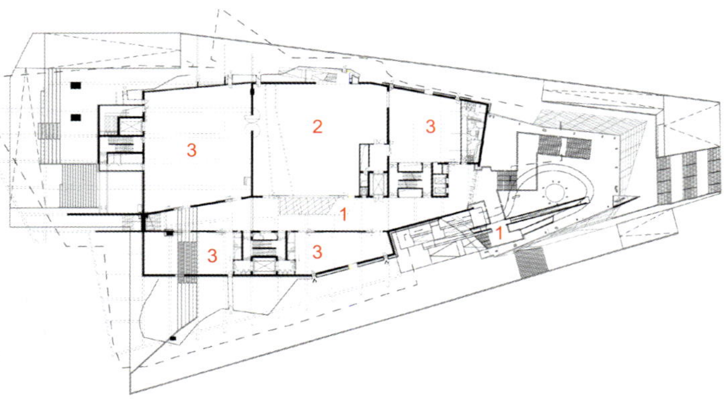

10

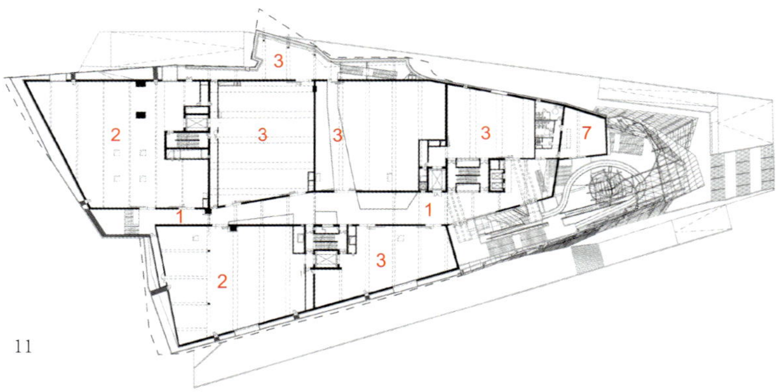

11

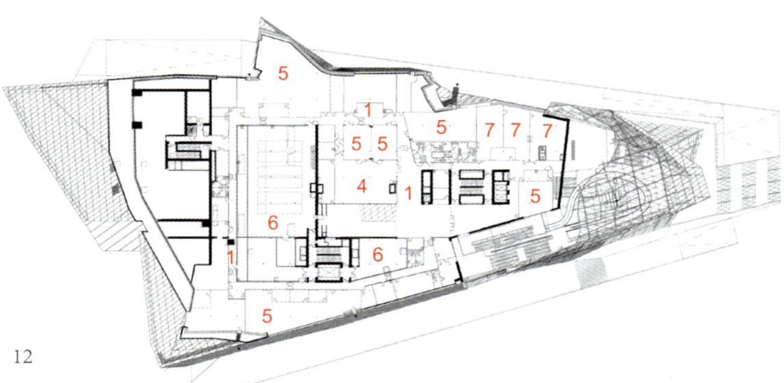

12

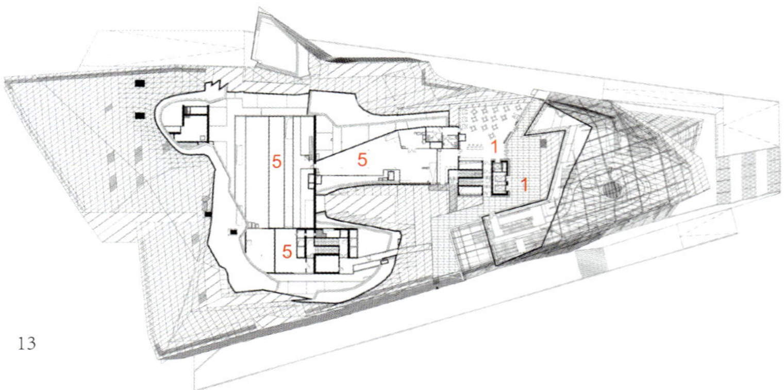

13

9. Floor plan: Level 00
10. Floor plan: Level +8.84
11. Floor plan: Level +15.64
12. Floor plan: Level +22.78
13. Floor plan: Level +27.03
14. The Crystal: Entrance Hall and Gravity Well
15. Underneath the Cloud

1. Circulation/reception hall
2. Permanent exhibition
3. Temporary exhibition
4. Restaurant
5. Administration office
6. Technical area
7. Workshop

REGIONAL FUND OF CONTEMPORARY ART PACA

Architect: Kengo Kuma, Toury Vallet
Location: Marseille
Completion Date: 2012
Visual Documents: Kengo Kuma, Toury Vallet

The project for the Regional Fund of Contemporary Art (FRAC) for the Provence-Alpes-Côte d'Azur region (PACA) is the 3D version of the "museum without walls" invented by the French writer and politician André Malraux. It is a moving and living museum in which the works are in constant flux in order to give the public the greatest chance to see and interact with them. The FRAC was designed as a landmark in the city to give a greater visibility to contemporary art. The building is a symbol with an original and clear identity. It is composed of two clearly defined parts whose shapes fit in to the complex geometry of the plot.

The main body, along Rue Vincent Leblanc, contains the exhibition spaces and documentation centre. A small tower with the auditorium and children's workshop offers an upper terrace on the main boulevard. These two entities are connected by a set of footbridges and are unified by the envelope

1

of a glass skin, composed of panels with changing opacity.

The project explores the theme of windows and openings on different scales, to give a feeling of welcome and a permanent link with the exterior. The architects wished to produce a living and creative space whose action and effect is felt on the entire city, as well as the surrounding district and neighbourhood. The building adheres to the High Environmental Quality (HQE) charter.

2

3

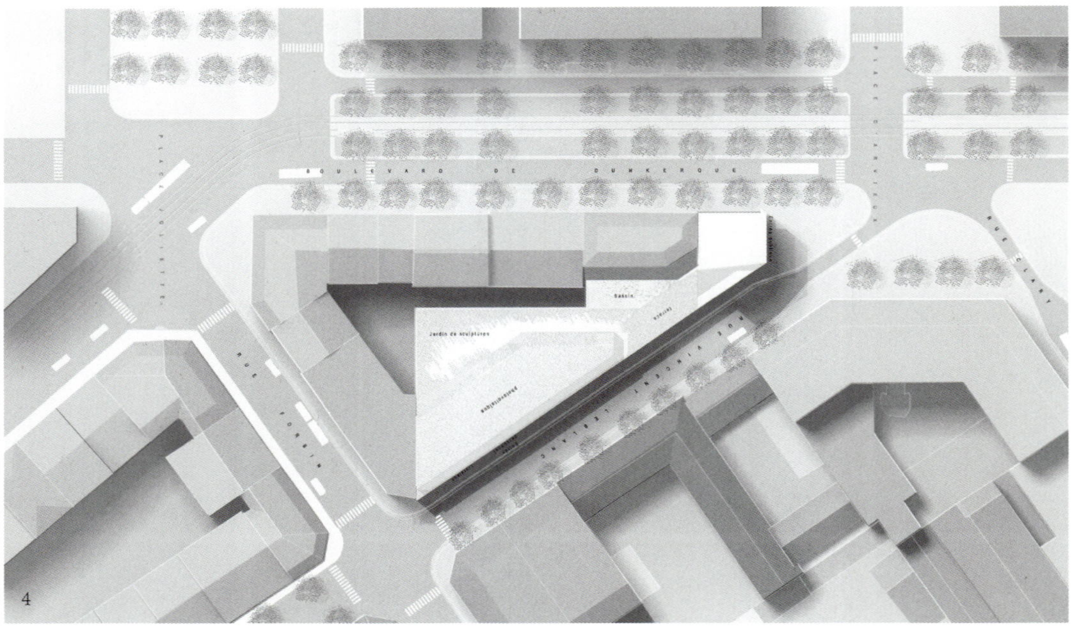

4

1. Exterior view
2. View of the entrance from the first exhibition room (large module): to the left of the staircase, the pool; to the right the reception desk; at the back, the staircase leading to the second exhibition room (proposals module)
3. View from Rue Vincent Leblanc
4. Master plan

5. Bird's eye view of the urban terrace from Arvieux Square
6. Prow of the edifice: study of the inclination of glass panels on the façace (pivoting on a horizontal axis of pixels)

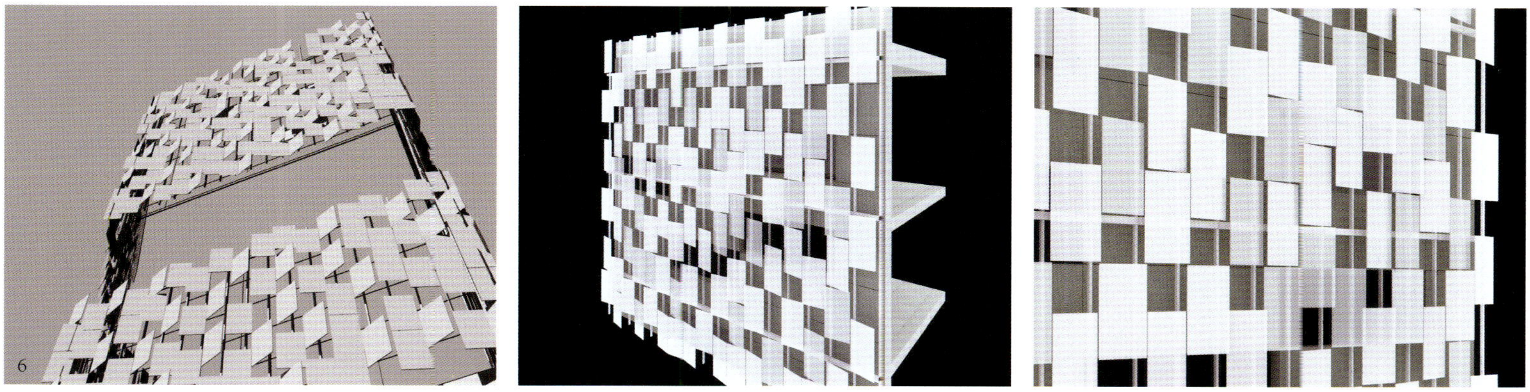

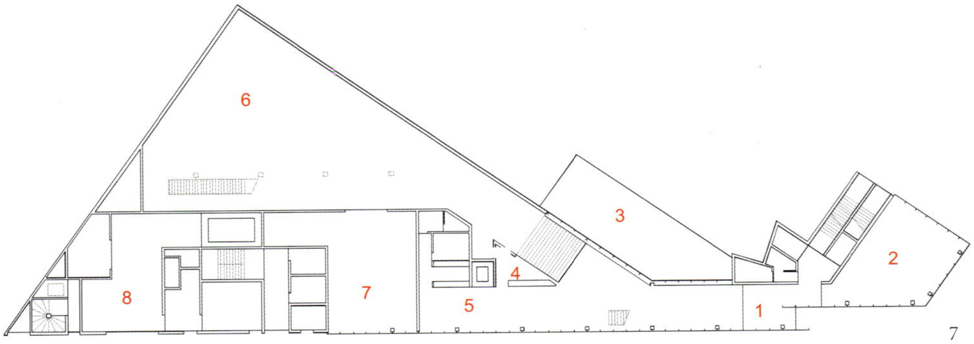

7

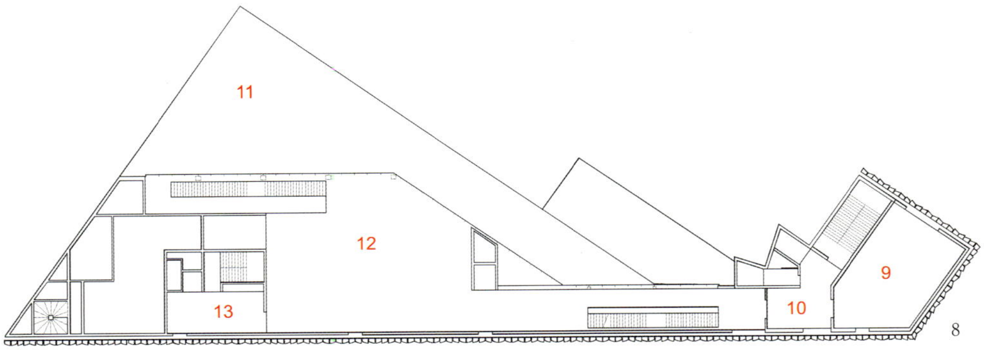

8

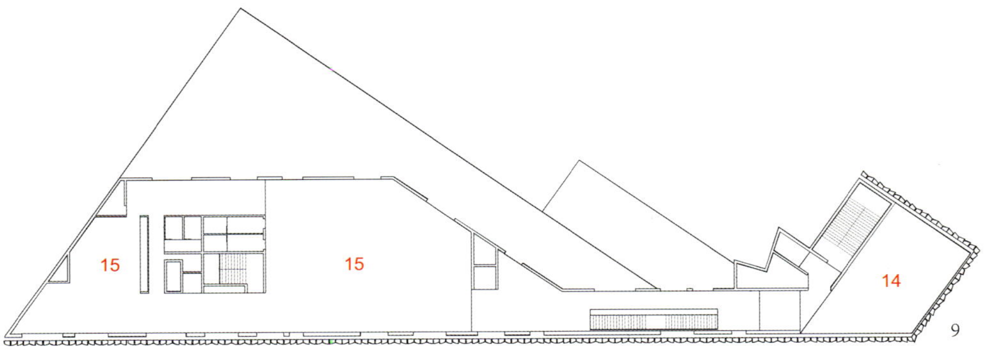

9

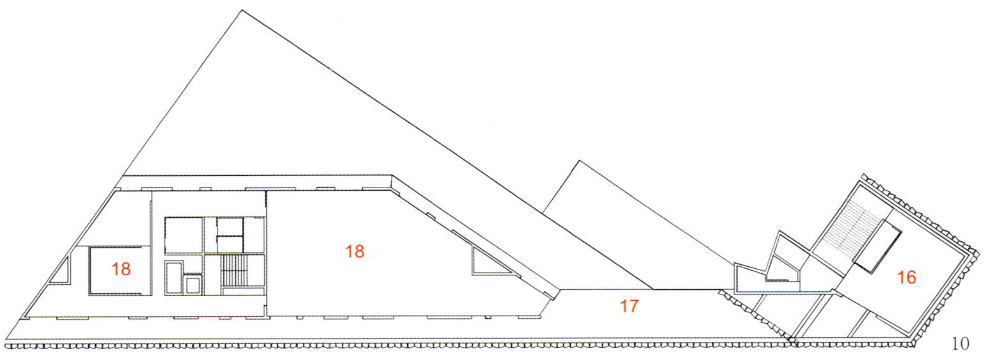

10

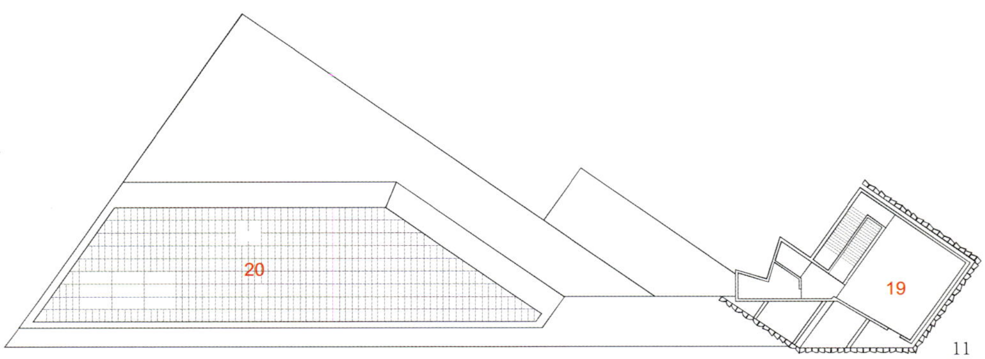

11

7. Ground floor plan
8. 1st floor plan
9. 3rd floor plan
10. 4th floor plan
11. 5th floor plan
12. View of the entrance from the bookshop and reception desk
13. View of the reception desk from the entrance

1. Entrance
2. Café
3. Pool
4. Reception
5. Shop
6. Exhibition room 1
7. Workshop
8. Deliveries
9. Conference room
10. Foyer
11. Sculpture garden
12. Exhibition room 2
13. Mounting
14. Urban terrace
15. Resource centre
16. Educational workshop
17. Terrace
18. Offices
19. Exhibition room 3
20. Roof with photovoltaic panels

12

13

14. Proposals module
15-16. Resource centre
17. Resource centre reception
18. Longitudinal section
19. Arrival at the proposals module

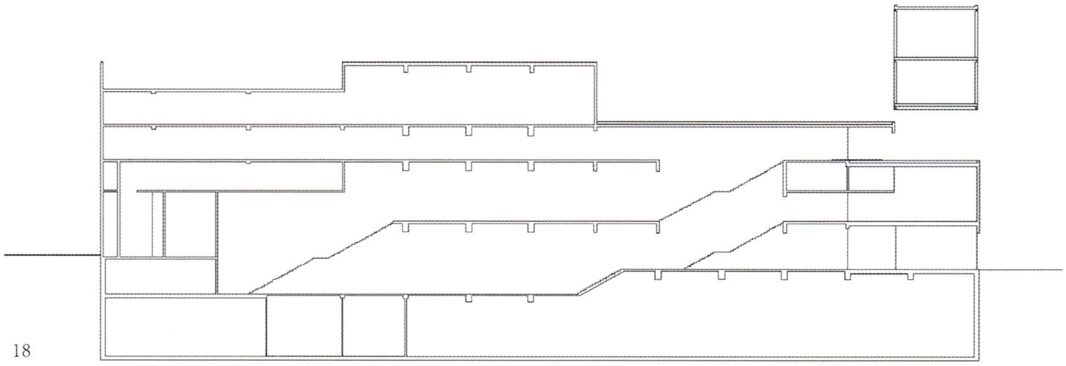

18

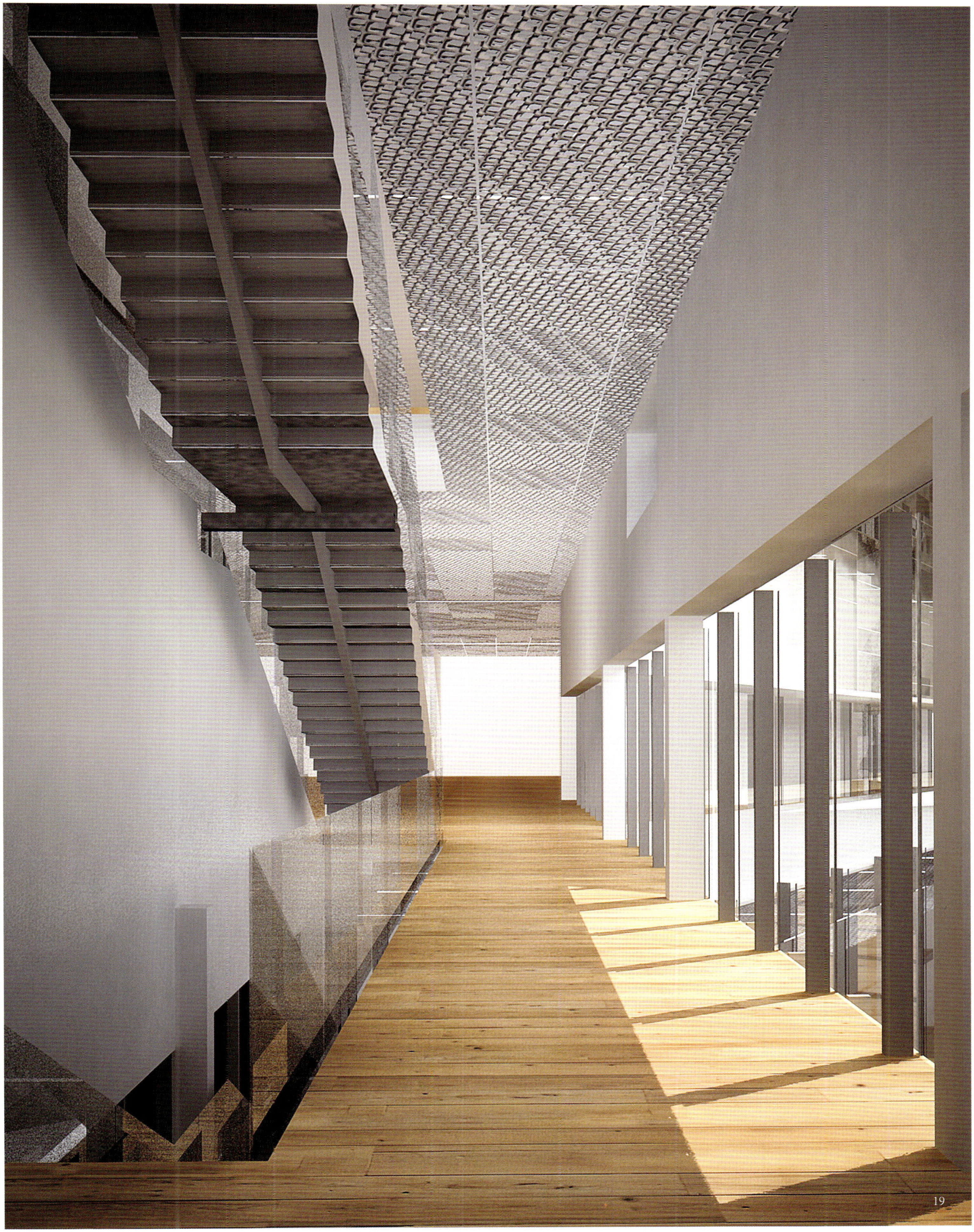
19

MARSEILLE HISTORY MUSEUM

Architect: Roland Carta,
with Studio Adeline Rispal (Exhibition architects)
Location: Marseille
Completion Date: 2013
Visual Documents: Roland Carta Architectes & Associés, Studio Adeline Rispal

In the heart of France's oldest city, the Marseille History Museum traces the history of the Phocean city from its foundation, in 600 B.C., to the present day. After the restoration of the adjoining Garden of Archaeological Remains and the establishment of this as the site of the Ancient Port, the museum itself is preparing for change as part of Marseille European Capital of Culture 2013. Around the central theme of seafaring, which has given the daily life of the city its rhythm over the centuries, the new museographic itinerary is divided into 13 historical sequences.

The museum building suffered from a lack of depth and of ceiling height, and there was a dichotomy between the scientific programme and the display area available: "Too many objects, not enough space." It was necessary to generate breathing spaces, vary the ceiling heights and create surprises to strengthen the strong museum sequences. This was done through bringing forward the façade of the

Mediterranean Centre for International Business (CMCI) wing to provide a double-height circulation area; enclosing the west walkway that was previously on the outside of the building; placing the archives in the triple height area under the glass roof; and expanding the garden-level space between the current entrance and the carpark fire escape.

The museum furniture is made up of modular elements called "bales" piled up like merchandise on the port. These

CENTRE BOURSE

3

ENTRE BOURSE
Musée d'Histoire de Marseille
Musée d'Histoire de Marseille
Musée d'Histoire de Marseille

4

1. Main entrance on Rue Henri Barbusse
2. Start of the walkway
3. The garden of archeological remains
4. Entrance to the museum from the archeological site
5. Architectural treatment of the walkway

elements on a human scale will allow life to settle in to the museum, just like the port in the shadow of the great ships. With order and disorder, various time schemes, that of the sea and that of the land, ships and men, the museum expresses all the facets of Marseille life over the course of its history. Tactile and interactive multimedia screens, children's itineraries, resting places to contemplate what one has seen, watch the films that are projected, experience, dream... this furniture can be adapted to all the visitors needs over time.

6. Entrance to the museum from the business centre
7. Display cases punctuate the space and direct visitors towards the ancient port
8. Reception area
9. The architectural display cases are lined up like boats in port

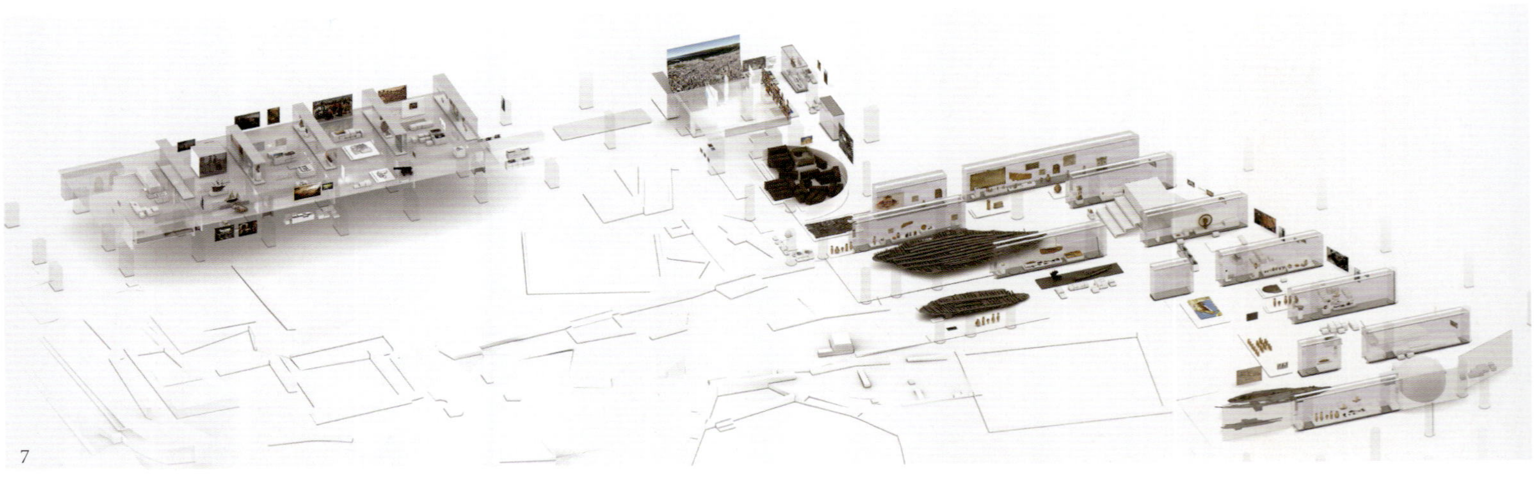

8

9

10

11

12

10. The ancient wrecks are displayed as if they are in a naval shipyard
11. A double-height space links the modern and contemporary galleries
12. The new façade frames views of the city
13. Spatial organisation of the permanent exhibition rooms

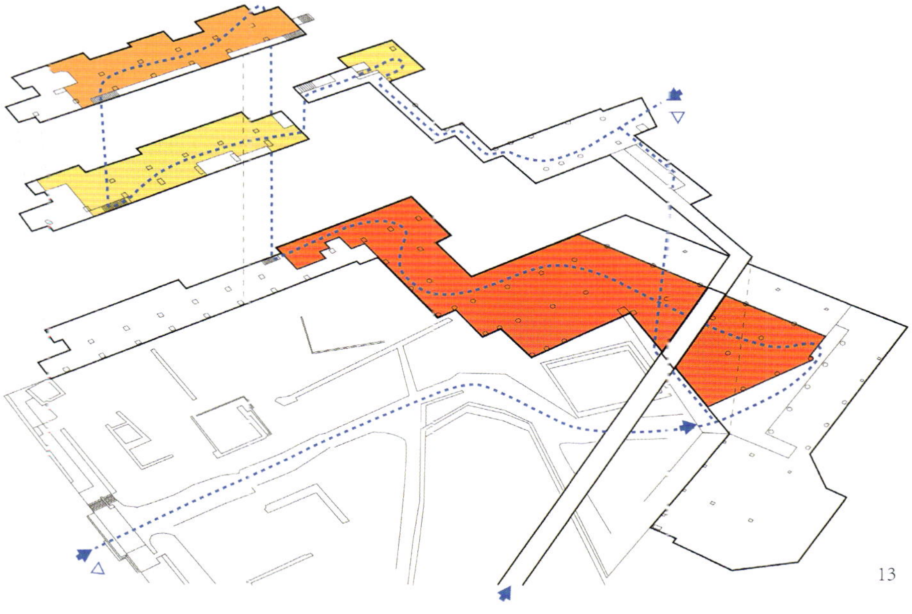

13

MUSEUM OF THE CIVILISATIONS OF EUROPE AND THE MEDITERRANEAN

Architect: Rudy Ricciotti, Roland Carta, Studio Adeline Rispal (Exhibition architects)
Location: Marseille
Completion Date: 2013
Visual Documents: Agence Rudy Ricciotti, Lisa Ricciotti

The Museum of the Civilisations of Europe and the Mediterranean (MuCEM) will be launched in 2013 as part of Marseille's year as European Capital of Culture. A major project of 40,000m^2, it is spread over three sites at the entrance to the Old Port. The heart of the museum will be the new 15,000m^2 building, constructed on the old J4 jetty by the architect Rudy Ricciotti and linked to the Saint-Jean fort by a footbridge. The foundation of the project is an urban vision that carves out its identity in strong lines. The ground floor with its sociological functions will face the sea esplanade and the Mediterranean wholesale market, and the volumetry will be horizontal so as not to rival the Saint-Jean fort.

Views, sea, sun and stone had to be orchestrated in a unifying and well-conceived programme for this museum.

1

First of all, a perfect 72m square. In this square, another, 52m square, is drawn, to contain the exhibition and conference rooms that are the heart of the museum. Around this, above and below, are the service areas. But the empty spaces between the two all look to the central square and form connections, following the paths of the old lanes of the town. Lured by the view of the fort, the sea or the port, most visitors will choose this

2

3

4

5

1. Perspective drawing – view from the sea
2. Façade
3. Perspective drawing – footbridge
4. Perspective drawing – view of the interior
5. Master plan
6. Perspective drawing – between two exterior footbridges

route to arrive at the museum. Taking one of the two interlaced ramps, they will then plunge into an imaginary Tower of Babel or ziggurat in order to climb up to the roof and, in the mind's eye, all the way up to the Saint-Jean fort. This peripheral fault offers a breathing space that takes one momentarily away from the museum, in the salty scent from the nearby seawater ditches, in order to chase away any doubts one might have about the way the history of our civilisations has been used.

The tectonic choice of a high quality concrete straight from the latest French industrial research makes its mineral mark on the high ramparts of the Saint-Jean fort. A single material with the dun colour of dust softened by the golden light, it is a eulogy for the dense and fragile environment around it. The MuCEM will seem to rise up from a landscape of stone, and look east through its shadows. But on the harbour basin side at the height of the pontoon, a bright slanting light casting silver reflections on the blue water will penetrate this territory so close to the sea.

7. The museum under construction, view from the sea – May 2012
8. Exterior view – latticework panel
9. Construction details

8

Index of Museums

Bliesbruck-Reinheim Gallo-Roman Baths
Structure Muséale des Thermes Gallo-romain
1 rue Robert Schuman 57200 Bliesbruck
T +33 (0)3 87 35 02 20
F +33 (0)3 87 35 02 29
bliesbruck@cg57.fr
www.archeo57.com

Bonnard Museum
Musée Bonnard
16 boulevard Sadi Carnot 06110 Le Cannet
T +33 (0)4 93 94 06 06
F +33 (0)4 92 18 24 41
contact@museebonnard.fr
www.museebonnard.fr

Cartier Foundation for Contemporary Art
Fondation Cartier pour l'art contemporain
261 boulevard Raspail 75014 Paris
T + 33 (0)1 42 18 56 50
http://fondation.cartier.com

Champollion Museum - Scripts of the World
Musée Champollion - Les Écritures du Monde
Place Champollion 46100 Figeac
T +33 (0)5 65 50 31 08
F +33 (0)5 65 50 16 79
musee@ville-figeac.fr
www.musee-champollion.fr

City of the Ocean
Cité de l'Océan
1 avenue de la Plage 64200 Biarritz
T +33 (0)5 59 22 75 40
www.citedelocean.com

Comic Book Museum
Cité Internationale de la Bande Dessinée et de l'Image
121 rue de Bordeaux BP 72308
16023 Angoulême Cedex
T +33 (0)5 45 38 65 65
musee@citebd.org
www.citebd.org

Confluences Museum
Musée des Confluences
28 boulevard des Belges 69006 Lyon
T+33 (0)4 72 69 05 00
museedesconfluences@rhone.fr

Courbet Museum
Musée Courbet
1 place Robert Fernier 25290 Ornans
T +33 (0)3 81 86 22 88
courbet.musee@doubs.fr
www.musee-courbet.fr

Éric Tabarly City of Sailing
Cité de la Voile – Éric Tabarly
Base de sous-marins de Keroman
56623 Lorient Cedex
www.citevoile-tabarly.com
T +33 (0)2 97 65 56 56
F +33 (0)2 97 65 59 22

Fabre Museum
Musée Fabre
39 boulevard Bonne Nouvelle 34000 Montpellier
T +33 (0)4 67 14 83 00
F +33 (0)4 67 66 09 20
musee.fabre@montpellier-agglo.com
www.museefabre.montpellier-agglo.com

Historial Charles de Gaulle
Hôtel National des Invalides
129 rue de Grenelle 75007 Paris
T +33 (0)8 10 11 33 99
accueilnord-ma@invalides.org
www.invalides.org

Institute of the Arab World
Institut du Monde Arabe
1 rue des Fossés Saint-Bernard / place Mohammed V
75236 Paris Cedex 05
T +33 (0)1 40 51 38 38
F +33 (0)1 43 54 76 45
www.imarabe.org

International City of Lace and Fashion
Cité Internationale de la Dentelle et de la Mode de Calais
135 quai du Commerce 62100 Calais
T+33 (0)3 21 00 42 30
cite-dentelle@mairie-calais.fr
www.cite-dentelle.fr

International Perfume Museum
Musée International de la Parfumerie
2 boulevard du Jeu de Ballon 06130 Grasse
T +33 (0)4 97 05 58 00
F +33 (0) 4 97 05 58 01
www.museesdegrasse.com

Jean Cocteau Museum
Musée Jean Cocteau
2 quai Monléon 06500 Menton
T +33 (0)4 89 81 52 50
www.museecocteaumenton.fr

Jean-Frédéric Oberlin Museum
Musée Jean-Frédéric Oberlin
25 montée Oberlin 67130 Waldersbach
T + 33 (0)3 88 97 30 27
F + 33 (0)3 88 97 32 21
oberlin@musee-oberlin.eu
www.musee-oberlin.com

La Maison Rouge
10 boulevard de la Bastille 75012 Paris
T +33 (0)1 40 01 08 81
info@lamaisonrouge.org
www.lamaisonrouge.org

Languedoc-Roussillon Regional Museum of Contemporary Art
Musée Régional d'Art Contemporain Languedoc-Roussillon
146 avenue de la Plage BP4 34410 Sérignan
T +33 (0)4 67 32 33 05
F +33 (0)4 67 76 99 09
museedartcontemporain@cr-languedocroussillon.fr
http://mrac.languedocroussillon.fr/

La Piscine – Museum of Art and Industry
La Piscine – Musée d'Art et d'Industrie
23 rue de l'Espérance 59100 Roubaix
T +33 (0)3 20 69 23 60
F +33 (0)3 20 69 23 61
lapiscine.musee@ville-roubaix.fr
www.roubaix-lapiscine.com

Lille Modern Art Museum – LaM
Musée d'Art Moderne de l'Agglomération Lilloise (LaM)
1 allée du Musée 59650 Villeneuve d'Ascq
T +33 (0)3 20 19 68 88
F +33 (0)3 20 19 68 99
info@musee-lam.fr
www.musee-lam.fr

Malraux Museum
Musée Malraux
2 boulevard Clémenceau 76600 Le Havre
T +33 (0)2 35 19 62 62
museemalraux@lehavre.fr
www.muma-lehavre.fr

Marseille History Museum
Musée d'Histoire de Marseille
Square Belsunce - Centre Bourse 13001 Marseille
T +33 (0)4 91 90 42 22
F +33 (0)4 91 90 43 78
musee-histoire@mairie-marseille.fr
www.marseille.fr

Matisse Museum
Musée Matisse
Palais Fénelon
59360 Le Cateau-Cambrésis
T +33 (0)3 59 73 38 00
F +33 (0)3 59 73 38 01
http://museematisse.cg59.fr/
museematisse@cg59.fr

Meaux Country Museum of the Great War
Musée de la Grande Guerre du Pays de Meaux
Rue Lazare Ponticelli 77100 Meaux
T +33 (0)1 60 32 14 18
www.museedelagrandeguerre.eu

Mobile Art Pavilion
Pavillon Mobile Art
Institute of the Arab World (Institut du Monde Arabe)
1 rue des Fossés Saint-Bernard
Place Mohammed V
75236 Paris Cedex 05
T +33 (0)1 40 51 38 38
F +33 (0)1 43 54 76 45
www.imarabe.org

Museum of the Civilisations of Europe and the Mediterranean
Musée des Civilisations d'Europe et de Méditerranée (MuCEM)
Caserne du Muy
21 rue Bugeaud 13003 Marseille
www.mucem.org

Nancy Museum of Fine Arts
Musée des Beaux-Arts de Nancy
3 place Stanislas 54000 Nancy
T +33 (0)3 83 85 30 72
F +33 (0)3 83 85 30 76
mbanancy@mairie-nancy.fr
http://mban.nancy.fr

Orangerie Museum
Musée de l'Orangerie
Jardin des Tuileries 75001 Paris
T +33 (0)1 44 77 80 07
information.orangerie@musee-orangerie.fr
www.musee-orangerie.fr

Orsay Museum
Musée d'Orsay
62 rue de Lille 75007 Paris
T +33 (0)1 40 49 48 14
www.musee-orsay.fr

Pompidou Centre
Centre Pompidou
Place Georges Pompidou 75004 Paris
T +33 (0)1 44 78 12 33
www.centrepompidou.fr

President Jacques Chirac Museum
Musée du Président Jacques Chirac
19800 Sarran
T +33 (0)5 55 21 77 77
F +33 (0)5 55 21 77 78
musee.president@cg19.fr
www.museepresidentjchirac.fr

Quai Branly Museum
Musée du Quai Branly
37 quai Branly 75007 Paris
T +33 (0)1 56 61 70 00
communication@quaibranly.fr
www.quaibranly.fr

Quimper Museum of Fine Arts
Musée des Beaux-Arts de Quimper
40 place Saint-Corentin 29000 Quimper
T +33 (0)2 98 95 45 20
F +33 (0)2 98 95 87 50
musee@mairie-quimper.fr
www.mbaq.fr

Regional Fund of Contemporary Art PACA
Fond Régional d'Art Contemporain PACA
1 place Francis Chirat 13002 Marseille
T +33 (0)4 91 91 27 55
F +33 (0)4 91 90 28 50
infos@fracpaca.org
www.fracpaca.org

Strasbourg Museum of Modern and Contemporary Art
Musée d'Art Moderne et Contemporain de Strasbourg
1 place Hans Jean Arp 67000 Strasbourg
T +33 (0)3 88 23 31 31
www.musees.strasbourg.eu

Tomi Ungerer Museum
Musée Tomi Ungerer
Villa Greiner
2 avenue de la Marseillaise
67076 Strasbourg cedex
T +33 (0)3 69 06 37 27
F +33 (0)3 69 06 37 28
www.musees.strasbourg.eu

Val-de-Marne Museum of Contemporary Art
Musée d'Art Contemporain du Val-de-Marne (Mac-Val)
Place de la Libération BP 147
94404 Vitry-sur-Seine Cedex
T +33 (0)1 43 91 64 20
F +33 (0)1 43 91 64 30
contact@macval.fr
www.macval.fr

Valence Museum of Fine Arts and Archeology
Musée des Beaux-Arts et Archéologie
4 place des Ormeaux 26000 Valence
T +33 (0)4 75 79 20 80
F +33 (0)4 75 79 20 84
info@musee-valence.org
www.musee-valence.org

Vesunna Gallo-Roman Site-Museum
Vesunna, Site-Musée Gallo-Romain
Parc de Vésone
20 rue du 26e Régiment d'Infanterie
24000 Périgueux
T +33 (0)5 53 53 00 92
F +33 (0)5 53 35 40 12
vesunna@perigueux.fr
www.perigueux.fr

Würth Museum
Musée Würth
Z.I. Ouest
Rue Georges Besse BP 40013
67158 Erstein Cedex
T +33 (0)3 88 64 74 84
F +33 (0)3 88 64 74 88
www.musee-wurth.fr
mwfe.info@wurth.fr

Index of Architects

Amplitude Architectes
14 rue Génissieu 38000 Grenoble
T +33 (0)4 76 12 25 84
F +33 (0)4 76 12 90 36
contact@amplitude-architectes.com
www.amplitude-architectes.com

Architecture Studio
10 rue Lacuée 75012 Paris
T +33 (0)1 43 45 18 00
F +33 (0)1 43 43 81 43
as@architecture-studio.fr
www.architecture-studio.fr

Ateliers 234
234 rue du Faubourg Saint-Antoine 75012 Paris
T +33 (0)1 55 25 15 10
234@fbg234.com
www.a234.fr

Ateliers AFA – Adrien Fainsilber & Associés
69 rue Barrault 75013 Paris
T +33 (0)1 45 65 50 90
F +33 (0)1 45 65 50 91
agence@ateliers-afa.eu
www.ateliers-afa.eu

Atelier de l'Ile
3 rue Dagorno 75012 Paris
T +33 (0)1 48 06 22 00
F +33 (0)1 48 06 91 75
paris.atile@atile.fr
www.atile.fr

Beaudouin-Husson Architectes
3 rue de la Monnaie 54000 Nancy
T +33 (0)3 83 36 49 46
F +33 (0)3 83 36 80 30
elb@beaudouin-architectes.com
www.beaudouin-architectes.fr

Bodin & Associés
33 rue des Francs-Bourgeois 75004 Paris
T +33 (0)1 44 59 21 40
F +33 (0)1 44 59 21 45
33@bodin.fr
www.bodin.fr

Brochet Lajus Pueyo
Hangar G2 - Quai Armand Lalande 33300 Bordeaux
T +33 (0)5 57 19 59 19
F +33 (0)5 57 19 59 10
architectes@brochet-lajus-pueyo.fr
www.brochet-lajus-pueyo.fr

Riland Carta Architectes & Associés
20 rue Saint Jacques 13006 Marseille
T +33 (0)4 96 10 29 00
F +33 (0)4 96 10 29 09
agence@cplust.eu
www.cplust.eu

Clément-Vergely Architectes
7 quai Général Sarrail 69006 Lyon
T +33 (0)4 72 65 91 44
F +33 (0)4 72 65 92 47
atelier@vergelyarchitectes.com
www.vergelyarchitectes.com

Coop Himmelb(l)au
Wolf D. Prix & Partner ZT GmbH
Spengergasse 37
1050 Vienna, Austria
T +43 (0)1 546 60
F +43 (0)1 546 60-600
communications@coop-himmelblau.at
www.coop-himmelblau.at

ECDM – Emmanuel Combarel Dominique Marrec
7 passage Turquetil 75011 Paris
T +33 (0)1 44 93 20 60
F +33 (0)9 58 72 33 21
contact@ecdm.fr
http://ecdm.eu/

Ferrero & Rossi
4 avenue de la Résistance 06140 Vence
T +33 (0)4 93 58 15 03
F +33 (0)4 93 58 21 38
contact@ferrero-architecte.com
contact@rossi-architecte.com
www.ferrero-architecte.com

Jacques Ferrier architectures
77 rue Pascal 75013 Paris
T +33 (0)1 43 13 20 20
F +33 (0)1 43 13 20 21
communication.ferrier@agencejfa.com
www.jacques-ferrier.com

Manuelle Gautrand
36 boulevard de la Bastille 75012 Paris
T +33 (0)1 56 95 06 46
F +33 (0)1 56 95 06 47
contact@manuelle-gautrand.com
www.manuelle-gautrand.com

Zaha Hadid Architects
10 Bowling Green Lane
London EC1R 0BQ United Kingdom
T +44 20 7253 5147
F +44 20 7251 8322
press@zaha-hadid.com
www.zaha-hadid.com

Steven Holl Architects
450 West 31st street 11th floor
New York, NY 10001, USA
T +1 212 629 7262
F +1 212 629 7312
nyc@stevenholl.com
www.stevenholl.com

Frédéric Jung
20 rue Fredérick Lemaître 75020 Paris
T +33 (0)1 42 02 04 84
F +33 (0)1 42 02 03 10
jung.architecture@free.fr

Kuma & Associates Europe
16 rue Martel 75010 Paris
T +33 (0)1 44 88 94 90
F +33 (0)1 42 46 23 55
kuma@kkaa.co.jp
http://kkaa.co.jp

Christophe Lab (Atelier)
21 rue de Tanger 75019 Paris
T +33 (0)1 53 26 56 57
57 Familistère aile gauche 02120 Guise
T+33 (0)3 23 09 25 39
atelierlab@wanadoo.fr

Moatti-Rivière
22 rue de Paradis 75010 Paris
T +33 (0)1 45 65 44 04
communication@moattiriviere.com
www.moatti-riviere.com

Moget-Gaubert Architectes
7 rue Suger 75006 Paris
T +33 (0)6 21 33 52 56
T +33 (0)6 16 79 73 75
pierre.moget@free.fr

Jean Nouvel (Ateliers)
10 cité d'Angoulême 75011 Paris
T +33 (0)1 49 23 83 83
F +33 (0)1 43 14 81 15
info@jeannouvel.fr
www.jeannouvel.com

Renzo Piano Building Workshop
34 rue des Archives 75004 Paris
T +33 (0)1 44 61 49 00
F +33 (0)1 42 78 01 98
france@rpbw.com
www.rpbw.com

Jean-Paul Philippon
6 rue de Braque 75003 Paris
T +33 (0)1 42 71 02 96
F +33 (0)1 42 71 94 43
j.p.philippon@wanadoo.fr
www.philippon-architecte.fr

Projectiles
8 Passage Brûlon 75012 Paris
T +33 (0)1 58 30 82 61
F +33 (0)1 43 67 86 47
atelier@projectiles.net
www.projectiles.net

Jacques Ripault Architecture
43 rue des Tournelles 75003 Paris
T +33 (0)1 44 54 29 30
F +33 (0)1 44 54 29 39
architectes@ripaultarchitecture.fr
www.jacquesripault.com

Rudy Ricciotti
17 boulevard Victor Hugo 83150 Bandol
T +33 (0)4 94 29 52 61
F +33 (0)4 94 32 45 25
rudy.ricciotti@wanadoo.fr
www.rudyricciotti.com

Adeline Rispal (Studio)
23 rue du Faubourg Saint-Denis 75010 Paris
T +33 (0)1 43 56 91 45
contact@adelinerispal.com
www.adelinerispal.com

Rogers Stirk Harbour + Partners
Thames Wharf, Rainville Road
London W6 9HA United Kingdom
T +44 (0)20 7385 1235
F +44 (0)20 7385 8409
enquiries@rsh-p.com
www.rsh-p.com

Toury Vallet Architectes
14 rue Lauzin 75019 Paris
T+33 (0)1 44 75 37 69
F+33 (0)1 44 75 38 40
mail@touryvallet.fr
www.touryvallet.fr

Wilmotte & Associés SA
68 rue du Faubourg Saint-Antoine 75012 Paris
T+33 (0)1 53 02 22 22
wilmotte@wilmotte.fr
www.wilmotte.com

This edition published in January 2013

Design Media Publishing Limited
20/F Manulife Tower
169 Electric Rd, North Point
Hong Kong
Tel: 00852-28672587
Fax: 00852-25050411
E-mail: Kevinchoy@designmediahk.com
www.designmediahk.com

Editorial Consulting: ICI CONSULTANTS
Direction: Chia-Ling CHIEN
Communication/Documentation: Nicolas BRIZAULT
English Translation: Alison CULLIFORD
Design/Layout: Karine de La MAISON
Wijane NOREE

ISBN 978-988-15662-3-2

Printed in China

Antique Advertising

Country Store Signs and Products

Rich Bertoia

Schiffer Publishing Ltd®
4880 Lower Valley Road, Atglen, PA 19310 USA

Library of Congress Card Number:
2001089632

Designed by Bonnie M. Hensley
Cover design by Bruce M. Waters
Type set in Bulmer BT/Korinna BT

ISBN: 0-7643-1450-5
Printed in China
1 2 3 4

Published by Schiffer Publishing Ltd.
4880 Lower Valley Road
Atglen, PA 19310
Phone: (610) 593-1777; Fax: (610) 593-2002
E-mail: Schifferbk@aol.com
Please visit our web site catalog at **www.schifferbooks.com**
We are always looking for people to write books on new and related subjects. If you have an idea for a book please contact us at the above address.

This book may be purchased from the publisher.
Include $3.95 for shipping.
Please try your bookstore first.
You may write for a free catalog.

In Europe, Schiffer books are distributed by
Bushwood Books
6 Marksbury Ave.
Kew Gardens
Surrey TW9 4JF England
Phone: 44 (0) 20 8392-8585; Fax: 44 (0) 20 8392-9876
E-mail: Bushwd@aol.com
Free postage in the U.K., Europe; air mail at cost.

Contents

DON'T MONKEY
WITH
OTHER GROCERY MEN WHILE
CAMPBELL
IS IN TOWN
HE IS THE CHEAPEST AND BEST
1909 January 1909

FRANCISCO AUTO HEATER
Summer Here all the Year
FRANCISCO HEATER

Acknowledgments

I wish to thank Mr. Bob Lyons for unselfishly allowing his personal country store to be photographed and recorded, and all without reservation or limits. The three books detailing this incredible collection represent a lifetime of masterful searching which further adds to the honorable gesture by Mr. Lyons. Legends in antiquing are built around the principle of sharing one's rare finds with others with the same interest, and it is with pride that I place Bob Lyons in such a distinguished class of collectors. The staff of Schiffer Publishing deserves high marks for their truly professional work on these books, and I am sure, they also wish to thank Bob for the opportunity of working around such great objects, and the man who put them together. Finally, a never ending thanks to all who have helped promote these books: without your help, the pages would never be opened.

Preface

A third and final visit into the incredible finds of the Bob Lyons' country store actually brings me back to the start of this series, as the advertising to be found in this edition devotes the attention to the marketing of the products pictured on many of the former pages. A closer look at the wonderful graphic depictions help recall the equally wonderful products they were meant to help sell. Clever and attractive signs were the only tools available to even the wealthiest of early companies. To insure instant success, advertising campaigns involved seeking the best of artists and the sharpest of copywriters. Together with the proper placement of products on the shelves, people had to be drawn to the merchandise by color, shape, size, and an occasional false claim of the product's miraculous properties. This was quite different from TV commercials of today, but still had the same bottom line of attempting to sell products to an awaiting and growing society. The collection, in my opinion, can rest its highest merits on the fact that it is fully representative of our society in its buying infancy. Without the advantage of multimedia, and sophisticated national campaign networking, early advertising agencies were able to perform minor miracles, through the simple magic of beautiful graphics and effective copy. Nothing escaped the imagination of these ad companies: if it had a surface, it could be stenciled or printed upon. The goal was to create a flood of the company name and product keeping it in front of the public at all times.

Bob Lyons' country store contains an important cross section of the various mediums and extravagant items used to promote merchandise and to help get it carried into every American household. The hours spent on chronicling this country store has been a privilege that few aficionados of collecting ever get to experience, and I hope the book's character reflects my warmest thanks for a collection well done.

Introduction

Country store advertising signs have been produced in a plethora of shapes, sizes and thematic portrayals. While some border on the inanely comical, others border on truly great works of art. The art market was not an open and easy endeavor for many of America's talent pool, thus working as an artisan for a major advertising company meant a steady paycheck for the very gifted. Many of the classic signs were sketched by famous artists of the day, and their beauty is still marveled at today. This book does not categorize signs or products, as I feel a visual tour of Bob's store commands a more unique grazing with a surprise on every page. A walk through the store allows the eyes to wonder at the multitude of distinct items displayed, and the book will follow this same pattern. By dissecting the store into individual pictures, we are able to examine each piece with a more focused appreciation of the goods. While one of the country store's shelves may have contained boxes, signs, or tin cans, the book will also feature a random selection of mixed goods and the signs that drew attention to their contents. It has been a very rewarding and enlightening experience to put together this book, and the two previous volumes, and my hope is that it provides genuine enjoyment and added knowledge to collectors of all levels.

Chapter One

Art in Advertising

We begin with a splash of color, and a look into the master work of early American graphic magic. With the advent of tin lithography, great works of art were easily transformed into exciting visuals that helped make simple products into household names. It is easy to view these signs with awe and amazement, to imagine the creativity that went into the design, taking what was once just a thought in the mind of a young artist and copywriter and transforming it into moving image and word. Many of these signs indeed unfold before our eyes as truly great masterpieces. Great minds work together, and the use of cardboard, paper, tin, porcelain, or glass was the job of the layout specialist employed by countless ad agencies. The importance of the success of any single sign becomes apparent when considering the complexity of the early chromolithograph process and the time consuming stone shaving methods utilized. As you view the following signs, remember this, and appreciate the true artistry of the trade.

Even the sign painter had to advertise. This is a reverse painted glass sign, typical of elaborate workmanship.

Opposite page: A sign with artistic visuals making the product almost secondary to the total look. 15" x 20". Card stock. The Universal Food Chopper. $400-600

THE
UNIVERSAL
FOOD
CHOPPER
UNIVERSAL
NO. 2.
FOOD CHOPPER
PAT. OCT. 12. 1897.
And
A few of the things
it chops.
MANUFACTURED BY
LANDERS, FRARY & CLARK,
NEW BRITAIN, CONN.,
U.S.A.

Both pages: A captive view of artistry in advertising. Most of these artists probably found their craft slightly inhibited by the demands of the commercial world, but the rewards of living a comfortable life-style may have outweighed unlimited potential. These signs may range from $300-700

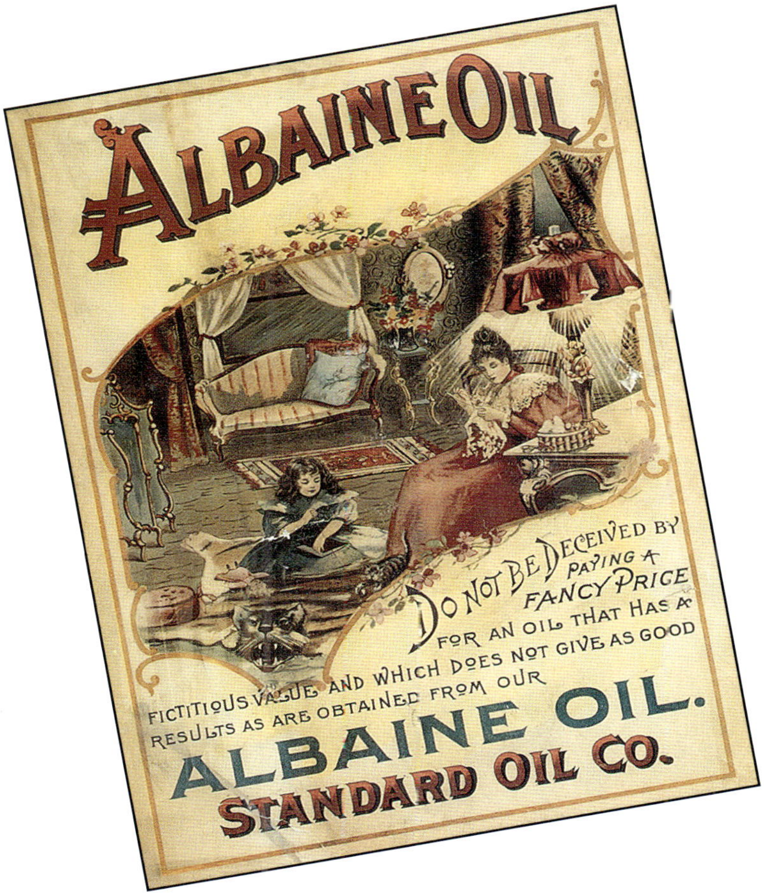
ALBAINE OIL
DO NOT BE DECEIVED BY PAYING A FANCY PRICE
FOR AN OIL THAT HAS A FICTITIOUS VALUE AND WHICH DOES NOT GIVE AS GOOD RESULTS AS ARE OBTAINED FROM OUR
ALBAINE OIL.
STANDARD OIL CO.

J. I. CASE
THRESHING MACHINE CO.
RACINE, WIS.,
U.S.A.

BORAX
STARCH GLAZE

Both pages: A difference in mediums, but always the same eye catching results. Pictured are: wood, paper, and lithographed tin signs.

MY ELGIN'S ALL RIGHT
The Meyercord Co. Chicago.

Both pages: Five examples of an artist's work together with a graphic artist's advertising creation. These die-cuts are in great scale and exacting lifelike detail. $300 to $800 for larger examples. The Twin Oaks has retailed recently for over $1000.

1908
JANUARY
FEBRUARY
APRIL
MAY
JUNE
JULY
AUGUST
OCTOBER
NOVEMBER
DECEMBER

LATHER FROM 1 OZ
LENOX SOAP
IN HARD WATER.
PROCTER & GAMBLE
LENOX
SOAP.
LATHERS FREELY IN HARD WATER

EN-AR-CO & EN-AR-CO PENN MOTOR OIL
1937 FEBRUARY 1937
SUN MON TUE WED THU FRI SAT
1 2 3 4 5 6
7 8 9 10 11 12 13
14 15 16 17 18 19 20
21 22 23 24 25 26 27
28
EVEN THE GROUND HOG HAS A COMING OUT PARTY
WHITE ROSE GASOLINE
SOUTH DELTA OIL CO.
H. A. Gillespie, Prop.
Phone SSS-145 DELTA, OHIO

USE
Bell's Buffalo Soap.

FROM
Nos.
TRADE MARK

PRIDE OF KENTUCKY
WHISKEY
PRIDE OF KENTUCKY
HAND MADE
SOUR MASH
WHISKEY
THE WEIDEMAN-HOLMES CO
CLEVELAND, OHIO.

Both pages: Diminutive masterpieces in trade card form. These examples would surely make amazing paintings. $20-45 each

WE SELL
EGG-O-SEE
"Dere aint gon'er be no leavin's"
EGG-O-SEE.

Largest Exclusive Ball Plant in the World
HOOVER STEEL BALL COMPANY
ANN ARBOR MICHIGAN

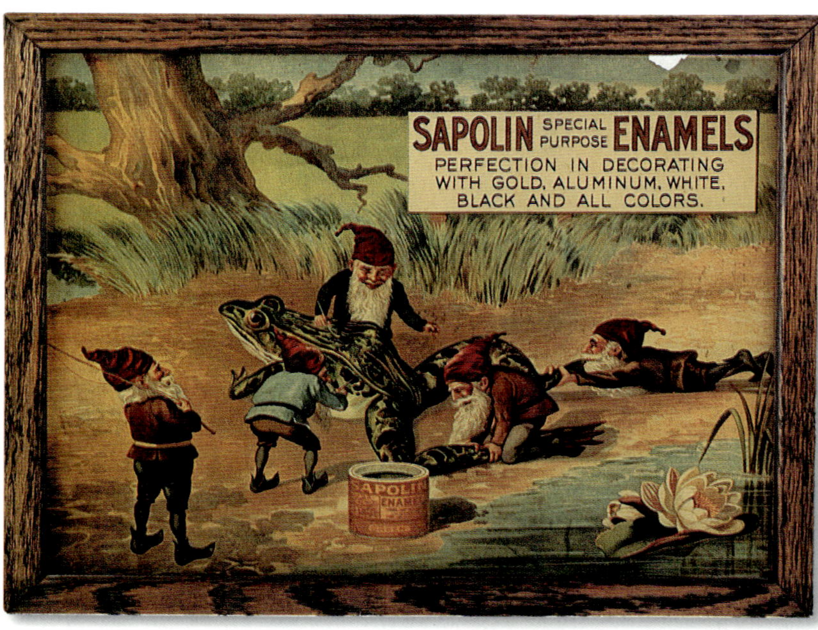
SAPOLIN SPECIAL PURPOSE ENAMELS
PERFECTION IN DECORATING
WITH GOLD, ALUMINUM, WHITE,
BLACK AND ALL COLORS.

Both pages: Framed with dignity and an obvious air of importance. Any product displayed so proudly was sure to be viewed as the pinnacle in its class. Very effective advertising, and again, completed by a very skilled artist. Prices may range in the range of $1000-$2000

Both pages: Any artist worth his weight in marbles can paint a great portrait, and we find people in a variety of favorite ad signs and products. $300-$600

ATI ENQUIRER.
Remarkable Success!
WIEDEMANN'S BEERS
TO THE FRONT.
FACTS.
FROM THE
GEO. WIEDEMANN
BREWING CO. INC
NEWPORT, KY.

Compliments of
Ed. V. Price & Co.
Merchant Tailors
Chicago.
Who's your Tailor?
My Turn Next
1908

NEBUCHADNEZZAR
or the story of a MULE
Price 10 cents
LITH AND PRINTED BY THE FORBES CO. BOSTON.
COPYRIGHT, 1887, BY C.AULTMAN & CO.

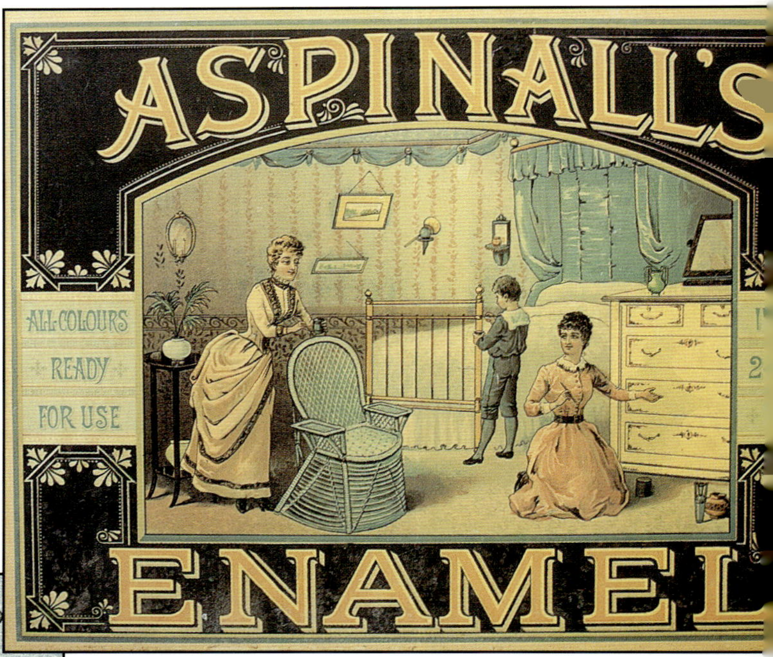

Elaborate advertising pictorials, both in paper and tin. Prices vary widely for these examples, but interesting to note that signs with an automobile theme have consistently commanded strong prices. $400-$800

RAIL CROSSING ROAD
COAST TO COAST REFRIGERATOR CO.
LAST YEAR
2485 KILLED
6804 INJURED
24% ran into side of trains
HELP LESSEN CROSSING ACC DENTS THIS YEAR
GS CAUTIOUSLY

NECK AND NECK TO THE WIRE.

SALZER'S SUPERIOR ONION SEED FOR PROFIT.
SALZER'S KING OF THE EARLIEST PRICE - Pkg. 10¢ oz. 20¢ ¼ lb. 50¢ 1 lb. $1.00 4 lbs. $7.00
AUTUMN KING PRICE - Pkg. 10¢ oz. 20¢ ¼ lb. 35¢ 1 lb. $1.30 4 lbs. $5.00
THE TWO GREAT MONEY MAKING ONIONS
AUTUMN KING 2507 BUS. FROM 3 ACRES.
KING OF THE EARLIEST READY FOR MARKET JULY 10TH
KING OF THE EARLIEST
AUTUMN KING 1108 BUS. PER ACRE.
JOHN A. SALZER SEED CO.
LA CROSSE, WIS.

ASK FOR
CANDEE RUBBERS
MADE BY L. CANDEE & CO.
THE OLDEST MANUFACTURERS IN THE WORLD

Two cigar signs that relied more on the copy then the concept. They are, although, very interesting and effective ads. $125-$400

Doodles for the artist, but a masterpiece for optimum advertising. These Brownies are busy working for the company. $500-$750

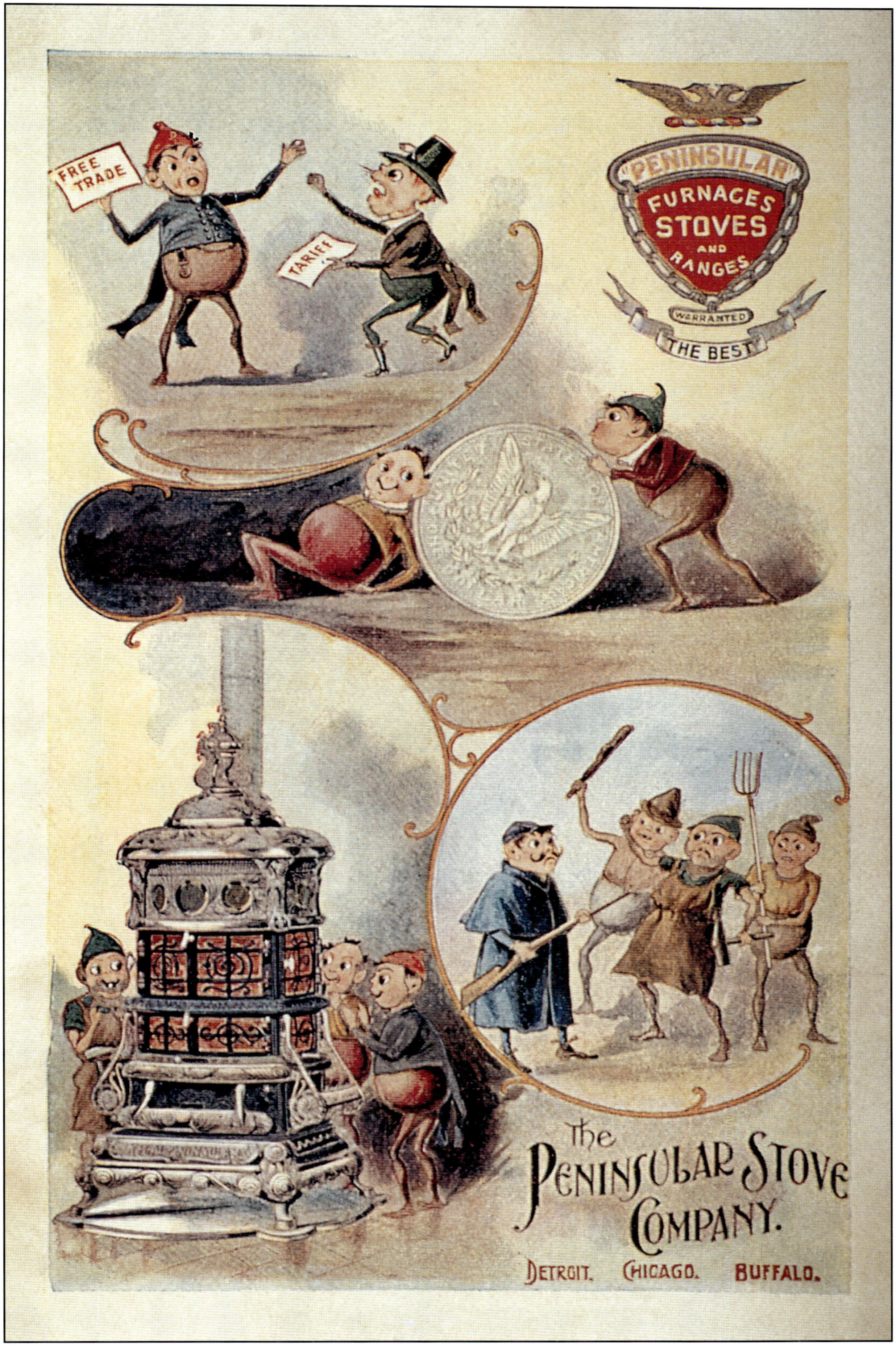

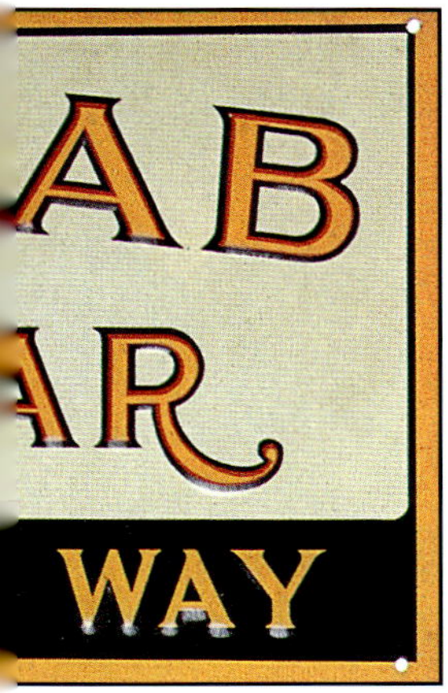

VELVET SKIN SOAP and POWDER,
FOR THE
Belles Boudoir
and the Baby's Basket.

Buy

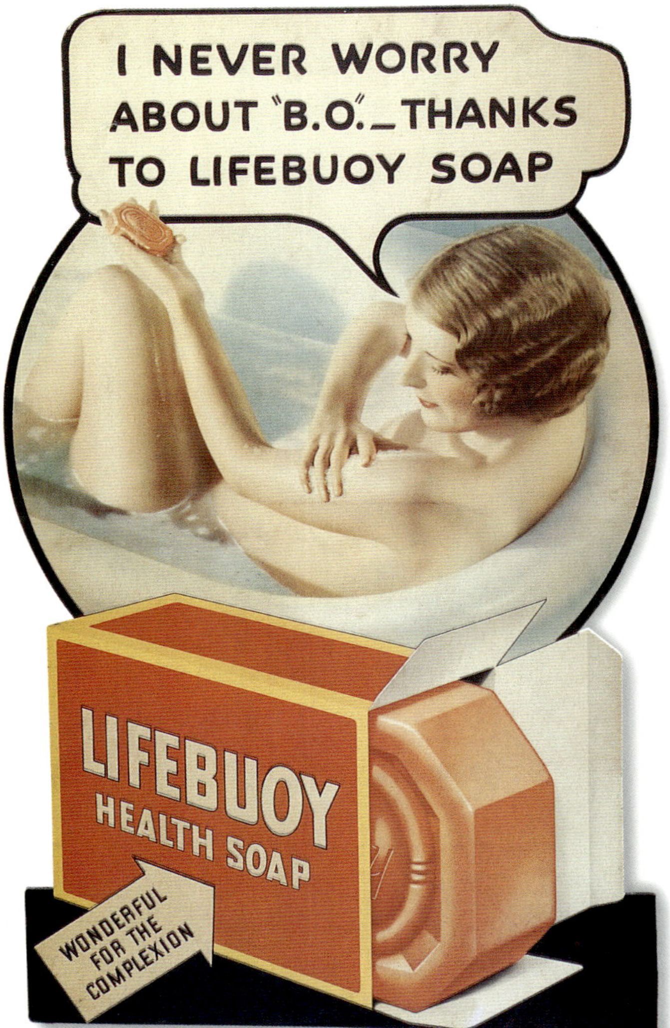
I NEVER WORRY
ABOUT "B.O."_THANKS
TO LIFEBUOY SOAP
LIFEBUOY
HEALTH SOAP
WONDERFUL FOR THE COMPLEXION

L. Z. Foerster Brewing Co.,
YPSILANTI, MICH.

Both pages: What could be more eye catching then the beauty of a woman. Advertisers used this natural phenomenon to their advantage. This is a great sampling of classic advertising beauty. $100-300

Both pages: Only the enchantment of happy children could have a wider appeal, and create more advertising dollars for the promoters

WESTBURN
Finest Quality
By Appointment
Sugar Refiners & Purveyors to
His Majesty The King
Highly Refined
GOLDEN SYRUP
"Chairing the Favourite".
THE WESTBURN SUGAR REFINERIES LTD
GREENOCK.

I TALK
FOR
MINARD'S LINIMENT

Both pages: The bread winners of their day would find these advertisements worth a pause. A gifted artist could easily present a simple product as a must-have, fun-to-be-around purchase.

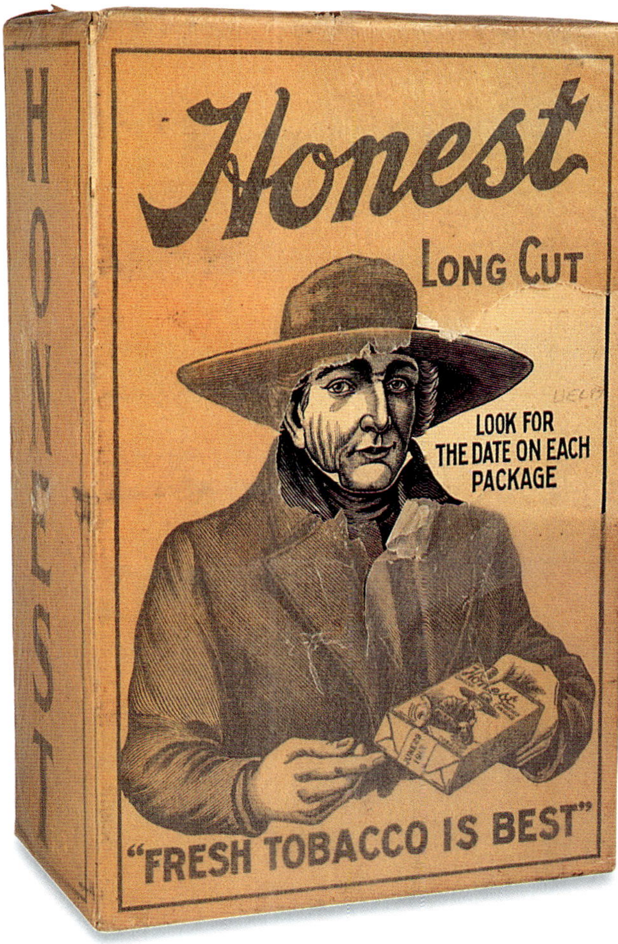
HONEST
Honest
LONG CUT
LOOK FOR
THE DATE ON EACH
PACKAGE
"FRESH TOBACCO IS BEST"

We Install the
BOYCE
MOTOMETER
" Free "

MAYO'S
PLUG
LIGHT
DARK
SMOKING
COCK O'THE WALK

J.I. CASE
THRESHING MACHINE CO.
RACINE, WIS.,
U.S.A.

Both pages: The animal kingdom cid its fair share of selling merchandise. These signs show the strength of a well-drawn figure, and how our eyes seem to observe the entire area of the sign. $200-400

Action advertising at its best. The movement of the eyes stops only to read the product advertised.

This Dutch Boy figure became an advertising icon, which is still used on Dutch Boy paints today.

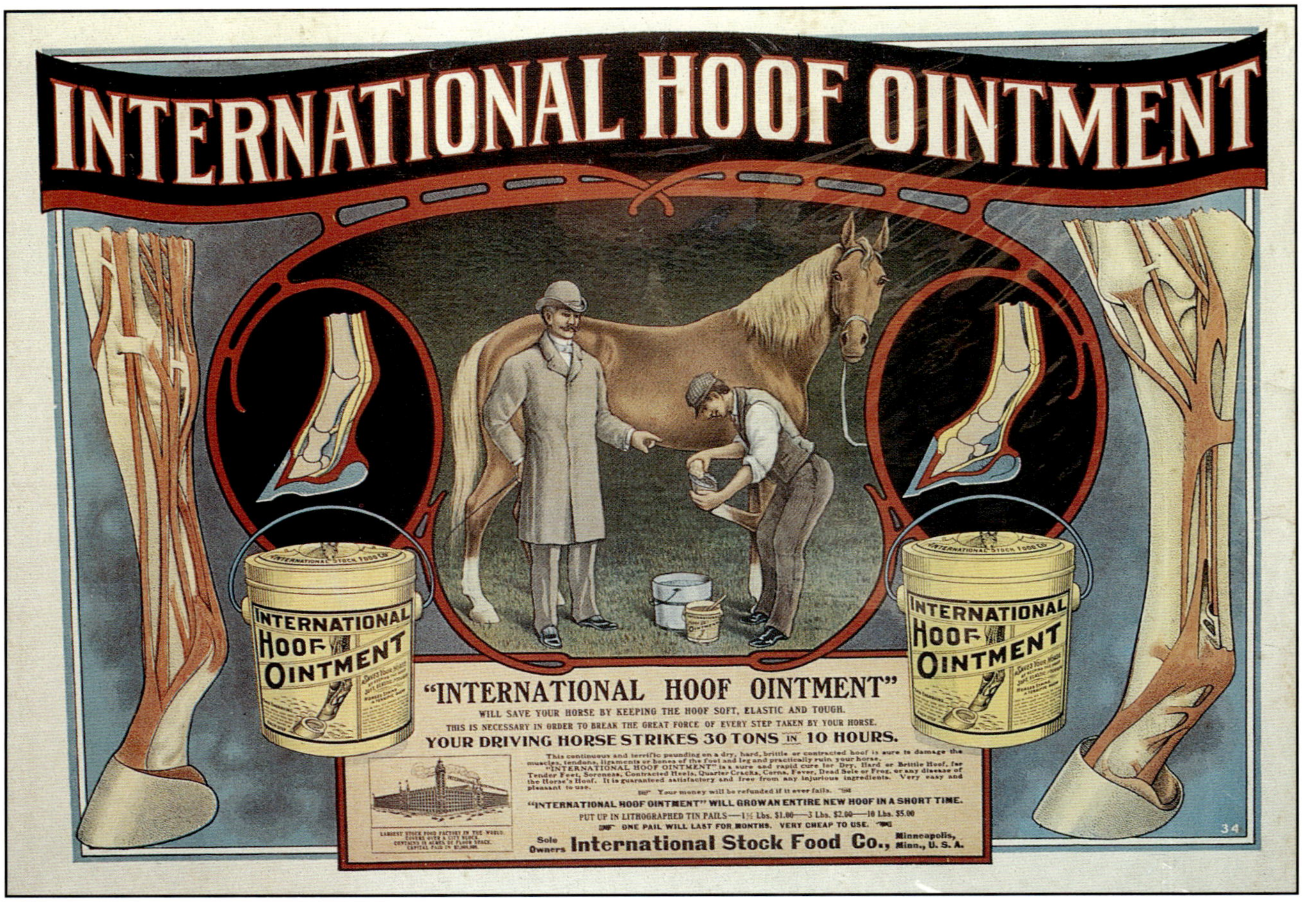

Both pages: More misdirection with intentional results. While these animal prints keep us captivated, the products name becomes embedded in our minds. Great graphics such as these command the attention of collectors today. $200-400

DO YOU WANT
A 25 LB. PAIL OF THIS ANIMAL TONIC
GUARANTEED TO MAKE YOU $7.00
BY AIDING DIGESTION, QUICK GROWTH, HEALTH.
3 FEEDS FOR ONE CENT
WON HIGHEST MEDAL
AT PARIS IN 1900
INTERNATIONAL STOCK FOOD
It Will Make Every One of Your Cows
Give Two to Three Quarts More Milk
Every Day During Winter and Spring.
By purifying the blood, invigorating the entire system and by giving better digestion and assimilation "International Stock Food" will increase the milk production of your cows and keep them perfectly healthy and free from disease. It makes the milk more healthful for human use and gives a better quality of cream and butter. "International Stock Food" and skim milk will keep your Calves healthy and make them grow as rapidly as new milk. "International Stock Food" is the greatest Animal Tonic known and will Fatten Calves, Cows or Steers in 30 days less time than your usual plan of feeding. It saves grain by aiding digestion so that all animals will obtain more nutrition from all grain eaten. The average farm animal digests about 55 per cent of the average farm feeds. The use of "International Stock Food" increases this up to 70 and 75 per cent.
29 Per Cent Increase in Milk
International Stock Food Co., Minneapolis, Minn. Mankato, Minn.
Dear Sir:—About a month ago, at the request of Mr. W. W. P. McConnell, former Minnesota State Dairy and Food Commissioner, I made some experiments in feeding a mixed lot of cows on his Minneopa Park Farm, Mankato, Minn. I commenced with six cows, feeding the same ration for ten consecutive days and received an aggregate of 990 pounds of milk. At the end of the ten days I continued for ten days longer the same feed, and the same conditions, personally milking the cows—the only change was an added quantity of International Stock Food. During the ten days that we fed International Stock Food the same cows gave 1277 pounds of milk, an increase of 287 pounds in favor of the last ten days.
Yours very truly, JOHN C. PFISTER, Herdman.
Saves $2.50 Per Week for Ten Cows
International Stock Food Co., Minneapolis, Minn. Sedan, Kan.
Gentlemen:—I received your International Stock Food and found it all right. Its use saved me $2.50 per week in feed on ten milk cows and we got more milk.
Yours truly, H. P. MOSER.
Marvelous Increase in Milk Production
International Stock Food Co., Minneapolis, Minn. Belfield, Va.
Gentlemen:—Will say that we are running a dairy of about sixty cows and when we commenced to use International Stock Food we were milking about 40 to 45 cows and only getting 50 to 60 gallons of milk per day. We are now milking a less number of cows and getting from 80 to 90 gallons of milk per day and our cows are in much better condition than before. We expect to continue using International Stock Food.
Yours very truly, T. J. ROBBINS.
LARGEST STOCK FOOD FACTORY IN THE WORLD
CAPITAL PAID IN $5,000,000
INTERNATIONAL STOCK FOOD CO., Minneapolis, Minn.
MORE MILK?
96

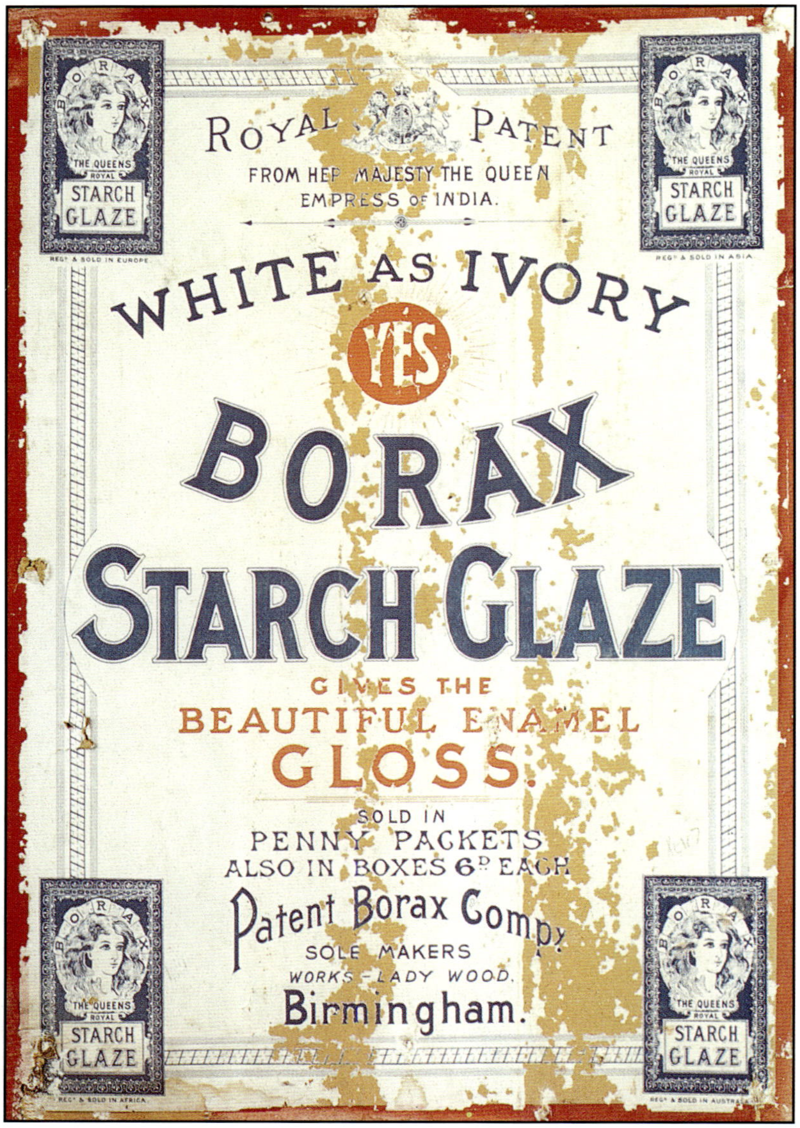
ROYAL PATENT
FROM HER MAJESTY THE QUEEN EMPRESS OF INDIA.
WHITE AS IVORY
YES
BORAX
STARCH GLAZE
GIVES THE BEAUTIFUL ENAMEL GLOSS.
SOLD IN PENNY PACKETS ALSO IN BOXES 6D EACH
Patent Borax Compy
SOLE MAKERS
WORKS - LADY WOOD.
Birmingham.
THE QUEENS ROYAL STARCH GLAZE

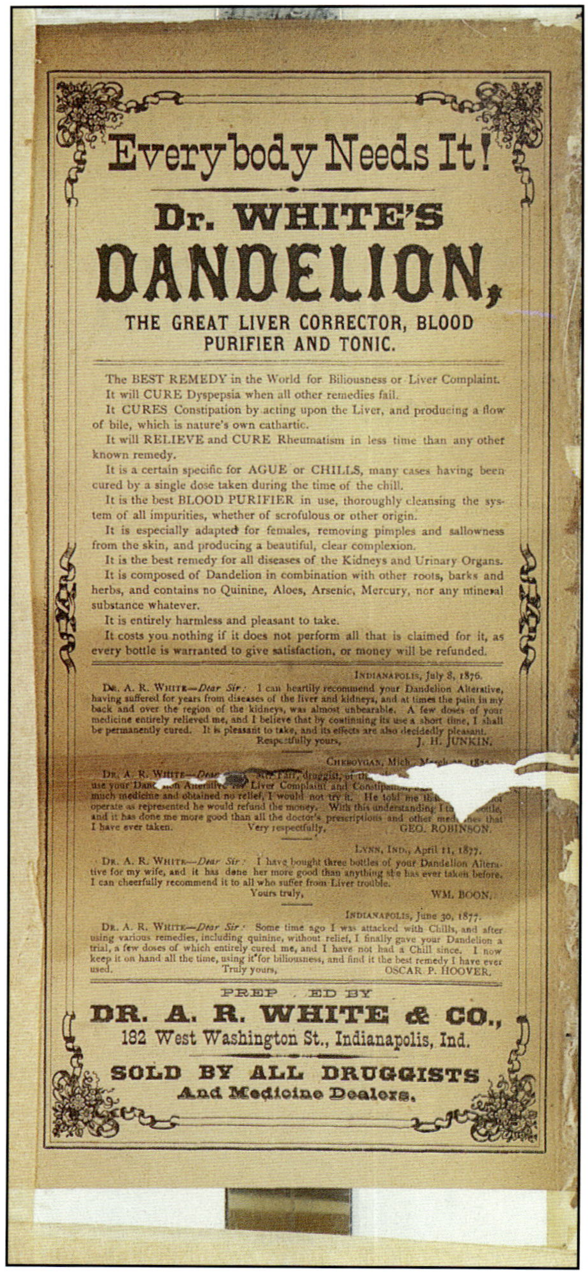
Everybody Needs It!
Dr. WHITE'S
DANDELION,
THE GREAT LIVER CORRECTOR, BLOOD PURIFIER AND TONIC.
The BEST REMEDY in the World for Biliousness or Liver Complaint.
It will CURE Dyspepsia when all other remedies fail.
It CURES Constipation by acting upon the Liver, and producing a flow of bile, which is nature's own cathartic.
It will RELIEVE and CURE Rheumatism in less time than any other known remedy.
It is a certain specific for AGUE or CHILLS, many cases having been cured by a single dose taken during the time of the chill.
It is the best BLOOD PURIFIER in use, thoroughly cleansing the system of all impurities, whether of scrofulous or other origin.
It is especially adapted for females, removing pimples and sallowness from the skin, and producing a beautiful, clear complexion.
It is the best remedy for all diseases of the Kidneys and Urinary Organs.
It is composed of Dandelion in combination with other roots, barks and herbs, and contains no Quinine, Aloes, Arsenic, Mercury, nor any mineral substance whatever.
It is entirely harmless and pleasant to take.
It costs you nothing if it does not perform all that is claimed for it, as every bottle is warranted to give satisfaction, or money will be refunded.
INDIANAPOLIS, July 8, 1876.
DR. A. R. WHITE—Dear Sir: I can heartily recommend your Dandelion Alterative, having suffered for years from diseases of the liver and kidneys, and at times the pain in my back and over the region of the kidneys, was almost unbearable. A few doses of your medicine entirely relieved me, and I believe that by continuing its use a short time, I shall be permanently cured. It is pleasant to take, and its effects are also decidedly pleasant.
Respectfully yours, J. H. JUNKIN.
CHEBOYGAN, Mich.
DR. A. R. WHITE—druggist, Liver Complaint and Constipation, much medicine and obtained no relief, I would not try it. He told me operate as represented he would refund the money. With this understanding and it has done me more good than all the doctor's prescriptions and other I have ever taken.
Very respectfully, GEO. ROBINSON.
LYNN, IND., April 11, 1877.
DR. A. R. WHITE—Dear Sir: I have bought three bottles of your Dandelion Alterative for my wife, and it has done her more good than anything she has ever taken before. I can cheerfully recommend it to all who suffer from Liver trouble.
Yours truly, WM. BOON.
INDIANAPOLIS, June 30, 1877.
DR. A. R. WHITE—Dear Sir: Some time ago I was attacked with Chills, and after using various remedies, including quinine, without relief, I finally gave your Dandelion a trial, a few doses of which entirely cured me, and I have not had a Chill since. I now keep it on hand all the time, using it for biliousness, and find it the best remedy I have ever used.
Truly yours, OSCAR P. HOOVER.
PREP ED BY
DR. A. R. WHITE & CO.,
182 West Washington St., Indianapolis, Ind.
SOLD BY ALL DRUGGISTS
And Medicine Dealers.

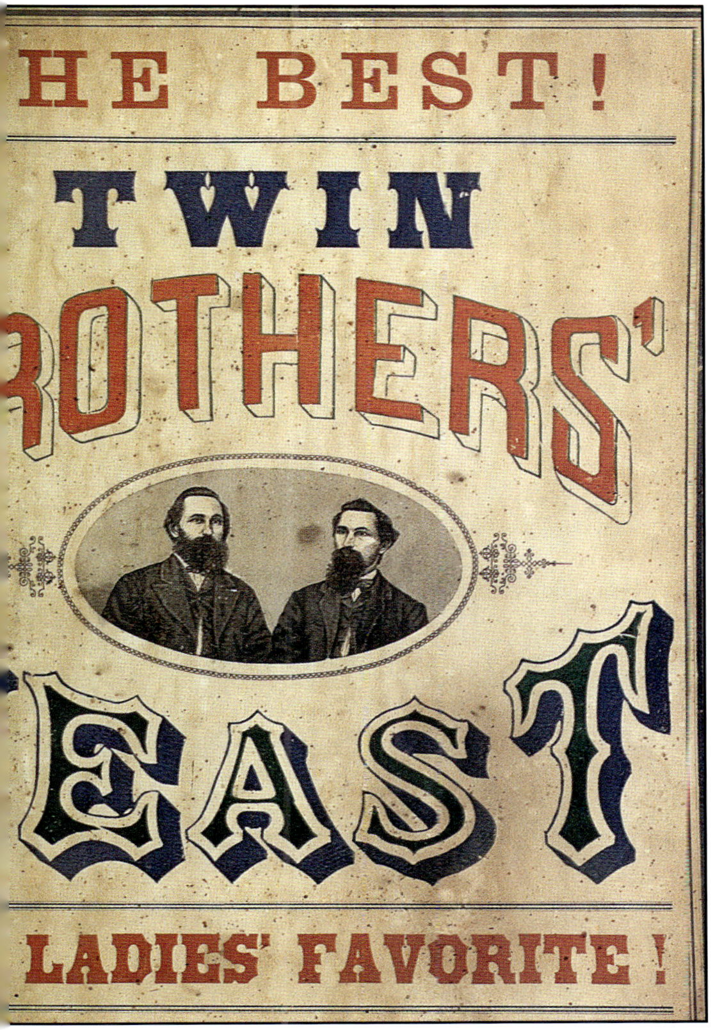

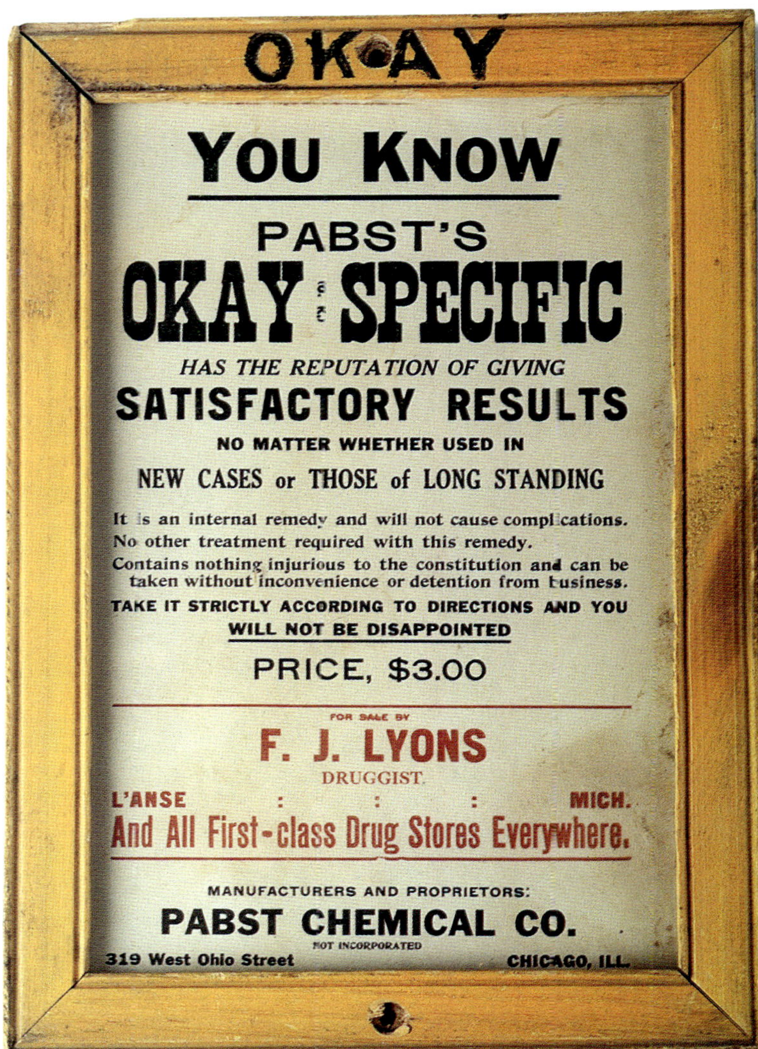

Both pages: Four examples of earlier signs demonstrating a no-frills approach to consumer awareness. $200-300

Both pages: It soon became apparent that advertising pays off and the product was best remembered by its packaging, and not just the ingredients.

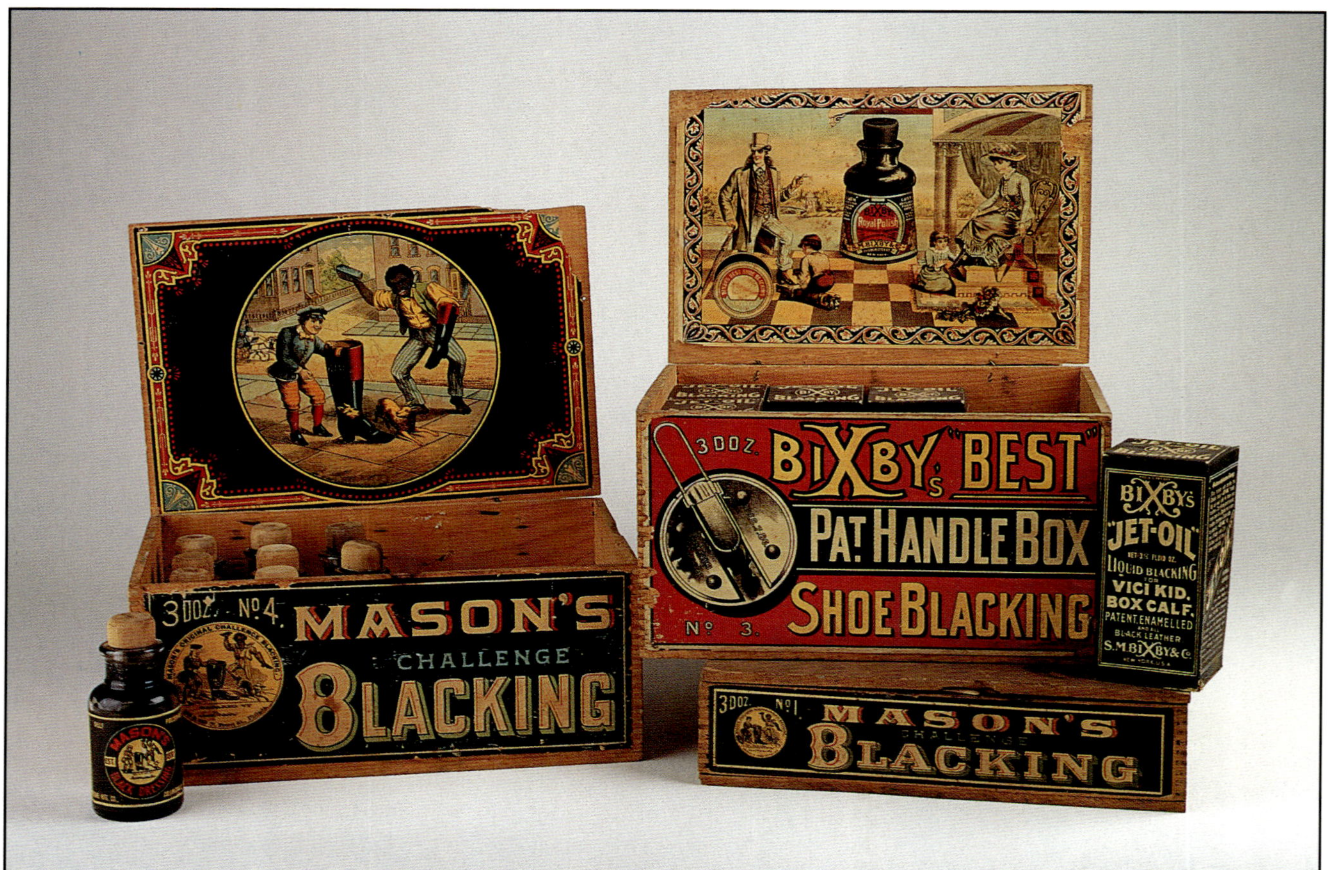

LUCKY STRIKE
"IT'S TOASTED"
A Merry Christmas
R.A. PATTERSON TOBACCO CO
LUCKY STRIKE
RICH'D VA
LUCKY STRIKE
CIGARETTES
flat
LUCKY STRIKE
"IT'S TOASTED"
CIGARETTES
fifties

ROI-TAN
CIGARS
An auto a day
is given away
A BRAND NEW
1939 CHEVROLET
An Auto a Day
is Given Away
BY
ROI-TAN
CIGARS
Write Your Entry Here
(or use a plain piece of paper)
MAN TO MAN—SMOKE ROI-TAN BECAUSE
Name
Street
City
State
SEE OTHER SIDE FOR COMPLETE DETAILS

Fitch's
REG. U.S. PAT. OFF.
DANDRUFF
REMOVER
SHAMPOO
Alcoholic Content 49.5%
Six Fl. Oz.
Active Ingredients
Methyl Salicylate
Potassium Carbonate
Potassium Bicarbonate
Oil of Lavender
Oil of Rosemary
Cocoanut Oil
(Saponified)
REMOVES DANDRUFF
OR MONEY BACK
The F.W. Fitch Mfg. Co.
Fitch's
REG. U.S. PAT. OFF.
ALCOHOLIC CONTENT 49.5%
DANDRUFF REMOVER
SHAMPOO
GUARANTEED TO REMOVE
DANDRUFF OR MONEY BACK
Active Ingredients: Methyl Salicylate, Potassium Carbonate, Potassium Bicarbonate. Oil of Lavender, Oil of Rosemary, Cocoanut Oil (Saponified)
NET CONTENT 6 FL. OZ.
The F.W. Fitch Mfg. Co.
DES MOINES BAYONNE
LOS ANGELES
RECONDITIONS
AS IT
CLEANSES
PRINTED IN U.S.A.

Both pages: The trend to advertise with visual identification continues today, and is evidenced in these circa 1940 ads with products. $75-125

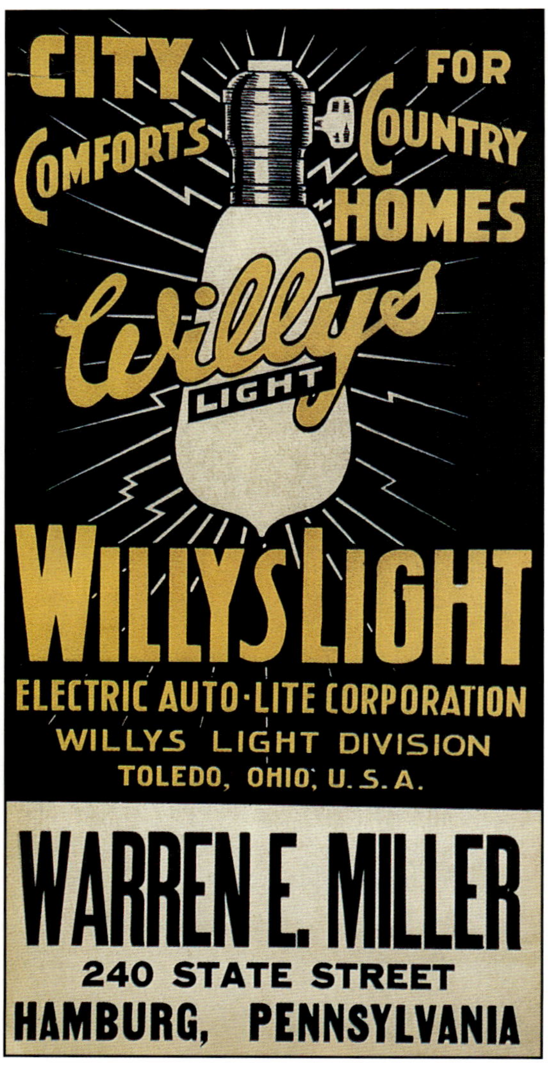

Both pages: Signs with product imagery. Placing the image of the merchandise on the sign helped people further remember the product. $150-200 each

NEED
SEAT COVERS?
Spradlings
INC.
BABY LABEL

GE
Fans
buy them here
PM-973

A different type of imagery. The graphics create an illusion that becomes easy to associate with the product itself. $100-175

The use of tin die-cuts or reverse glass signs add true importance and richness to any product. $125-175

Sign, 22" x 11", cardboard, Warner's Corsets. $400-600

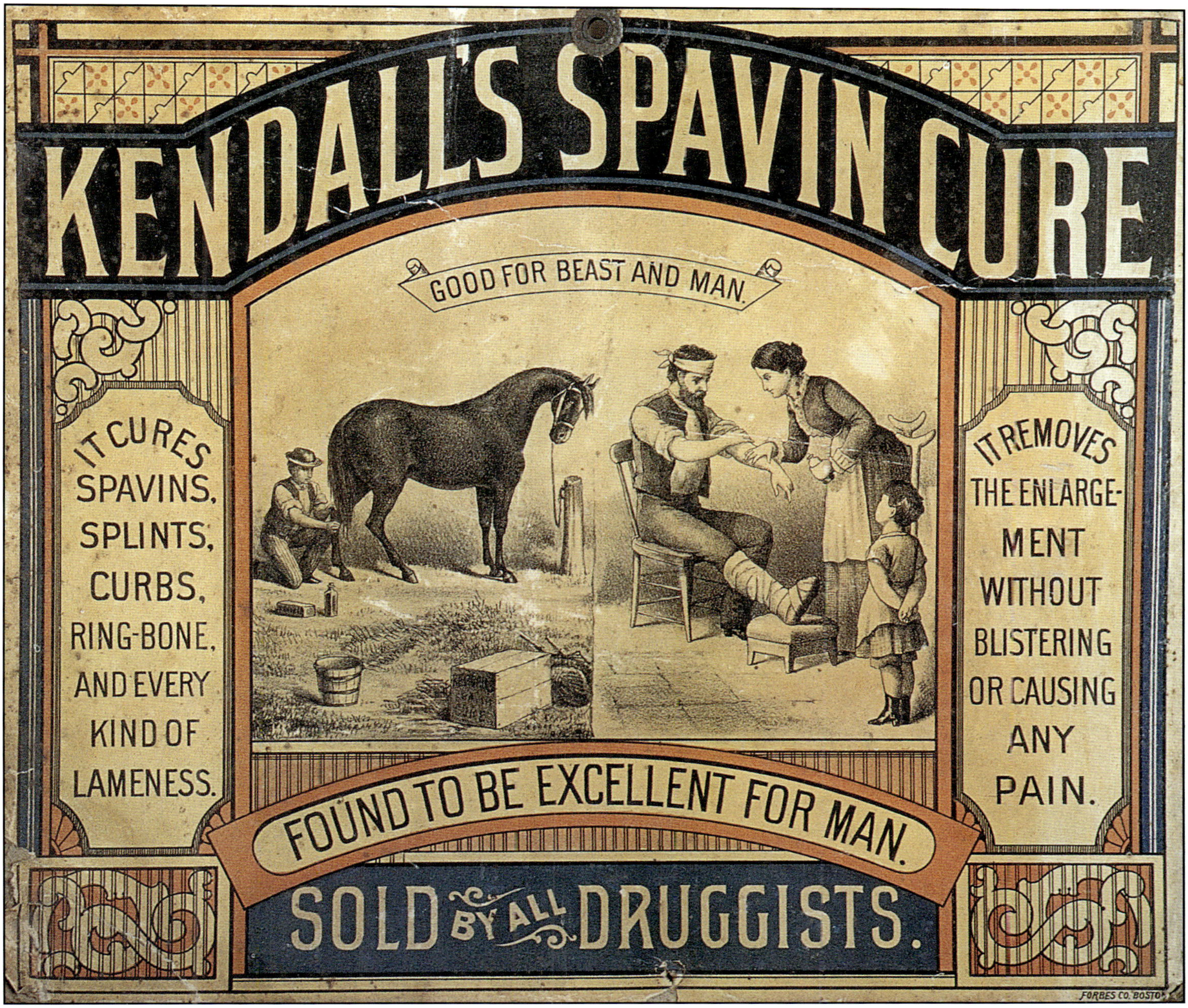

Advertising sign, Forbes Co., Boston, 9.25" x 12". $550-750

Cardboard, great image. $100-150

Impressive cardboard litho featuring an electric trolley. 51" long. $300-450

Sign, 10.5" x 15.5", cardboard, for Eveready Battery. $100-150

An early action scene on paper litho. $50-100

Tin lithographed sign, a definite classic. 18" x 40". $750-900

True cutting edge advertising. 9.75" x 19.75". $125-175

Another direct ad statement that really works on sight and mind. $60-90

A company that placed a lot of money into their ad campaign, and, although not nearly as successful as Coca-Cola, they are still around today. $175-250

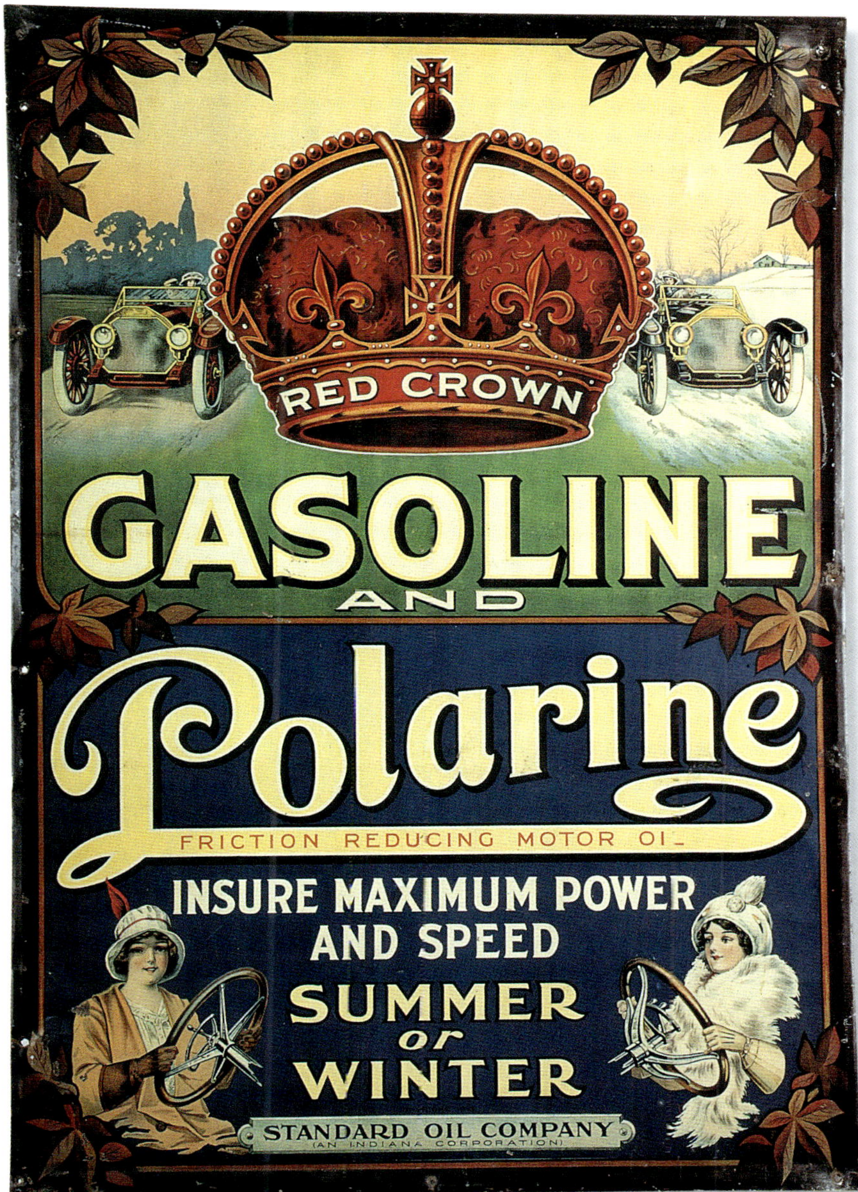

Spectacular graphics. Litho tin advertising sign, 27.5" x 19". $500-750

Yet another example of the mastery of the advertising artist. $100-125

Die-cuts were very effective eye catchers. $50-75

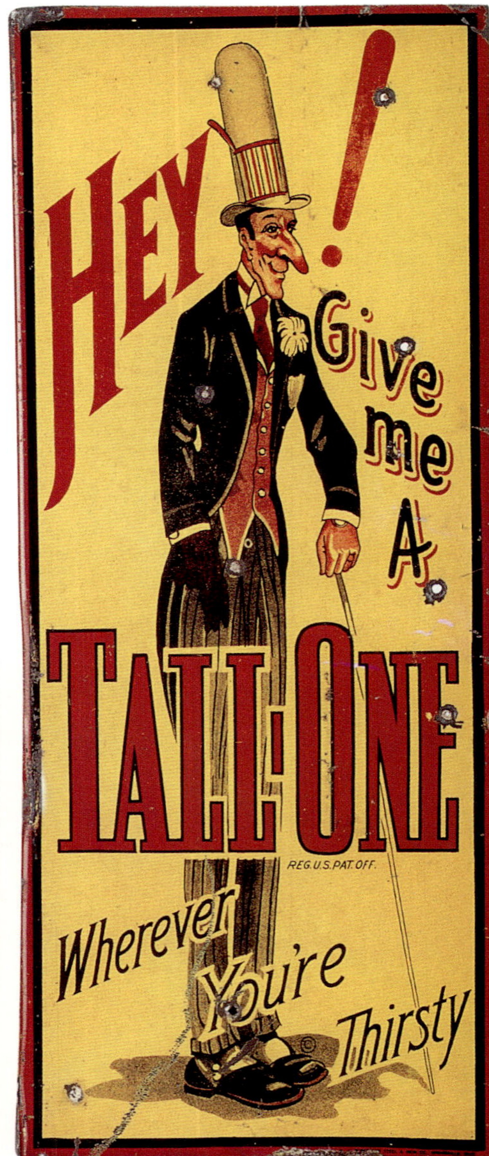

Advertising sign, Robertson Steel & Iron Co., Springfield, Ohio, two-sided, metal, 12" x 5". $125-175

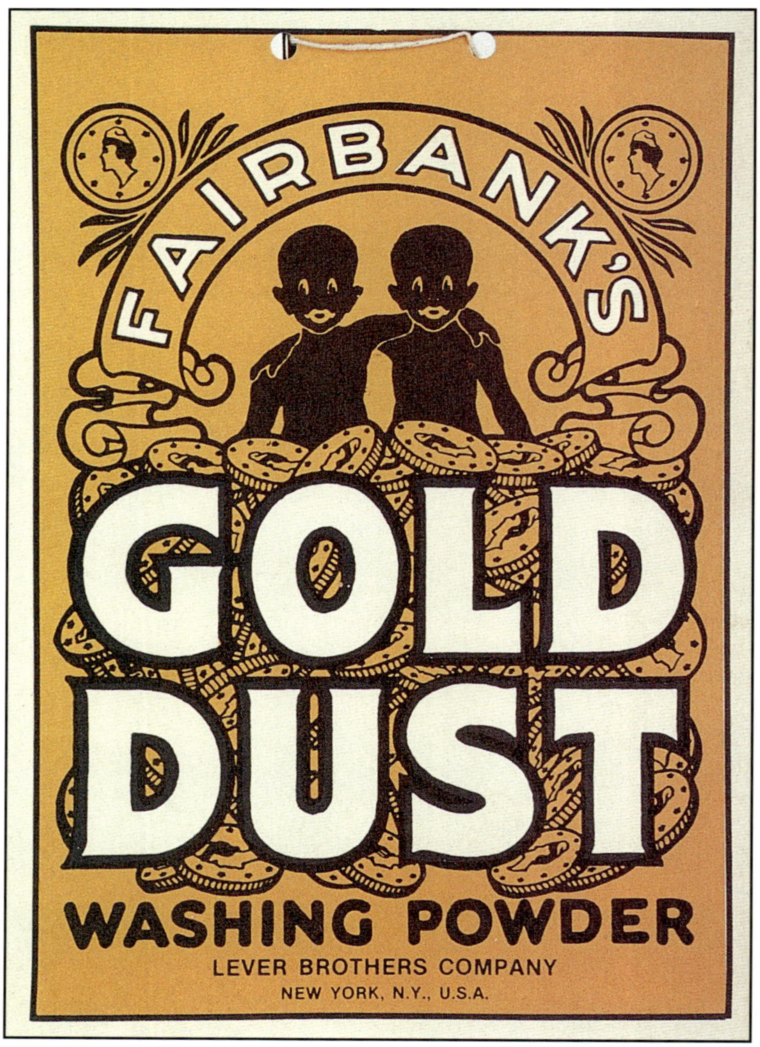

A very creative ad copy and a very popular sign with collectors today. $100-150

Advertising sign, The Henderson-Achert-Krebs Lith. Co., Cincinnati & Chicago, paper, 21" x 13.5". $125-175

Porcelain sign. 9" x 13". $200-350

Sign, 6" x 9", card stock. Forthoffer's Cola / Dole's Pineapple juice, standing display. $50- 75

Both pages: A potpourri of the mastery of art in advertising through simple calendars to large scaled signs.

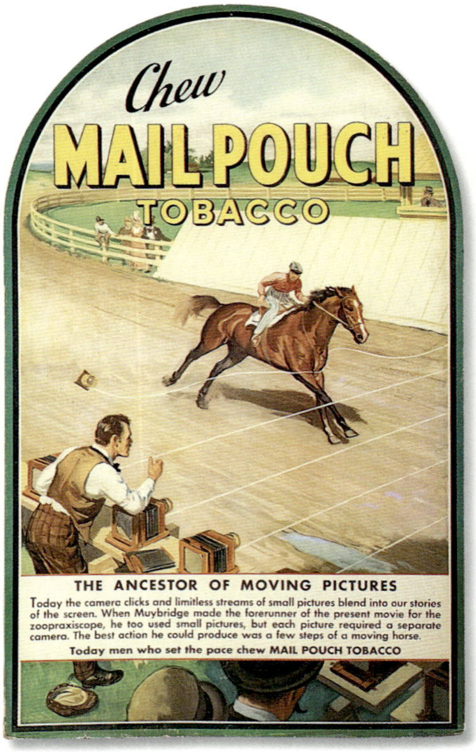

DONALD KENNEDY
KENNEDY'S MEDICAL DISCOVERY
AN ANGEL OF MERCY IN EVERY HOUSEHOLD
CURES SCROFULA, ERYSIPELAS, SCALDHEAD, SALTRHEUM, LEPRA, SCURVY, PIMPLES, ULCERS, CANKER AND EVERY DISEASE OF THE SKIN OF WHATEVER NAME OR NATURE.
ROXBURY MASS

TRIUMPH
NEW CLIPPER
D.S. MORGAN & CO.
MANUFACTURERS
Brockport, N.Y. & Chicago, Ill. U.S.A.

SHARPLES
SEPARATOR
1920 FEBRUARY 1920
SUN MON TUE WED THU FRI SAT
1 2 3 4 5 6 7
8 9 10 11 12 13 14
15 16 17 18 19 20 21
22 23 24 25 26 27 28
29

CUSTER'S LAST FIGHT.
The Original Painting has been presented to the Seventh Regiment U.S. Cavalry
ANHEUSER-BUSCH, St. Louis, Missouri, U.S.A.
WORLD'S LARGEST BREWERY
Home of BUDWEISER and other ANHEUSER-BUSCH FINE BEERS

F. and P. DEPT. RECORD.

IT IS NEVER TOO HOT OR TOO COLD
FOR THE MAN WITH A THERMOS BOTTLE
212° ABOVE ZERO
10° BELOW ZERO
COPYRIGHT 1908 BY AMERICAN THERMOS BOTTLE CO. N.Y.

OSBORNE ALMANAC AND ENCYCLOPEDIA
INTERNATIONAL HARVESTER COMPANY OF AMERI
(INCORPORATED)
CHICAGO U S A
I H C ALMANAC AND ENCYCLOPEDIA
INTERNATIONAL HARVESTER LINES
THE BEGINNING AND THE END OF LIFE
Presented by
WILLIAM DEERING & CO. Chicago, Ill.
GRAIN & GRASS MACHINERY

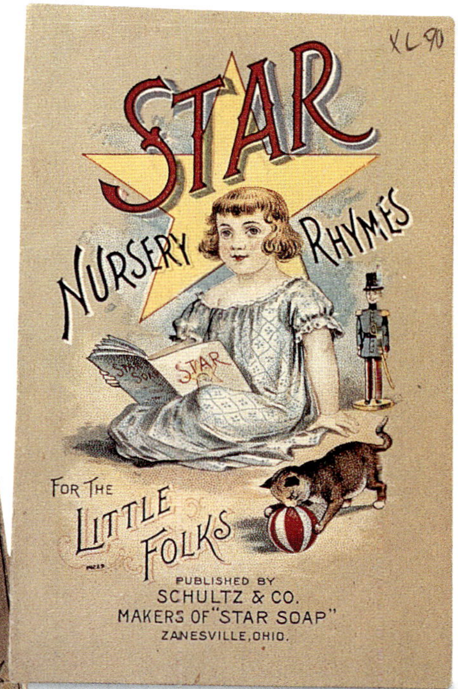

Both pages: A different type of mastery in booklet form, and drawn to lure in the consumer. $25-40

CORK
DISTILLERIES Co
LTD
WHISKY
PURE POT STILL
OLD IRISH WHISKY
CORK DISTILLERIES Co
GUARANTEED 10 YEARS OLD
PURE POT STILL WHISKY
CORK DISTILLERIES Co
IRELAND
JURORS AWARD - "VERY FINE FULL FLAVOR & GOOD SPIRIT."
JURORS AWARD - "UNQUESTIONABLY AS FINE A SPECIMEN AS ONE COULD WISH TO SEE."

BRILLIANTSHINE
Cleans & Polishes all Metals easily!
Aluminum Brass Copper Nickel
THE WORLD IS BOUND TO
J. W. Bennett's
BRILLIANTSHINE
METAL POLISH
MADE IN U.S.A.
PRODUCES THE BRIGHTEST AND MOST

Both pages: More classic examples of great early advertising signs.

An appropriate ad for every year, especially in the welcoming of the third millennium.

Chapter Two

It's All in the Name

In addition to great graphic appeal, the target product always needs a catchy name: one that just can't be forgotten and is easily recognized at a glance. Names were sometimes made to closely relate to everyday conversational colloquialisms or idiomatic expressions. This technique made it possible for people to mention a product's name without any subliminal triggers. Clever wording, common language, and the hook for free advertisement was in place. The following chapter highlights many of the popular brand products, and the many slogans associated with their success. We are instantly able to measure the success of some of these companies, as the products are still popular today, and their names have become household words.

The importance of a company's name is paramount to its longevity. Names that were too long or too difficult to pronounce were simply ignored by customers. Nobody likes to ask for a product they can't pronounce. Some of the trade names became so popular and familiar, that just the copy on a nicely framed tin or porcelain sign was enough of a draw for its purchase. Judge for yourself as to which signs have the appeal to make you give them a second stare, a concentrated study, or a quick dismissal of unimportance, and remember, this is exactly how we shopped a hundred years ago.

The letters are easy to remember–SSS, and the slogan is a natural in ordinary conversation. $40-60

The sign spells success, and is pictured here with a rich looking tin litho product can. $20-30

A classic product with an almost unforgettable name. This company utilizes extensive advertising signs and die-cuts in their fight for prosperity. These boxes may range from $35-75

A name that mentions the product's properties, a natural ad trick. $40-75

Two products with powerful names that reek of importance. $100-$200

The perfect advertising sign in every sense of the word. 32" x 14", porcelain enamel, die cut, Independent Lock Co. Fitchburg, Mass. $150-200

This ad box would have been impossible to miss in the store. Pan-Handle Scrap Tobacco box. 16.5" x 11" x 5". $150-250

Both pages: A few examples of "its all in a name." Which of these products can you quickly note are still a part of our everyday vocabulary?

SUN OILS
SUNOCO
THE DISTILLED OIL

ASK FOR
STERLING
MOTOR OIL
TRADE MARK
REG.U.S.PAT.OFF.
QUALITY
MEMBER OF PENNSYLVANIA GRADE CRUDE OIL ASSOCIATION
Guaranteed
100% PURE
PENNSYLVANIA
OIL
PERMIT NO. 1
Made from the highest grade crude oil in the world
THE BEST OIL IN ANY CASE

Sales and Service
Ford AND Fordson
Cars Trucks and Tractors

AGENCY
CHASE & SANBORN'S
TEAS AND COFFEES

INTERNATIONAL
MOTOR TRUCKS
C. I. LAUDENSLAGER & SONS
VALLEY VIEW, PA.

ROAD HORSE POWER
DEFIANCE
MOTOR TRUCKS

POLARINE
OIL AND GREASES
BEST MOTOR LUBRICANTS

Both pages: No need for fancy graphics here, these products have earned the trust of shoppers for some time now. $50-100. Auto signs done in porcelain command higher prices, and are actively sought by collectors.

Signs with a real message

Finish the oatmeal and read some copy. $35-50

How cold it was gave rise to a hot new item. $200-500

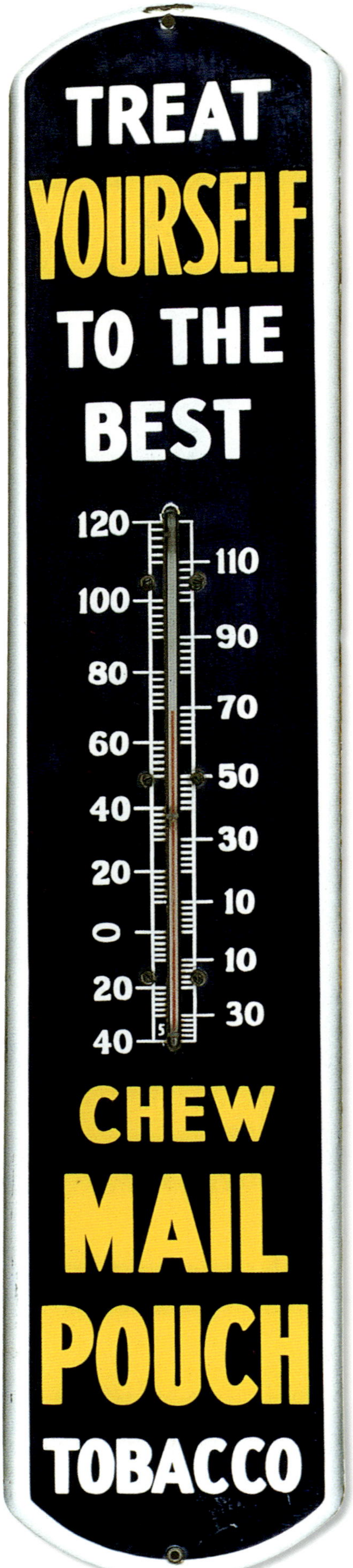

A popular and useful item to advertise a product. Tin litho ad tray. $300-500

Great images were possible on simple beer trays. $300-500

It would be difficult to miss the advertising message on these large trifold panels. Recognize the name? Probably not, maybe it was the ad?

The name is catchy, and kind of makes you want to know what's on the following pages.

Another simple, yet effective ad with eye appealing graphic image. $30-45

Wall hanging tobacco dispenser.
10.5" x 4.25". $75-125

Travel maps with real direction.

The possibilities for advertising on calendars was only limited to the imagination of the designer. 7.5" x 15.5", die cut cardboard, Campbell Grocery, 1909 calendar. $35-45

Nice image of auto, but can it be found at dealerships today?

A perfect example of the package selling the product.

This clever design could be used on a door push insuring every customer saw it on their way in.

An expensive sign whose image needs no copy. $300-400

Produce price guide, and made for plenty of stares. 12" x 7".

An outrageous point of purchase display for Armour's Quality Products. Cardboard. 30" x 76". $500+

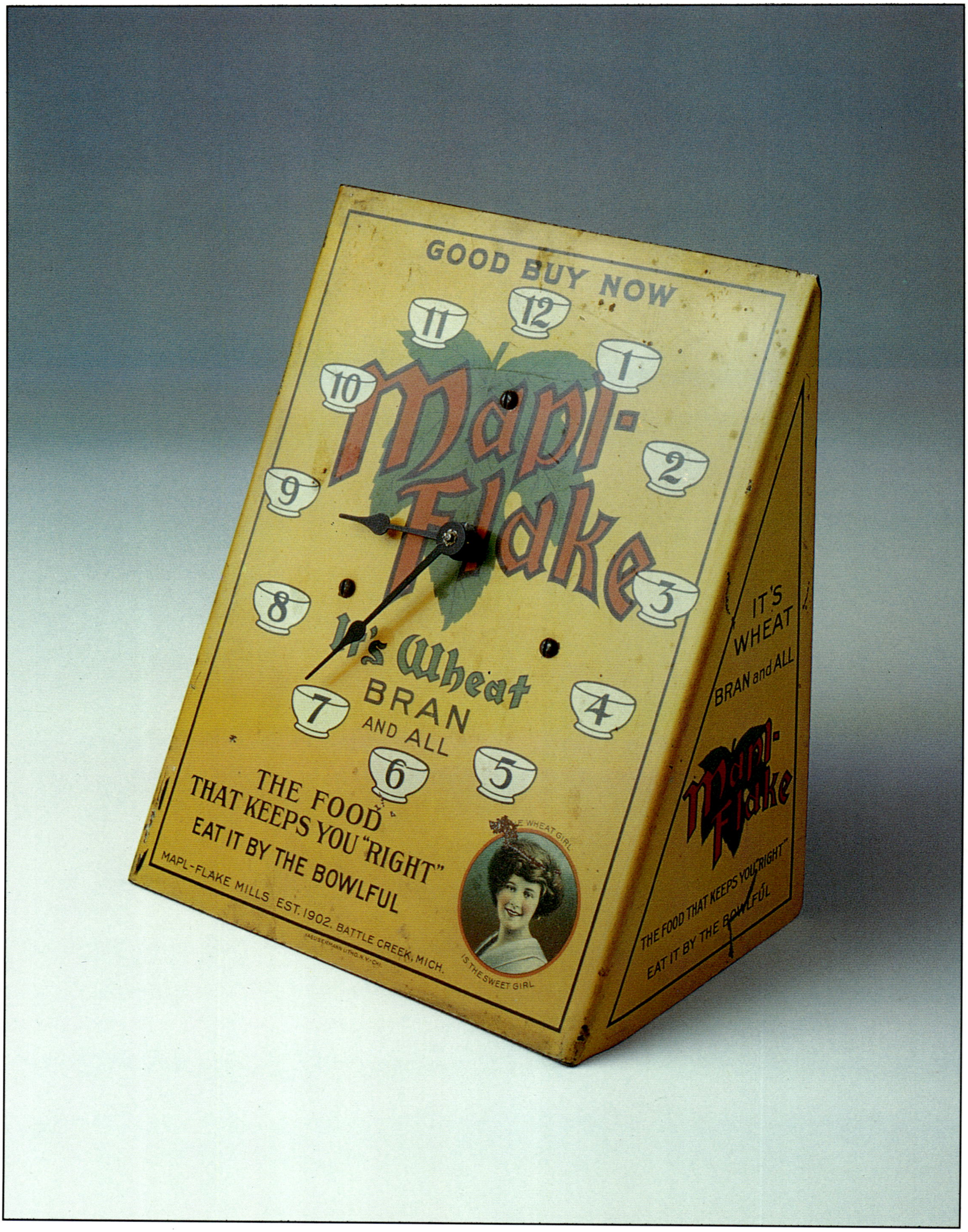

Clock advertising Mapl-Flake, "The Food That Keeps You 'Right'." Haeusermann Litho. N.Y.-Chicago. Lithographed tin. 8.5" x 6.75" x 4". $200-300

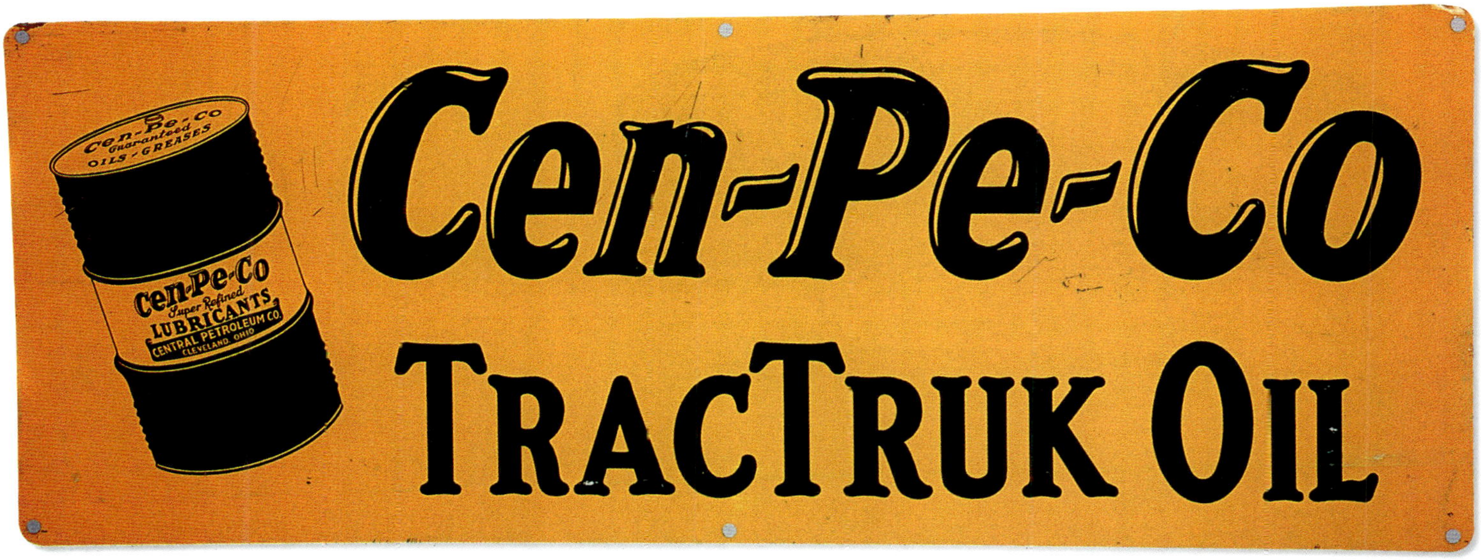

Obviously a very wordy name, and one that has been forgotten. $20-35

Not all signs were to sell a product, but to the point indeed.

Great execution of a simple ad drawing with plenty of draw. $35-45

A depiction not likely to be confused with any other product. $25-35

A simple camera box : transformed into a visual attraction. $100-125

The shapes of things to help the eye and the buyer remember the item.

Three of Bob Lyon's most appealing advertising products, and certainly family favorites.

All in a name continues with this now famous cereal ad sign. Simple, not flashy, but lets us know that food is serious and should not be anything more. $100-150

Great visuals with no confusion. Sign/box label, 11" x 8", paper, Hustler Brand. $25-35

Both pages: Classic signs that pack a big visual punch. $100-250

Power-lube
MOTOR OIL
SMOOTH AS THE TREAD OF A TIGER
Guaranteed
100% PURE
PENNSYLVANIA
OIL
PERMIT Nº127

BARNEY
OLDFIELD
TIRES
SERVICE STATION

FRED'K GAMASH
AUTOMOBILES
GENERAL SUPPLIES
FORD PARTS
NEWPORT · N. H.

L. P. CHARPIOT HDWE.
WEST UNITY - OHIO
GOOD YEAR TIRES
AUTO SUPPLIES

Overland
TRADE MARK REG.
Service
TINKELPAUGH BROS.
COBLESKILL

SCHENCK MFG. & SUPPLY CO.
PARKERS LANDING
AUTOMOBILE
SUPPLIES & REPAIRS
PREST-O-LITE

Both pages: A nice grouping of signs that lack in graphic appeal, but excel in name alone. $75-150.

This sign says it all. Price, properties, and powerful product name. 14" x 10", embossed tin, Colt Acetylene generators. $75-125

Both pages: Shaped for attention. Paper litho ads made to fit anywhere, or used as handouts. $25-50

Both pages: These flange signs were very useful for awkward walls or special attention. $75-125

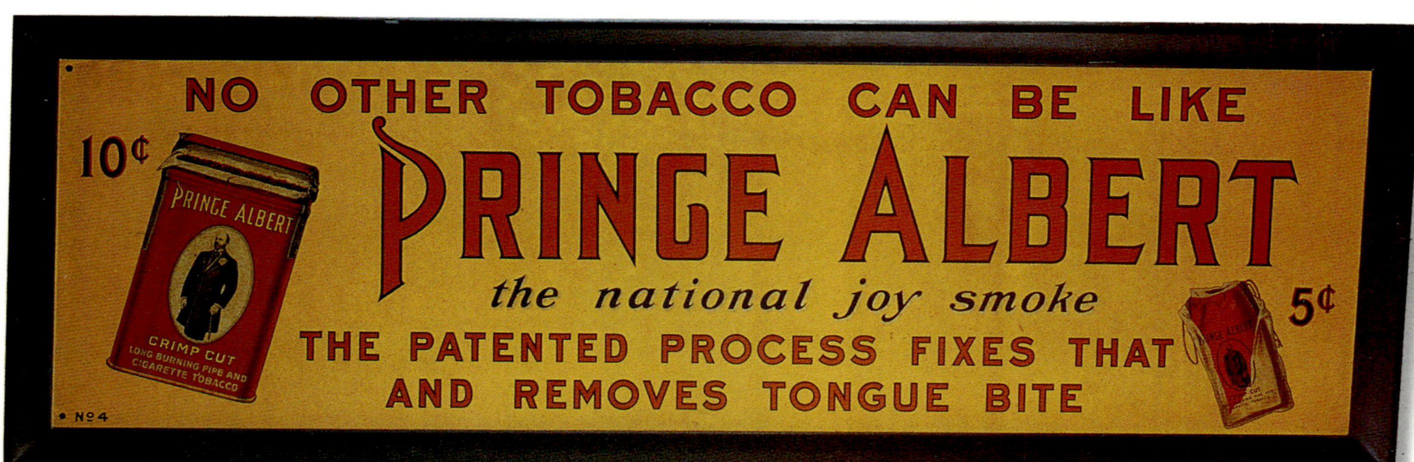

GAY COCK
BRAND
Stanley Levinson Co.
LOS ANGELES, CALIFORNIA

The R. OVENS BRANCH
·U·S· BAKING CO.
CAKES
CRACKERS
BISCUITS
TRADE MARK
159 to 167
·BUFFALO·N·Y·
ELLICOTT ST.

The Worlds Greatest Fire Insurance Company
FIRE THEFT COLLISION
AUTOMOBILE INSURANCE
WE HOLD THEE SAFE
ROYAL
INSURANCE
COMPANY
LIMITED
AUTO
INSUR

"The axes of the world are Collins" is a powerful ad statement that makes me want to buy one! $75-125

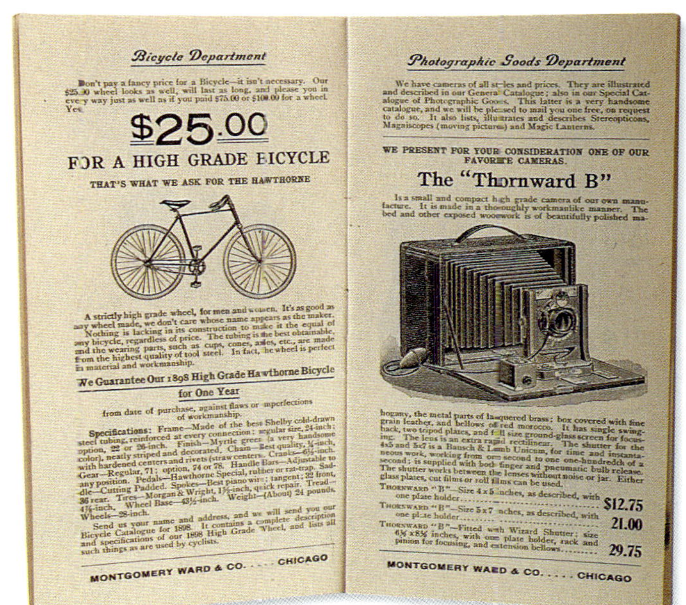

Both pages: The advantage of paper advertising was the ability to fold and crease in order to add that third dimension to the visual effect. $15-35

A captivating ad, and close-up of the extensive detail to the artwork. $20-30

While photo images may make effective ads, they don't feature the same crispness as the following paper litho ads.

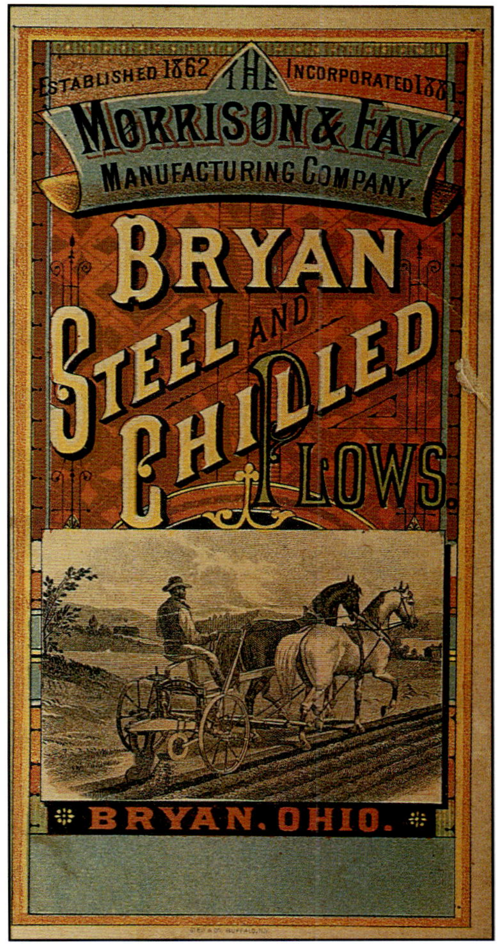

It doesn't get any finer in detail.

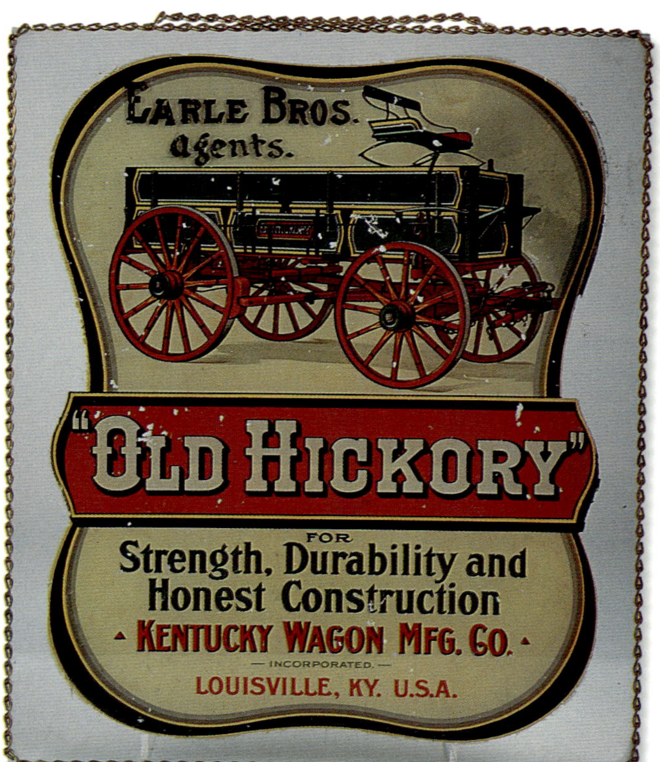

Both pages: The proper use of color and the many faces that a subtle change in the artists palate was capable of creating.

GGS
TO-DAY
2 9
CENTS
OW KING
KING POWDER
d Baking Powder since 1873."

KETCH-ALL
AUTOMATIC MOUSE TRAP
WORLD'S BEST ··· NO BAIT NEEDED!
CATCHES UP TO 15 MICE IN ONE SETTING
Wind and place trap with either entrance two inches from wall or object
KNESS MANUFACTURING CO. ALBIA IOWA
PAT. NO. 4233918

MICHIGAN AVENUE
MATA
U.S. 112
TOURIST ASSOCIATION

Examples of lithographed celluloid backed mirrors: the perfect company handout. $75-175

Place yourself in this ad . $75-125

The true definition of an ad campaign.

A chance to interact with the ad, pull on the string to see what will pop-out. $50-75

Book marked for advertising success. $75-150

Spending time at the store just browsing through the latest catalogs must have been a part time job.

Both pages: There was no end to the placement of advertising on ordinary objects. From a glass ashtray, to a child's train car, to the surface of boxes and pamphlets, society changes, but the need to read with our eyes never changes.

"SCANDINAVIA"
TRANSMISSION LINING
for FORD CARS
"SCANDINAVIA"
P.O.B. No 20
"One-Shot"
GAUGE FLUID
GUARANTEED CORRECT GRAVITY NON FADING
DIRECTIONS — TAKE ONE
ALEMITE
High pressure lubricating system
Special for Ford Automobiles
A product of THE BASSICK MANUFACTURING CO. Chicago, Illinois

HORSES, FARM AND PREPARAT
M.W. SAVAGE
INTERNATIONAL STOCK FOOD FACTORY
INTERNATIONAL STOCK FOOD COMPANY, Minneapolis, Minn.
CAPITAL PAID IN - $2,000,000
THE FIVE FASTEST
INTERNATIONAL STOCK FOOD CO.
MINNEAPOLIS, MINN. U.S.A.
3 FEEDS FOR ONE CENT
INTERNATIONAL STOCK FOOD
80% NET PROFIT
25 LARGE ILLUSTRATED STOCK BOOKS FREE.
ALSO $7.50 VALUE IN
TWO $3.75 NEW HORSE BOOKS FREE
IF YOU ORDER A $50 BILL BY RETURN MAIL

Chapter Three

Store Goods & Curious Stock Items

I call this the curiosity chapter because it certainly contains the items used in a more primitive, though still advancing society. The gadgets and products of the country store were sometimes promoted with a bigger budget then the actual cost of the ingredients, but that practice hasn't necessarily slowed down today either. What has changed though, is the information available to us as buyers of millions of products. Without the advantage of multimedia, young America was held hostage, in a sense, to the look of a product or the promise of its ease. This creates the chuckle effect when we examine some of these primitively styled contraptions, and we wonder how anyone could have been sold on its worthiness. We have come a long way, but, really, is their anyone who hasn't been trapped by a magic product billed on TV as the next wonder of the world, only to have it thrown into the trash after one or two uses? Don't feel bad or stupid, it's the allure of good advertising and, as buyers, we have never changed that much over the years. And we examine some of the merchandise that makes collecting early country store items a contagious habit.

Both pages: A quick entry with some canned good selections. $20-40

Pratts
POULTRY REGULATOR
ABSOLUTELY PURE
PRATTS POULTRY REGULATOR
MAKES LITTLE CHICKS GROW FAST
and develops them into
BIG LAYERS.
KEEPS FOWLS HEALTHY.
A SAFE REMEDY FOR
THEIR COMMON AILMENTS.
Pratts
Poultry Regulator
SUPPLEMENTAL MINERALS
A TONIC

HOOVEN
BLACK LABEL
TRIDENT TRADE MARK
CORN FLAKES
The Hooven Mercanti
DISTRIBUTORS
QUAKER
BRAND
PUFFED
RICE
Steam Explodec
8 times Normal Si
The Quaker Oats Company
Georgie
Porgie
Cereal
Kellogg's
TOASTED
CORN
FLAKES
THE ORIGINAL HAS THIS SIGNATURE
W.K. Kellogg
KELLOGG TOASTED CORN FLAKE CO.
BATTLE CREEK, MICH.
The sweetheart of the corn

MAKES EVERY WOMAN HAPPY
You Can Iron Dandy With
STARCH
TRADE MARK
IRON-DANDY
POLISH
CHAS. H. RATH CO., INC.
MANUFACTURING CHEMISTS
1347 North Front St., PHILADELPHIA, PA., U. S. A.
NO COOKING
NO STICKING
IVORY
TRADE MARK
REGISTERED
QUALITY FAR IN EXCESS OF OTHER STARCHES
STARCH
A MODERN INVENTION
PREPARED ON SCIENTIFIC PRINCIPLES
BEWARE OF IMITATIONS
THE BEATTY STARCH CO.
NEW HAVEN, CONN.

Both pages: And a few boxed goods. $20-50

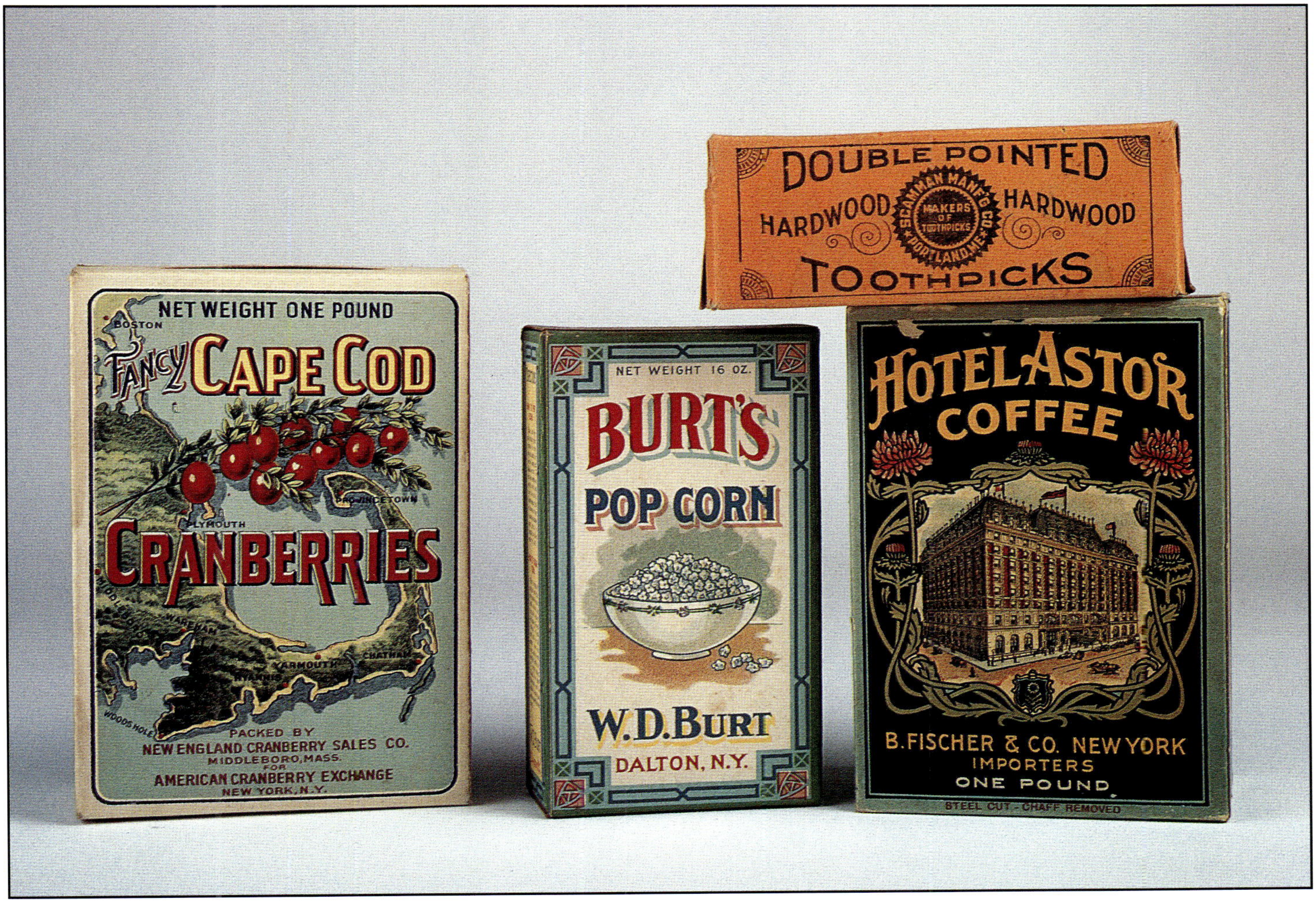

ECONOMY
HOD
ROBINSON'S PAT.
BATCHELOR
SAL-VET
BRAND
LICE POWDER
For LICE And MITES
Standard
Lice Killer
FOR DESTROYING VERMIN ON POULTRY AND ALL DOMESTIC ANIMALS.
60¢
KRONKINE
FEVERS AND INFLAMMATORY DISEASES OF HORSES
BUFFALO, N.Y.

GET RID
INSECT POWDER
FIVE IN ONE
FLIES, FLEAS,
COCKROACHES
BED BUGS,
ANTS
WHAT IS
Kill 'Em
F-L-U-I-D
Active Ingredients:
Kerosene, Carbon Tetrachloride,
Paradichlorbenzene, Cresylic Acid,
Methyl Salicylate.
BREWER & COMPANY, INC.
ONE PINT
BELL'S
KIL-ZEM
LIQUID
PRICE 35¢
QUICKLY DESTROYS BED BUGS
ROACHES AND MANY OTHER INSECTS
AND THEIR EGGS
BELL CHEMICAL CO.
CHICAGO, U.S.A.
Edgar A. Murray's
DOOM
Kills
FLIES
MOSQUITOES
MOTHS, ANTS, FLEAS,
BED BUGS & ROACHES
BUG

Both pages: A look at the mixed mediums of product packaging. From tin to glass, everything was either colorful or ornately embossed. $25-125

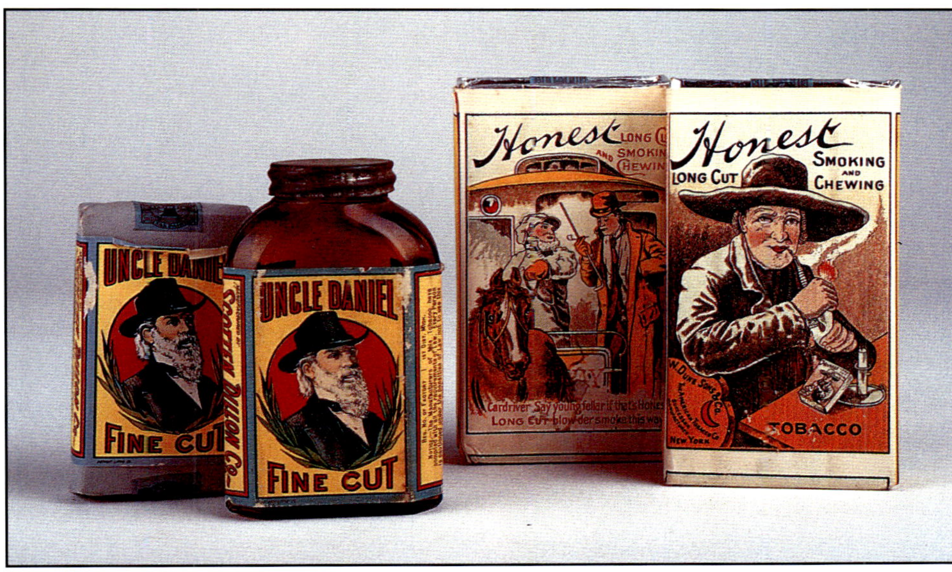

Both pages: Covering products with colorful paper litho images was inexpensive and very easy to manufacture. $25-45

TALL BOY
VEGETABLE SOUP
HEART OF INDIANA
BRAND
DISTRIBUTED BY
JOHN S. MITCHELL, INC.
WINDFALL, IND.
General Jackson
MORGAN PACKING CO. AUSTIN, IND
FIRST QUALITY
PACKED BY
REEVES, PARVIN & CO.
BARE FOOT BOY
PACKED BY
NEW FEDERAL CANNING Co.
FRANKFORT, INDIANA.

THE ARGO
CAP MANTLE
UNITED
MANTLE

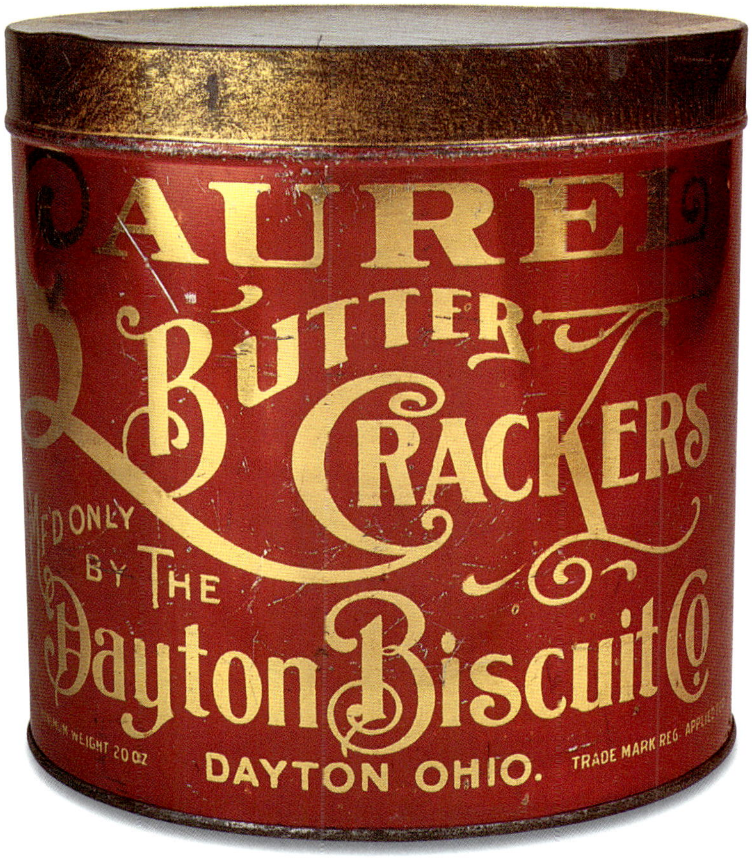

BUTTER CRACKERS
BY THE
Dayton Biscuit Co
DAYTON OHIO.

IMPERIAL
SHOE
POLISH
CROWN
DRESSING
FOR
LADIES AND
CHILDRENS
BOOTS & SHOES
TRAVELLING BAGS
&c. &c.
PREPARED BY
FRANK MILLER
& SONS.
NEW YORK
BROWN'S
CIRAGE FRANCAIS
OR
FRENCH
DRESSING
FOR
LADIES' AND
CHILDREN'S
BOOTS & SHOES,
TRUNKS, HARNESS,
CARRIAGE TOPS &C.
MANUFACTURED BY
B. F. Brown
BOSTON, MASS.
BLACK
CAT
SHOE
DRESSING
FOR ALL
LADIES
AND
CHILDRENS
SHOES
MANUFACTURED BY
THE
Black Cat Polish Co.
BUFFALO, N.Y.
A Renovator
for all
Cordovan Shoes
MASON'S
CORDOVAN SHINE
CLEANER
JAS. S. MASON CO.
PHILADELPHIA, PA.

GLO-
REG. U.S. PAT. OFF.
REG. TRADE MARK
ALUMINUM
Cleanser and Polisher
Makes Utensils Glow
GLO
Makes
Utensils
Glow

Both pages: The bottled selection was also quite inviting. $20-40

Mayo's
Cut
Plug
TRADE MARK
MAYO'S
TOBACCO
IS ALWAYS GOOD
REG'D SEPT. 1878
FOR SMOKING AND CHEWING

OJIBWA
FINE CUT
MANUFACTURED BY
SCOTTEN DILLON CO.,
DETROIT, MICH.
DARK
OJIBWA
FINE CUT
CHEWING TOBACCO
SCOTTEN-DILLON CO.
DETROIT, MICH.
OJIBWA
DARK FINE CUT
TOBACCO
SCOTTEN DILLON CO., DETROIT, MICH.

BRIGHT
TIGER
CHEWING TOBACCO
5 CENT PACKAGES
BRIGHT
TIGER
CHEWING TOBACCO
5 CENT PACKAGES
TIGER
CHEWING TOBACCO
5 CENT PACKAGES

Both pages: Tobacco tins and large store bins are probably the most collected of all the early country store products. The variety is unending. $75-500

A mix of early boxed merchandise makes for a great start-up country collection. $10-20

Many collectors are hooked on boxed only toys. Early dominos, $20-30

A simple bottle of cleaner polish with these graphics becomes highly collectible, and still very affordable for all levels of collectors. 4" h. $20-35

The size and uniqueness of these two wooden oil barrels with taps can add instant variety to a collection 10.5", 13.25". $50-100

EAT IT FOR HEALTH
FLEISCHMANN'S YEAST
KEEP IN REFRIGERATOR
KINGSFORD'S
CORN STARCH
EXPRESSLY FOR FOOD,
T. KINGSFORD & SON.
PERFECTLY PURE.
CORN PRODUCTS REFINING CO.
RED POPPY
BRAND
SELF RISING
BUCKWHEAT
FLOUR
PACKED EXPRESSLY FOR
JAS. P. GALLIGAN & CO.
TAUNTON, MASS.
PURITY
JAPAN
TEA
THE PURE TEA LEAVES
FRANK FORTUNE
JEFFERSON, OHIO
DOVE
BRAND
SELECTED
LEAF
MARJORAM
THE FRANK TEA & SPICE CO.
CINCINNATI, OHIO
WILLIAMS' ROOT BEER
EXTRACT.
STRONGEST AND BEST EXTRACT IN THE WORLD.
WILLIAMS & CARLETON, PROPRIETORS, HARTFORD, CONN.
LILY
GLOSS
STARCH
OTTUMWA STARCH CO. OTTUMWA, IOWA.
GOLDEN RULE
CO.
TEA

NEAR'S
FLY OIL
PROTECTS YOUR STOCK
FROM FLIES, LICE AND VERMIN.
TRADE
MARK
NEAR'S FOOD CO.,
AUBURN, N.Y. U.S.A.
ONE GALLON
KROKEM
FLY SPRAY
KILLS
FLIES
DESTROYS
INSECTS
KELLOGG CHEMICAL COMPANY
5 POUNDS NET WEIGHT
EDGAR A. MURRAY'S
Roach Doom
(TRADE MARK "DOOM" REG. U.S. PATENT OFFICE)
Death to Roaches
Edgar A. Murray Company, Sole Manufacturers
DETROIT, MICH., U.S.A.
PRICE $1.25 PER POUND

Both pages: A potpourri of more co orful and affordable country store advertising tins and cans. $20-25

Both pages: These products couldn't be missed on the shelves. Their size overpowered other products, giving the impression that they were popular enough to be bought in bulk size. The true purpose was simply to advertise at point of purchase. $75-350

5 POUNDS NET WEIGHT WHEN PACKED.
GARLAND
BLEND
COFFEE
DISTRIBUTED BY
SEARS, ROEBUCK AND CO.
CHICAGO.
DALLAS, TEXAS. SEATTLE, WASH.

STANLEY
XMAS
FOR SAFETY SAKE
DEMAND "PROPP"
ELECTRICAL
DECORATIVE SETS
PROPP
XMAS TREE LIGHTING
OUTFIT
with MAZDA LAMPS
For Safety Sake
INDOOR & OUTDOOR
MULTIPLE LIGHTING
OUTFIT
NOMA
Decorative Lighting Outfit
FOR ALL OCCASIONS
GENERAL ELECTRIC
MAZDA
CHRISTMAS TREE
LAMPS

FIVE POUNDS NET
GEAR GREASE
MANUFACTURED EXPRESSLY FOR
PIERCE-ARROW
PACIFIC SALES CO., INC
SAN FRANCISCO, CALIF.
Moreland's
OILS AND GREASES
3 Cup Grease
PARAGON
Peak of Perfection
TRANSMISSION GREASE
TOLEDO, OHIO.
HANCOCK
OLD BLACK JOE
AXLE
GREASE
JOHN HANCOCK OIL CO.
TWIN CITIES

Whiz
ROADSIDE
HAND
CLEANSER
12 FL. OZ.
Whiz
FLY FUME
16 FL. OZS.
NO. 3 SIZE
WHIZ
WHIZ

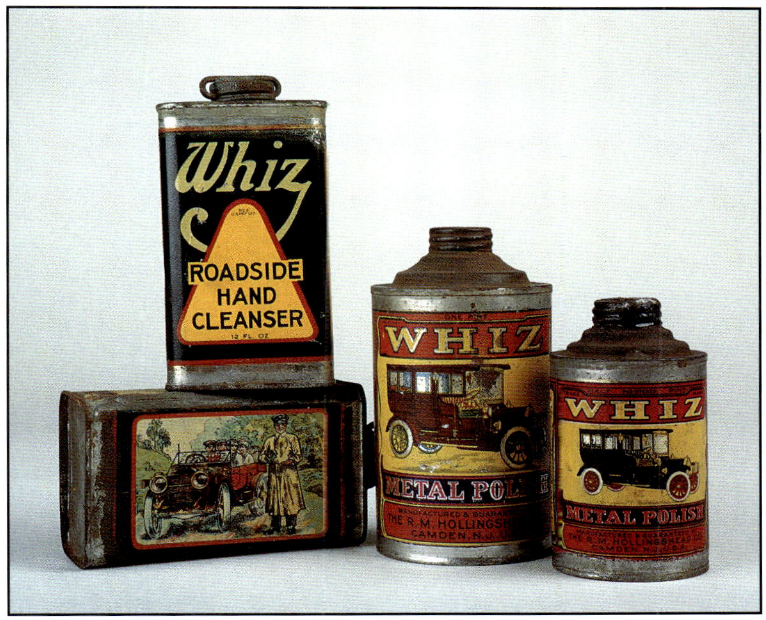

Both pages: This grouping depicts the diversity of the Bob Lyon's country store. The shelves are packed from ceiling to floor, and it gives an accurate detail of yesterday's mall.

Glass jars made popular counter displays, especially when filled with candy or peanuts. $100-175

Both pages: A different sort of candy and peanut vendor. They needed no storekeeper until it was time to refill them. $150-300

Spring 1896.
Special Premium Offer for 1896 see inside cover
Free with each order
John A. Salzer Seed Co., La Crosse, Wisconsin.

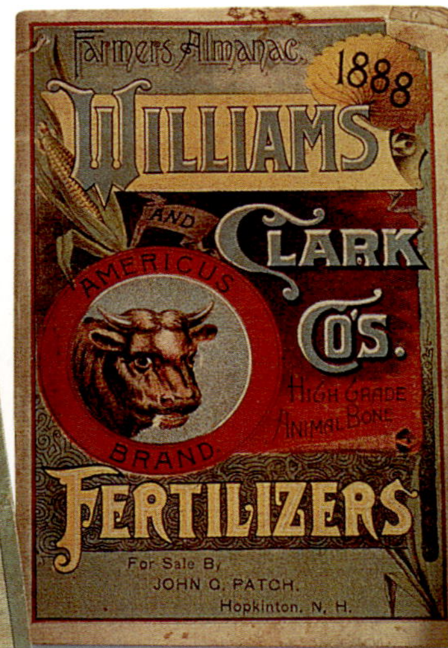
Farmers Almanac.
1888
Williams and Clark Co's.
Americus Brand
High Grade Animal Bone
Fertilizers
For Sale By
JOHN Q. PATCH.
Hopkinton, N. H.

Williams & Clark Fertilizer Co.
High Grade
Animal Bone
Fertilizers

E. R. Durkee & Co's
Gauntlet Spices
Cinnamon
Strictly Pure

Artificial Snow

Both pages: Fancy goods in beautiful boxes made great shelf appeal. $20-50

Both pages: Great tin lithographed canned goods.

A child's book with brilliant cover litho. $20-25

Wolverine Toy Wringer
WOLVERINE TOY WRINGER
Directions
The thumb screws of the clamps should be on the outside of the tub. When fastening to the tub do not screw too tight. Do not forget to put a few drops of oil in oil holes in upper bearing.
MADE ONLY BY
Wolverine Supply & Mfg. Co.
PITTSBURG, PA., U.S.A.

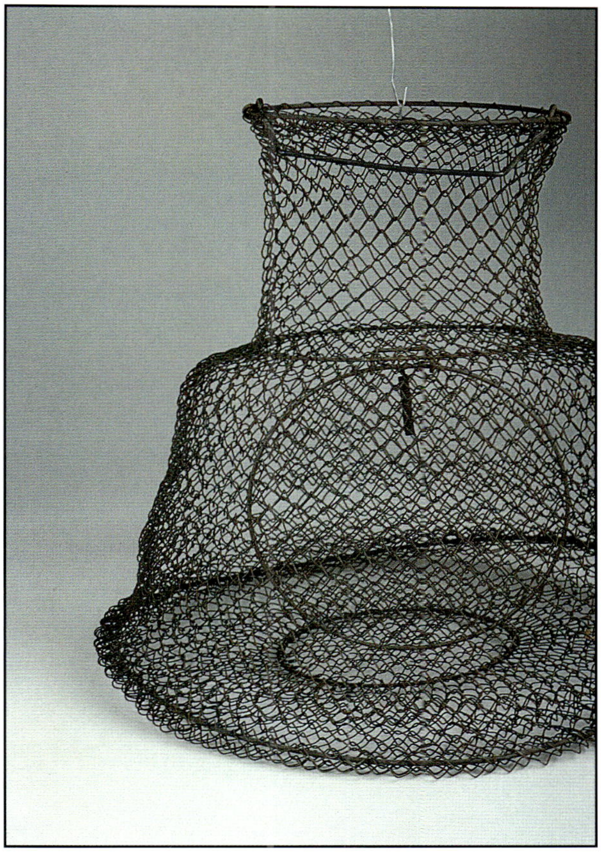

Both pages: A few of the necessities of the home, and always available at the country store. Whether you were planning to net some minnows, make a candle, grate some cheese, or wring out a fresh shirt, these lights could provide the candle power needed.

Maybe a special clock for the home or office. Anything could be advertised on these wall mount units, and it made them appear rather special.

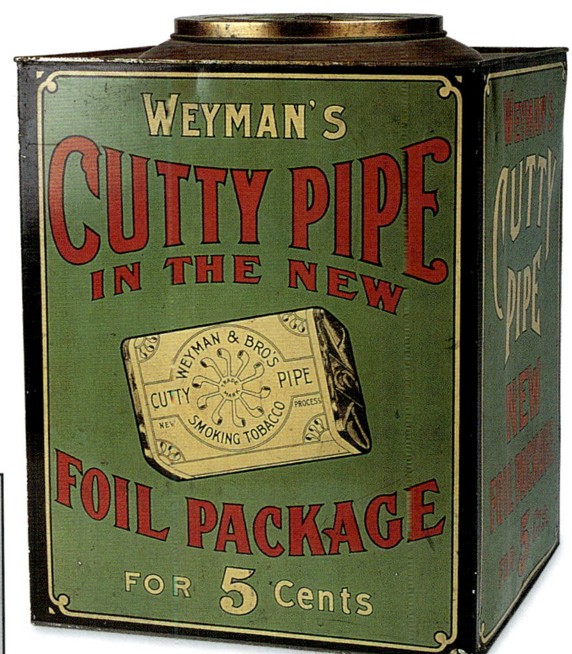

It would be hard to miss these large tobacco tins, even in a well-stocked store. $200-450

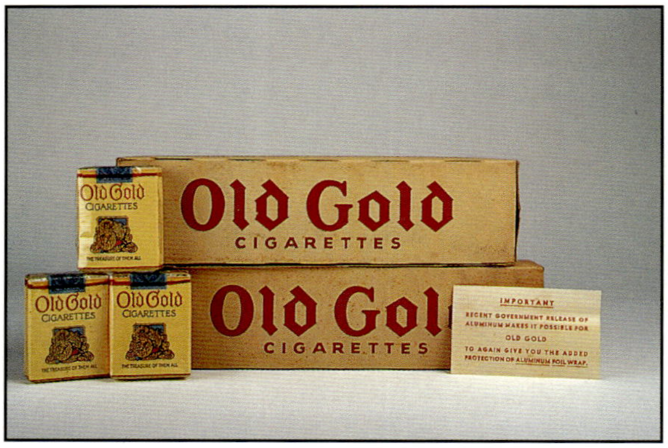

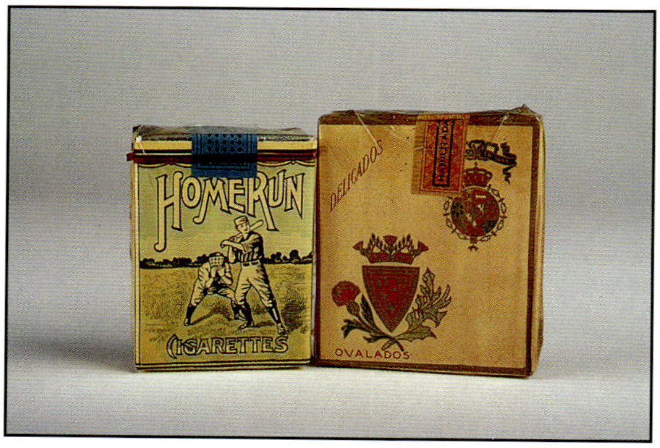

Both pages: American's have found these products quite addicting, and not only for their great packaging. When viewed in such a diverse grouping, it is easy to realize the stiff competition that must have had the giant companies scampering for the country's best artists and package designers. Prices for tin containers still reign king, but the paper covered canvas pouch bags make a most interesting and affordable collection. The examples available are still plentiful, and its curious to note that some companies marketed the same tobacco in varying titles, probably in search of a name that would finally capture the biggest draw.

PEACHEY
RIBBON CUT
SCRAP

CARDINAL
Duke's Mixture
ORPHAN BOY
SMOKING TOBACCO
TRUE SMOKE
LONG TOM
STUD

ARARAT
SAN FELICE
OJIBWA
SAN FELICE
BAGLEY'S
WILD FRUIT
TOBACCO

SPARK PLUG
CHEWING TOBACCO
YANKEE GIRL
PLUG TOBACCO
CHEW
TOBACCO
HORSE SHOE
PENN'S
SPELLS Quality
BRIGHT
CHEWING
TOBACCO
DAYS O WORK
APPLE
Fresh, Juicy and Mild

PIPER HEIDSIECK
CHEWING TOBACCO
CHAMPAGNE FLAVOR
LAREDO
CUT PLUG
OCEANIC
OUR FLAG CUT PLUG
TOBACCO

OCEANIC
PLUG
CIGARETTES

LUCKY STRIKE
CIGARETTES
flat fifties
LUCKY STRIKE
A Merry Christmas

DIXIE QUEEN
PLUG CUT
HUGH CAMPBELL'S
SHAG TOBACCO
DILL'S BEST
SMOKING TOBACCO

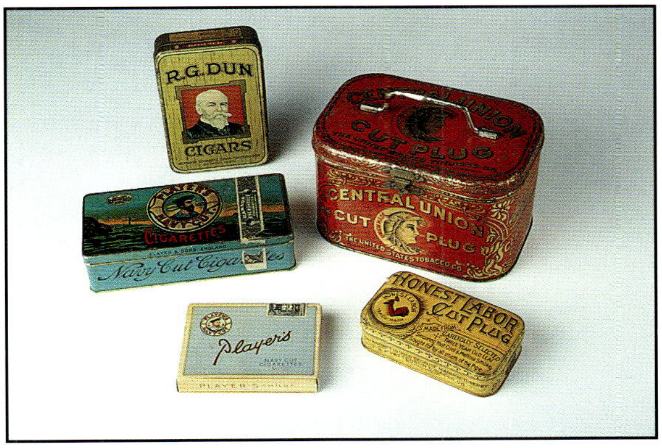
R.G. DUN
CIGARS
CUT PLUG
CENTRAL UNION
CUT PLUG
Navy Cut Cigarettes
Player's
HONEST LABOR
Cut Plug

YALE
SMOKING TOBACCO
BALTIMORE, MD.
YALE
BALTIMORE

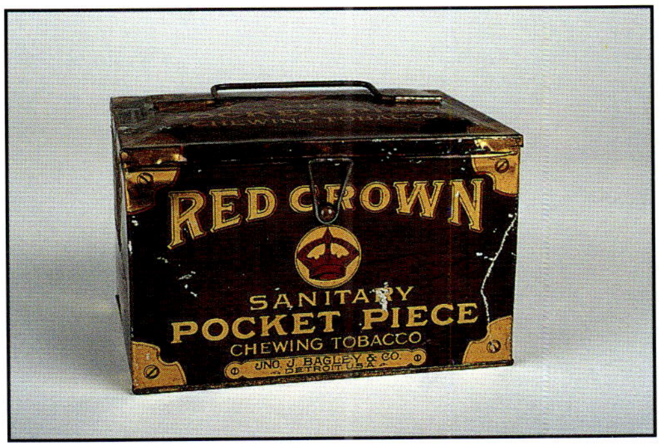
RED CROWN
SANITARY
POCKET PIECE
CHEWING TOBACCO

SMOKE
TOBACCO
SMOKE
TOBACCO

This sleek can of oil could be easily stacked, and not easily missed by a curious eye. $35-45

More colorful paper litho packaging to brighten the shelves. $20-30 each

The product is dull in comparison to the box container. Boot polish $15 each, as a complete box set, $50-75

Even match companies had plenty of ad competition, as demonstrated by these great examples. $10-15

Assortment of jar rubbers and rings made by various companies also competing for a slice of the American consuming pie. $5-15

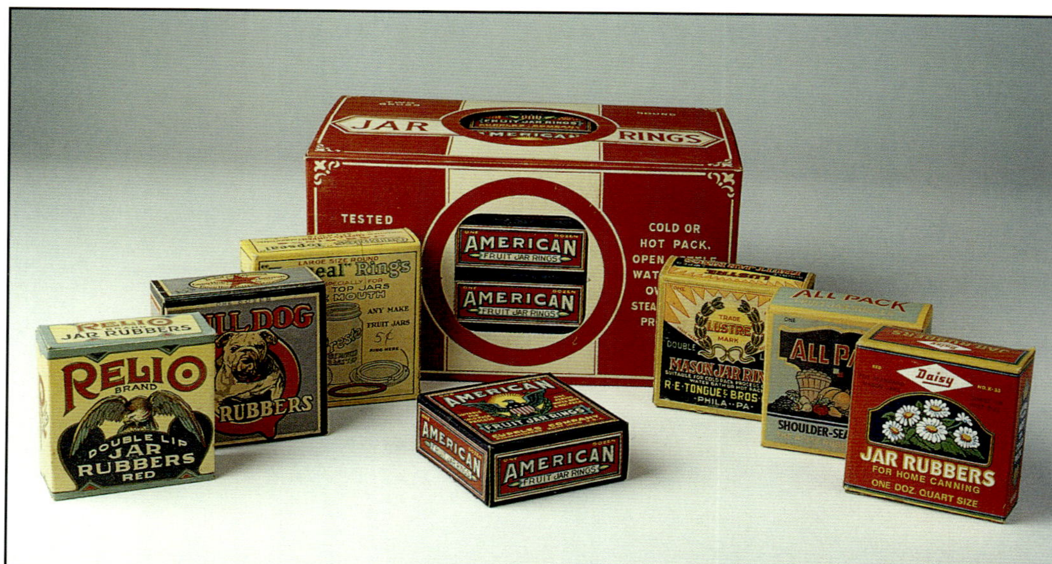

Grouping of assorted rolling papers flashing their own graphic mastery. $5-15

Which repellent would you choose from these two very interesting brands?

Let there be light, and always on hand at the store.

Pair of oil cans, hand painted. Tin. 7.75" high to spout.

Another in the unusual fire-driven devices. Kerosene blowtorch marked The Schneider Trenkamp Co., Cleveland, O. Metal and wood. 11" high.

A different sort of lighting appliance. Gas burner with cast iron base and knobs to adjust height of wicks, Gardner, Massachusetts. 10" x 7.25".

Very useful when natural lighting forces unleashed their own fury. Three lightning rod insulators. $75+ each

A glimpse into the ordinary products that have since been replaced by modern machinery, or improved ingenuity.

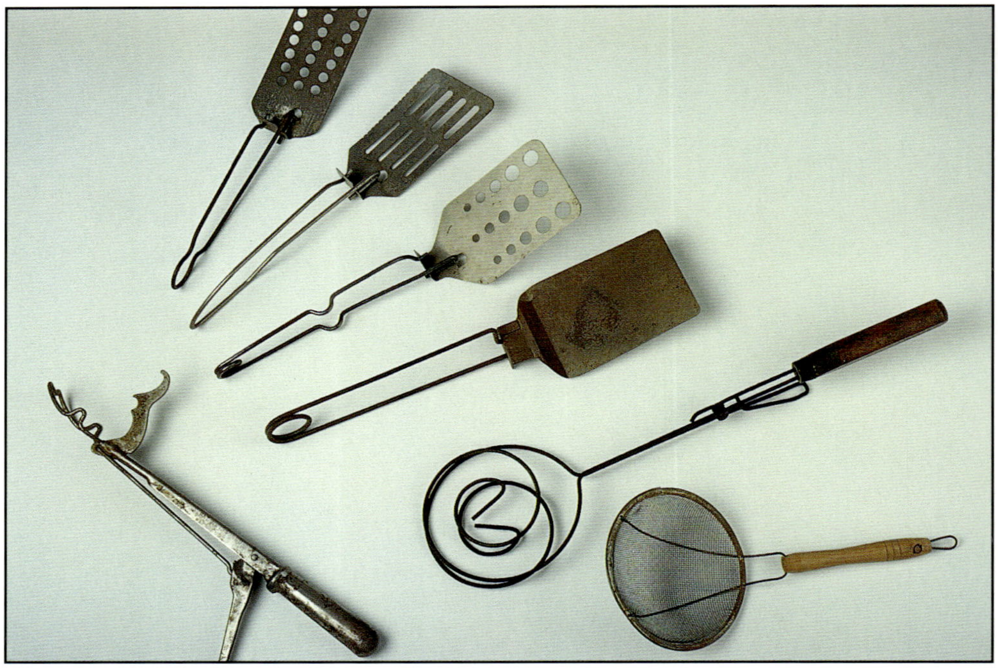

Metal kitchen utensils, in the days before Teflon.

Boot jacks cast in animal designs.

Today's versions of the supermarket vending machines replaced great casting effects with lights and electronic motions, but give me this example any day. Coin operated peanut dispenser, "Smilin' Sam from Alabam The Salted Peanut Man," 13.5".

Imagine the lucky secretary who got to use this model and eliminate trips to the health club in the process. Stapler, marked "Acme No. 2," "Made in U.S.A." Acme Staple Co. Metal. 7" high x 10" long.

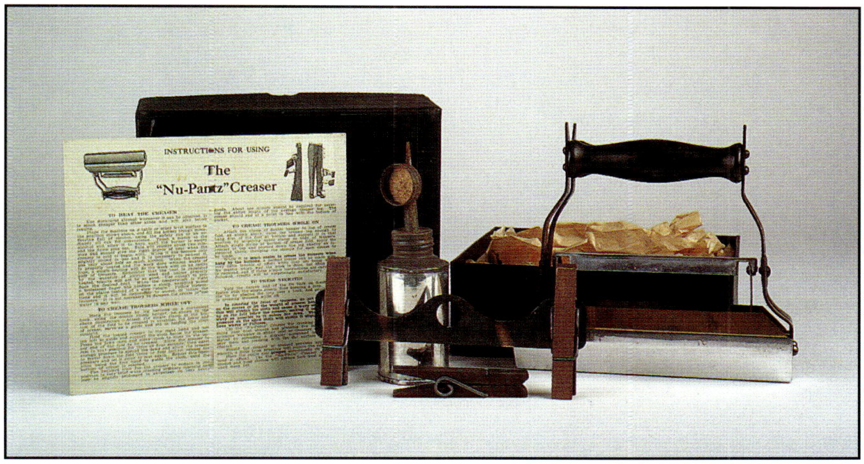

The "Nu-Pantz" Creaser. Yes it has been improved over the years. Have seen this similar model sell for $50. Makes a great decoration and conversation piece.

Home Shoe Button kit, rein spring, harness menders, shoe and harness repairing outfit, shoe waterproofer.

Salesman's samples of door hardware, mounted on wood.

Everything for the favorite horse.

And for the favorite car. Brass automotive gasket cutter.

For that favorite lady.

Store bought fishing tackle must have seemed like a luxury a hundred years ago.

Truly unusual, and difficult to price. The Aermore Exhaust Horn, "The Signal with a Smile." The Fulton Co., Milwaukee, Wisconsin. Iron and brass. 19" x 19".

The Bowser Self Measuring Oil tank, S. F. Bowser & Co., Fort Wayne, Indiana., 28" h. x 10" x 12".

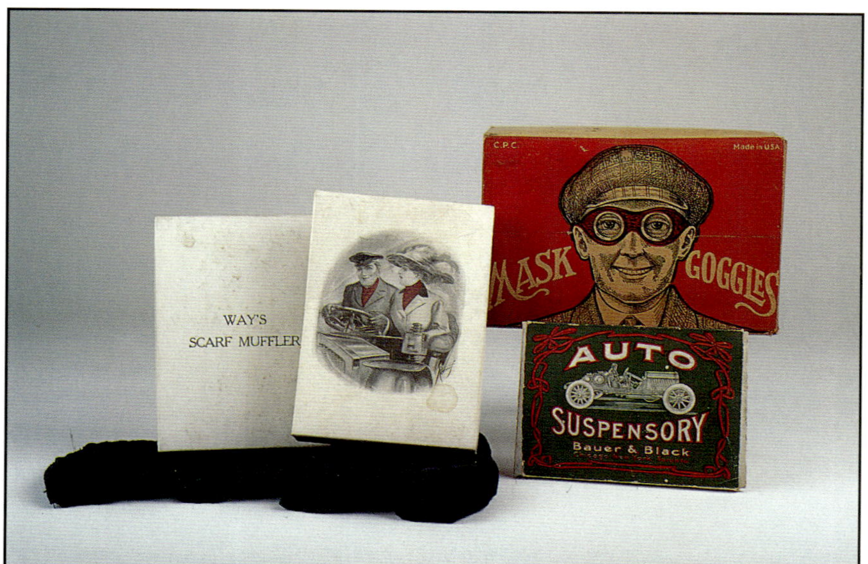

An interesting lot of auto accessories. Way's scarf muffler; mask goggles; Bauer & Black auto suspensory (jock strap). $35-75

A few items from an early automart. $20-35

Assortment of household and animal products, including clothes pins, carpet tacks, staples, and hog rings. $5-20

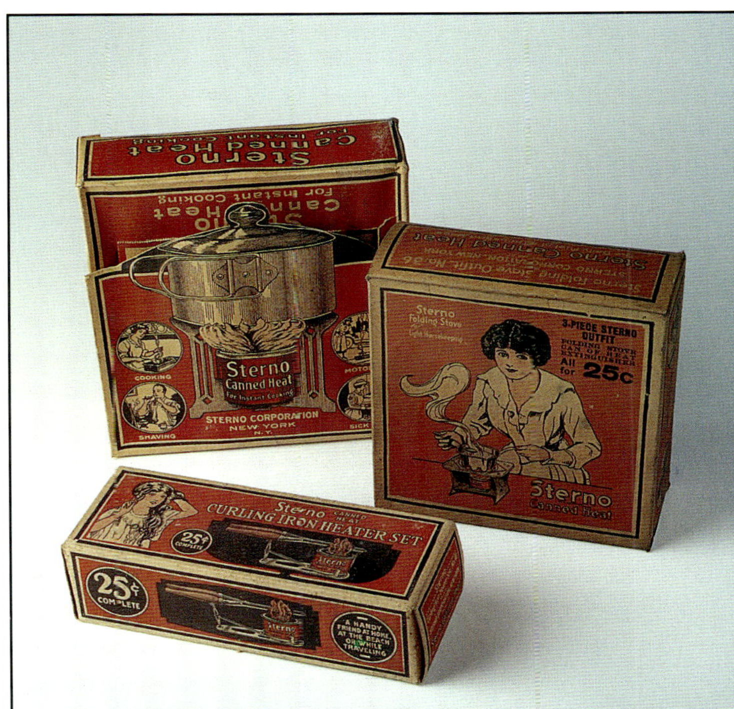

Here's a product that hasn't changed much over the years. Assortment of Sterno Canned Heat products. Sterno Corporation, New York.

Fancy goods was the real heartbeat of the country store, and the following canned goods from it's shelves give a good representation of the quality and quantity available to the general public.

Large, 10 pound tin for Buffalo Brand Fancy Salted Peanuts. F. M. Hoyt & Co., Amesbury, Massachusetts. Tin. 9" high, 8.25" dia. $450-600

An almost endless variety of tobacco products grace the shelves.

Drinks from a can, or maybe just a scam.

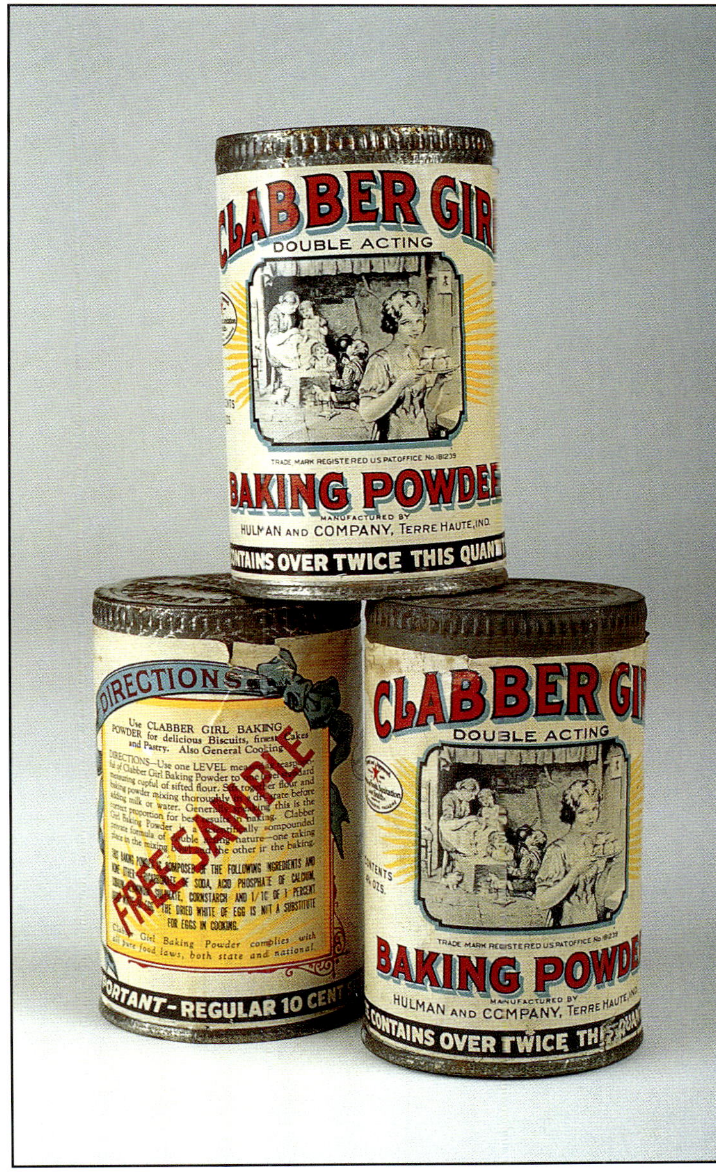

Baking needs and a few products to help clean up the mess afterwards. $15-25 each

SENECA POULTRY POWDER
MANUFACTURED BY THE SENECA COMPANY TIFFIN, OHIO.
THE SCIENTIFIC PREPARATION FOR CHICKENS, TURKEYS AND DUCKS. CONTAINS NO WORTHLESS FILLER BUT IS A HIGHLY MEDICATED COMPOUND.
PRICE 50 CENTS
INCREASED SIZE OF PACKAGE OVER OTHERS
SENECA INSECT POWDER
MANUFACTURED AND GUARANTEED BY THE SENECA COMPANY TIFFIN, OHIO.
FOR THE DESTRUCTION OF ALL KINDS OF LICE AND INSECTS THAT INFEST POULTRY, HORSES, CATTLE, SHEEP, HOGS AND OTHER ANIMALS.
PRICE 25 CENTS

SUPERIOR
CONDITION Powders
SCIENTIFIC COMPOUND
HORSES, CATTLE
DR. HESS STOCK TONIC
HOGS SHEEP.
FREE
SAMPLE
A Conditioner and Worm Expeller
BLUEBELL BRINGS BRIGHTNESS

THE BEST
MOSQUITO DESTROYER COILS
TRADE MARK
Camel
"THE CRATER"
SULPHUR CANDLE FUMIGATOR
BULL DOG BRAND FLY AND INSECT POWDER
DAISY FLY KILLER

INDEPENDENCE SAFETY MATCH
ONE
BOXES
GLOBE MAT
MADE BY
HE DIAMOND MATCH
THREE STARS
SAFETY MATCHES

RAT CORN
KILLS RATS AND MICE
WITHOUT ODORS
Botanical Mfg. Co.
Philadelphia Pa. U.S.A.
RAT CORN
KILLS RATS AND MICE
WITHOUT ODORS
Botanical Mfg. Co.
Philadelphia Pa. U.S.A.
CAUTION
POISON
RAT ANNIHILATOR
THE MODERN RAT DESTROYER
Kills and completely consumes the body of the Rodent, leaving no resultant odor
It really does what others claim to do
Harmless to handle but do not take internally
SAFE, SURE SANITARY
TRADE MARK
POISON!
TRADE MARK
GOPHER DEATH
(Tablets)
READY FOR USE
Manufactured by
Fort Dodge Chemical Co.
FORT DODGE, IOWA

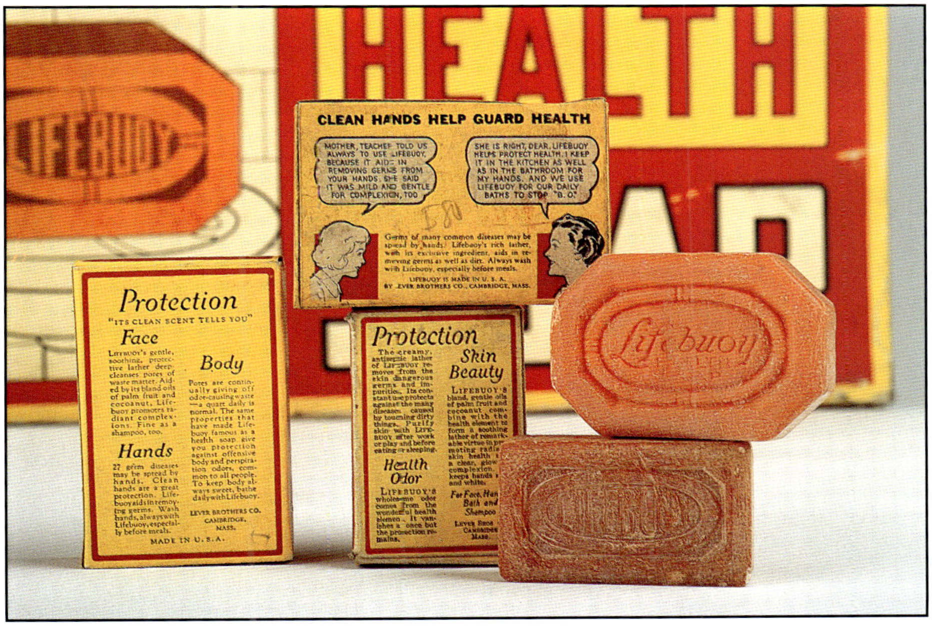

Both pages: If you could think it, the store probably carried it. Assortment of insecticides, mosquito destroyer, candle fumigator, fly and insect powders, matches, and much more.

THE COMPUTING SCALE CO.
MONEYWEIGHT

STOCK REMEDY
BRINGS BRIGHTNESS
SENECA POULTRY POWDER

Both pages: A few snapshots to show the true feeling of Bob Lyon's country store. Complete with scales, clocks, bag racks, and all the true look and feel of a working business.

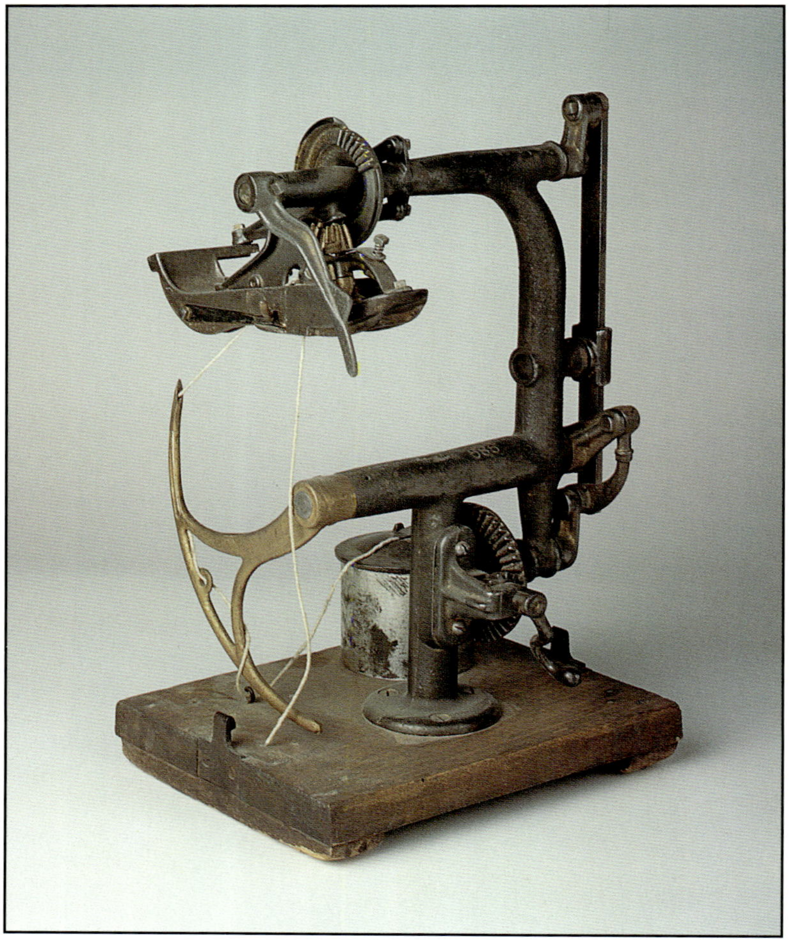

All the latest from the city slicker salesmen, and perfect for country life. Salesman's sample for a knotter (binds bales of hay). 14" high.

Cheese cover. Glass with wood base. 9.5" high, 16" dia. $125-175

A few toys for the kiddies.

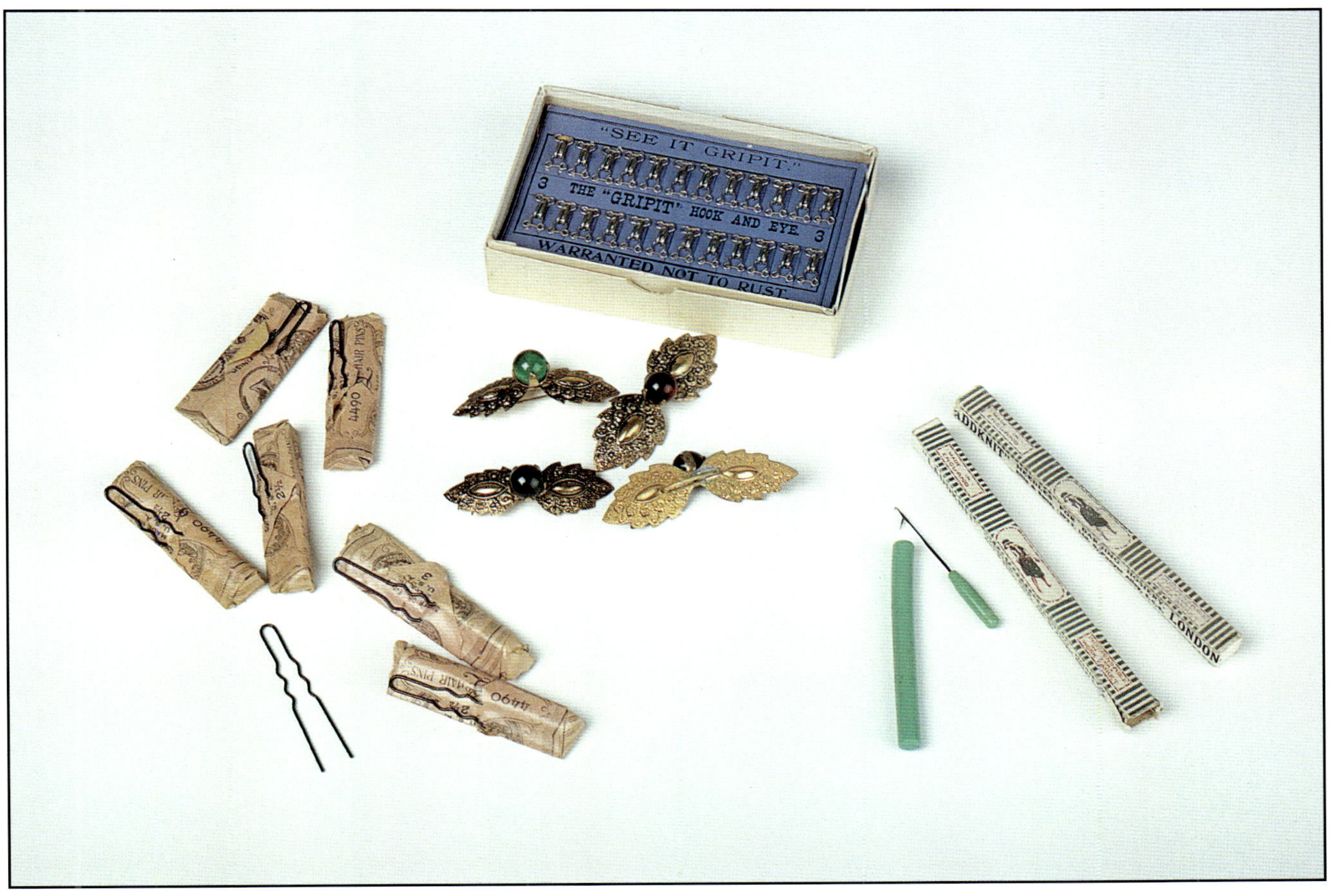

The end of this third book marks the start of the first, with two classic shots of the incredible Bob Lyon's Country Store collection.

Fancy glass jars for mom.